Another Country

GROWING UP IN '50S IRELAND

D0281690

By Gene Kerrigan

GENE KERRIGAN

Another Country

GROWING UP IN '50S IRELAND

GILL & MACMILLAN

Gill & Macmillan Ltd
Goldenbridge
Dublin 8
with associated companies throughout the world
© Gene Kerrigan 1998
0 7171 2745 1
Design and print origination by *Deirdre's Desktop*
Printed by ColourBooks Ltd, Dublin

This book is typeset in Goudy 11 on 14 point.

A catalogue record for this book is
available from the British Library.

3   5   4   2

For Cathleen Kerrigan

Thanks

This book being, of necessity, more personal than anything I had previously written, I depended on the perspective of friends to help me keep my bearings. As always, Julie Lordan read, listened and encouraged. Noel Murphy and Pat Brennan read the first draft and made useful suggestions. Evelyn Bracken not only read the second draft as a friend but did a thoroughly professional editing job, eliminating repetition, pointing out weaknesses and suggesting significant additions. Thank you all.

One

They take you back, those hymns, those chanted psalms, those supremely confident words sung to graceful music. *We will be true to thee 'til death.*

It's the second week of November, the daylight hours are shortening, the days are bright and cold, more often than not we light a fire in the evening, the sheets are cold when we go to bed. A bracing, almost enjoyable coldness. Up in the supermarket they're already selling Christmas wrapping paper, setting out the fake Christmas trees. In the shopping centres they're clearing spaces to set up castles and grottoes and cabins wherein Santa will hold court. The long run in to Christmas has begun. At this time of year it doesn't take a nostalgic soundtrack to stir memories, but for the past few days a warm sound has been billowing forth from the Sony speakers. Plaintiff notes strip back the years, unpeel clear memories and ambiguous emotions. The sounds define that other country where I was a child.

> Holy God we praise Thy name,
> Lord above we bow before Thee.
> All on earth Thy sceptre own,
> All in Heaven above adore Thee.
> Infinite Thy vast domain;
> Everlasting be Thy reign.

Faith of Our Fathers, the CD is called, subtitled *Classic Religious Anthems of Ireland*. 'Faith of Our Fathers', 'Sweet Heart of Jesus', 'The Bells of the Angelus', 'Queen of the May', 'O Sacrament Most Holy'. All familiar to those of us reared in the Catholic Ireland of the early 1960s and before. The album came out a few weeks back and it immediately shot to the top of the charts. The words of the hymns, the flowing lines, settle easily into grooves in our minds, comfortable scars long ignored but still traceable despite the decades that have passed since they were cut into our psyche. Along with the sounds comes unbidden the smell of damp rising from our rain-sodden clothes as we crouched in the Church of the Most Precious Blood, Canon Burke looking sternly down at us through his watery eyes, our sore knees shifting on the hard wooden kneeler.

Track 8 of the CD comes on and I discover that I can sing in Latin. My lips are moving, as they haven't done for thirty-five years, in synch with the words of 'Tantum Ergo'. Back then we made the church echo with our ragged sopranos, now the grave sounds of 'Tantum Ergo' come in perfect unison from the throats of the monks of Glenstal Abbey.

> Tantum ergo Sacramentum
> Veneremur cernui
> Et antiquum documentum
> Novo cedat ritui . . .

I didn't know back then what the words meant and I don't know now. I could easily find out, but that would spoil the magic. The meaning of the words never mattered much. What mattered was the seductive sound tethering our souls to a time and a place, a God and his Church.

> Blood of my Saviour, bathe me in Thy tide,
> Wash me in waters flowing from His side.

We didn't take the words as metaphor. The idea of washing ourselves in the waters flowing from His side created a fairly revolting image for kids to assimilate, but in our innocence we accepted that these were ancient words of sacred meaning, binding us to timeless truths.

> Deep in Thy wounds, Lord,
> Hide and shelter me.

An image to treasure.

They take you back, those hymns. When *Faith of Our Fathers* came on the market we went quietly in our tens of thousands and brought home this slice of our past and it went double platinum within days of its release. That time and place represented a point high up on the rising curve of ascendancy for a religious and political institution that aspired to rule our schools and hospitals and homes, our government and our souls. And those hymns were the soundtrack that accompanied our guilt-ridden little lives.

> O gentle, chaste and spotless Maid,
> We sinners make our prayers through thee;
> Remind thy Son that He has paid
> The price of our iniquity.

We iniquitous children, guilty and sorrowful for the part we played in crucifying Christ, sang our innocent hearts out. We knelt in supplication, made our Acts of Contrition and did our Penance. We crossed ourselves and every pain we suffered we Offered Up for the sake of the Souls in Purgatory. Above our respectfully bowed heads things were going on that we couldn't have imagined. We were innocents in a bleary-eyed world, taught to hunger for salvation, and offering in return our thoughts, words, deeds and any sense of ourselves as free beings. The sweetest fate we could hope for was death, sweeter by far than mere human love or contentment, as long as it was for the sake of our Father in Heaven. It wasn't that we were taught merely to endure suffering for our God, we were urged to long for it.

> Our fathers, chained in prisons dark,
> Were still in heart and conscience free;
> How sweet would be their children's fate
> If they, like them, could die for Thee.

3

How sweet it would be to die for the glory of God, how sweet it was that our ancestors lingered in chains as a result of religious conflict. It was an age when you could sing things like that in all seriousness, without blushing. An age of devotion to a stern god. An age when there was a lot of bowing and scraping and wallowing in obeisance.

For we who were children, it was an age of innocence, but an innocence hemmed in by fear and by guilt. The old men who presided over that society believed not only that they and their kind had a right to arrange every detail of our lives but that it always would be in their power to do so. It was a society that seemed set in stone, but when strong winds blew it began to flake, to quiver. The Church shook too, but it never broke apart. It just changed, as everything else did. It evolved, just as we children evolved, and just as we became different versions of ourselves, so the Church has become a different version of what it was.

The change required the adoption of more user-friendly rituals, and that meant ditching the florid declarations of how sweet it would be to be slaughtered for the faith. Now, some bright sparks have packaged those anthems of lost innocence and they're selling us back some remnants of a life we lived in a time gone and a place transformed.

They take you back, those hymns, they take you back. Play it again, Psalm . . .

* * *

'Miss?'

'Miss?'
'Miss?'
'Miss?'
'What's adultery, Miss?'

The young teacher was ready for the question. She was taking us through the Ten Commandments. And you don't take a class of

4

seven-year-old boys through the Ten Commandments without knowing that you're going to have to negotiate your way around a few awkward questions.

'Adultery is something that's not nice', said the young teacher, confidently, assuredly, and with finality, 'and it's hard for young children to understand it, but you needn't worry about it now, you'll find out all about it later on.' Having performed her neat sidestep she continued: 'Seventh, Thou Shalt Not Steal.'

'Miss?'

'Miss?'

'Miss?'

'Now, Thou Shalt Not Steal means that if something belongs to somebody else . . .'

We knew what stealing was.

'Miss?'

'Miss?'

'Miss?'

'Miss?'

'What's adultery, Miss?'

A huge difference between us and big people was that big people knew things. It wasn't just that they got to tell us what we could or couldn't do. That was okay, that was part of the natural order of things. They were bigger and they got to boss us around. That is the way the world works. We understood that in our bones. And there was nothing we could do about that until we grew up.

But there was something we could do about the fact that big people knew all about the world and we didn't. As soon as we could talk we began asking questions.

'Why is the moon up there?'

'It's just up there, because . . . that's where it is.'

'Is there something holding it up?'

'No, it's just up there.'

'Why doesn't it fall down?'

'Finish your dinner.'

'Why doesn't it fall down, but?'

The young teacher was nice. She had a lovely smile and she used it a lot. We liked her. We didn't start out to embarrass her. We just wanted a strange word explained.

'Miss?'

'Miss?'

'Adultery is a sin, and it's something that grownups . . . it's a bad thing and you'll learn all about it when you're older.'

'Miss?'

'Miss?'

'Miss?'

We couldn't wait until we were older. We needed to know now. This was important stuff. This was a Commandment. And it wasn't one of those nancy ones like Thou Shalt Keep Holy The Sabbath Day, which just meant not doing anything wrong on a Sunday unless you couldn't help it. Adultery was sandwiched in between Thou Shalt Not Kill and Thou Shalt Not Steal, so it had to be pretty serious.

We needed to know. If we didn't know what adultery was, how did we know that we mightn't at any moment commit it? And perhaps even commit it on a Sunday, inadvertently breaking two Commandments at the one time.

More than that. We now sensed something. We sensed that the young teacher was vulnerable. She was young and pretty and nice and we liked her but she was an adult and adults weren't often vulnerable and when we stumbled across something like this we pursued it, the way wolves pursue a bloody trail.

The young teacher pressed on to Eighth, Thou Shalt Not Bear False Witness Against Thy Neighbour, ignoring our raised hands and our chorus of 'Miss? Miss? Miss?'

As she explained about bearing false witness and telling lies, adultery drifted to the back of our minds. We wouldn't forget it, but there were other Commandments to be dealt with. Aware she had left blood on the trail, the young teacher distracted our attention while she put distance between herself and danger. She knew she was skirting dangerous territory with this next one, but she had her story ready.

6

'Ninth, Thou Shalt Not Covet Thy Neighbour's Wife.'

Covet, there was another new one. It sounded like cover, but that didn't make sense. Cover thy neighbour's wife. An image of me pulling a big, big tarpaulin over Mr Kavanagh's wife. No, that was not a sin I would be likely to commit.

'Miss?'

'Miss?'

'Miss?'

'Covet means to long for, to wish to have things that belong to someone else. It's a sin to be longing so much to have something that rightfully belongs to someone else.'

This seemed a somewhat superfluous Commandment. If you took something that belonged to someone else you were already marked for Hell because you'd broken Seventh, Thou Shalt Not Steal. And if you just longed for it, like I longed for a Chuck Connors *Rifleman* rifle like the one my friend Willie had, that could hardly be a sin.

And why would we long for someone's wife?

Still moving, distracting, the teacher was running towards safe ground, almost there now. 'Tenth, Thou Shalt Not Covet Thy Neighbour's Goods.'

Number Ten sounded like it was the same as Number Nine, except it was about our neighbour's goods, instead of his wife, which made a little more sense but not much.

'Miss?'

'Miss?'

'Miss?'

'What does coveting your neighbour's wife mean?'

And the young teacher made her mistake. 'The Ninth Commandment is much the same as the Sixth', she said, intending to wrap it up and tuck it away, instead slipping, losing her balance in full view of the wolves. 'Tenth, Thou Shalt Not Covet Thy Neighbour's Goods. Now, that just means . . .'

'Miss?'

'Miss?'

'Miss?'

'What's adultery, Miss?'

'I told you, you'll find out all about it when you grow up.'

'What is it, but, Miss?'

She tried again to fend us off with more assurances that we'd find out about it when the time was right. She hadn't prepared any more answers, assuming her authoritative assurances would be enough to keep us quiet. As our *Missmissmissmissmiss* persistence wore her down she tossed one more off-the-cuff explanatory remark at us before decisively moving on to something else. The young teacher, groping for words, found some that concisely summed up the feelings and beliefs of a young, decent, well-meaning and Catholic-to-the-bone convent school teacher in 1957. Forty years later, the words are clear in my mind.

'It's something dirty', she said. 'You'll find out about it when you grow up.'

The fact that adultery, whatever it might be, was so terrible a sin that they couldn't even tell us what it was made a huge impression and the young teacher's definition clung to a niche in the back of my mind through the next few years. The very word—adult with a bit tacked on the end—suggested the hidden activities of those in control. *Adult*ery: that which adults do. And now, whatever it was, we knew it was dirty.

Five years later, at the age of twelve, when I discovered what I would later learn were impure thoughts and my body did the things that bodies do in or around that time, the young teacher's words were still back there somewhere, filed away in my mind, waiting to connect with something grownup and dirty.

Bingo. This was it.

No one, priest or anyone else, ever told us about birds or bees or sinful thoughts, there was no preparation at all for coping with these feelings. Sex came upon us whole and unheralded, unexplained, for us to cope with as we might. And these mysterious urges, surges, flushes and fumblings were dirty, there could be no mistake about that. And in a month or two I'd be thirteen, a teenager, which was just a step below being grown up. So, this was it, this was grownup and it was dirty and that could mean only one thing: I'd committed adultery.

I'd broken a Commandment, committed a terrible sin. And when you committed a sin you had to confess it to the priest or risk Eternal Damnation. I thought about it and prepared myself. 'Bless me Father', I would say, 'It's been a week since my last Confession. I committed adultery. Twice.'

No, I couldn't do it. Here was the dreadful sin, the dirty sin, the horror that was so repulsive that they had a whole Commandment about it, so shocking that they couldn't even tell you what it was until you were grown up, and now I'd gone and committed it.

I missed Confession that week and agonised through the weekend and into the following week, but as Saturday came around again I had to face the fact that I would not be able to bring myself to confess my adultery to the priest. The pain of Eternal Damnation in the fires of Hell was preferable.

But you couldn't just not go to Confession for ever and ever. Questions would be asked. The weekly ritual of Confession and Communion was for us not a matter of choice but of routine. You could miss it once, now and again, by arranging your schedule so that chores or homework clashed with Confession, and you'd shrug and say, sure, won't I get it next week. But you couldn't pull that one indefinitely. So, I went to Confession and I told my trivial sins and I kept the big one a secret between me and God. I left the Confession Box and knelt to say my Penance, and I knew that somewhere up there all of Heaven was looking down at me with a big frown on its collective face.

And I slouched out of the church, a weight dragging on my soul, because I'd thought it through and I'd made a decision and the upshot was that I'd deliberately made a Bad Confession. There were few more terrible things a twelve-year-old could do than deliberately make a Bad Confession. And every other Confession I would make, next week and the week after that and all the way into the future, they would all be Bad Confessions, each one more

9

assuredly than the last damning me to eternal punishment, unless I confessed to making a Bad Confession, and that would mean confessing to my adultery and that just wasn't going to happen.

Sometimes now I wish I'd had the courage, so I would today have the memory of the priest's face as he peered out through the wire at the twelve-year-old confessing to adultery.

But I didn't have the courage, so Confession became an empty ritual. Worse than that, a damning one. I kept going to Confession, and the fact that I was damned, that every Bad Confession I made would on the Day of Reckoning shove me further into the depths of Hell, was something I didn't think about much. It was just there, my fate, a fiery punishment waiting somewhere past the other end of my life.

Which was okay, because when you're twelve or thirteen that's several eternities away.

*　*　*

There was school and there was home and there was the street. Each area of our lives had its own personnel, its rituals, its physical perimeters, its joys and its pains in the neck, the segments sometimes overlapping, people moving from one to another. And connecting and overlaying the various parts of our lives was the Church. The One, Holy, Catholic and Apostolic Church.

The Church was in our homes, through our parents and their religious emblems, in our Grace Before Meals and our Rosary before bedtime. The Church was on the street, physically dominating the neighbourhood, through which rang the stern sound of the Angelus bell twice a day. But most of all the Church ran the schools. Education started when you were six. There was Low Babies and High Babies and you then graduated to 1st Class, and these you attended in the convent school. Then, at age nine, to primary level, from 2nd Class to 6th Class, in national school, managed by the parish priest in the name of the bishop. Then, when you were about fourteen, there was secondary school (fee-paying, run by the Church) or technical school (state run, with a priest giving a Religious Instruction class), and then university. Hardly anyone from our neighbourhood went to third level, not a lot went to second level, and many of us never got much beyond primary. There was no sense of deprivation, just that this was how things were. Those going on to Secondary or to Tech were pitied, losers who had to spend more years behind bars.

> Finbar's School is a very old school,
> It's made of bricks and plaster.
> The only thing that's wrong with it
> Is the baldy-headed masters.

We sang it as we were marched from the Dominican Convent School, through the streets of Cabra West, to St Finbar's National School. It was the day of our graduation from convent school kids to national schoolboys, and our solemn march through the streets from one school to the other, in lines of two, was a ritual of transition.

We sang our impudent song quietly. You wouldn't want one of the baldy-headed masters to catch you insulting him. They didn't hit us in the convent—maybe a raised voice from time to time— but in the national school they were licensed to beat the shit out of us, and we all knew that.

The convent was all *mawla* (plasticine) and stories and paints smeared on sheets of newspaper and let's all sing a song, children. (Correction: *a pháistí*, they said, through the first national language. Let's all sing a song, *a pháistí*. And it was usually a hymn.) The transition from playing to learning was gradual, marked only by the rise from Low Babies to High Babies to 1st Class.

There was Mrs Vim and Miss Gardiner, and there was Sister Mary Gonsalvo, who was a dead ringer for Pope Pius XII, with his nose and his glasses. She was gentle, I know, but this far on I can't remember what exactly she did to make us love her. She had a group relationship with us, one of duty on her side, awe on ours.

11

There wasn't what you could call a personal relationship between us. The idea that you could have a personal relationship with one of those black-robed, pale-faced authority figures was a concept we were simply not capable of embracing. Probably, they couldn't either, poor sods.

On those rare occasions, apart from Angelus times, when the convent bell rang out across the neighbourhood we knew it meant that a nun had died. Each time I heard that bell, years later, I hoped (this was long after I'd stopped praying) that it wasn't for the beloved Sister Mary Gonsalvo.

'Will cad agum dull amok, mar shad du hall ay?' We didn't know what the individual Irish words meant, but that was what you said when you wanted to ask permission to go to the toilet. 'Why didn't you go during the break?', asked Mrs Vim, a lovely woman. My vocabulary didn't distinguish between want and need; and although I meant to say that I didn't need to go during the break, it came out as a cheeky 'I didn't want to', and Mrs Vim took offence and I trembled at her frown, her curt dismissal, her obvious anger. To be punished, even if only by being on the receiving end of a teacher's momentary bad mood, hurt all the more deeply for my innocence of any bad intent. Such slights, which an adult may be unaware of delivering, can linger in the child's memory, and in that part of us that remains a child, for decades.

Then there was the young teacher, who had the most effect and whose name is lost in the forty-year distance. She told us stories. She'd break them into daily episodes, taking perhaps a couple of weeks to get through each story. The most impressive, most memorable stories came from the movies. She came back from the cinema bubbling with tales to tell. She told us the story of *Around the World in 80 Days* and it lifted us out of 1950s Dublin and brought us to nineteenth-century England and France, the American Wild West, the Mysterious East and the concept of time zones, on which the kick in the ending of the story is dependent. The movie came out in 1956 (I just looked it up); so it probably got here in 1957, which means that we were aged seven when we came to understand global time zones. Not bad going for a young teacher (twenty, twenty-two, at a guess; a child's eye estimating an adult's age means she could have been anything from eighteen to thirty-eight).

And years later, when I saw the movie, everything was just as the young teacher had told us. Phileas Fogg and Passepartout looked just as she described them, and the gentlemen's club where the bet was made, and the belief that the bet was lost (the disappointment that flooded that room in the Dominican Convent, Cabra West, was numbing—how could Phileas lose, after all his efforts, after all those adventures, where was the happy ending?), and the date on the newspaper and Phileas realising his mistake and the dash to the club and at the last second the bet was won, and there was a happy ending. There is a power in stories that enchants, teaches, awakens, and it stretched across the years, from the pen of the long-dead Frenchman Jules Verne, through the camera of brash Hollywood producer Mike Todd (who would die in a plane crash a year later), through the young teacher in a room in a Dublin convent school, to little minds eager to conquer the vast empire of ignorance to which each child is heir.

Childhood is a smalltime world in which every new street you visit, every journey on which you are taken, every new word and idea, enlarges you; every story adds another few precious yards of familiar territory to the small space in which you feel at ease; every answered question colonises ground from the great unknown that is the domain of the grownups. Growth involves a succession of achievements: strength (feel that muscle), height (I'm getting bigger and bigger), ability (look what I can do), possessions (I want that, and that, and that), territory (that's my seat), knowledge (betcha didn't know that) and language (all of the above). As adults we see the cuteness in such striving; as kids we take for granted the persistent struggle to expand the territory of the known, the familiar, the reliable, the conquered.

The Ten Commandments (which according to some sources were given to humanity by God) came to us from epic movie director Cecil B. De Mille, via the young teacher. She came back from her visit to the cinema with a serial story that lasted weeks, of Moses and the bullrushes and the chases and the fights and the tablets of stone, the golden calf and the parting of the waters. (When, years later, I saw the movie the parting of the Red Sea wasn't half as impressive on the screen as from the young teacher's lips—her special effects were far superior to Cecil's.)

Having told us how the Ten Commandments came into being, from God through Charlton Heston, the young teacher had to, of course, tell us what they were. The Commandments: First, no false gods; Second, no taking the name of God in vain; Third, keep holy the Sabbath; Fourth, honour your mother and father; Fifth, no killing; and, of course, Sixth, Thou Shalt Not Commit Adultery.

Which is where we came in.

*   *   *

We had to attend training courses in preparation for making our First Holy Communion. (In the normal course of events one would 'receive' Holy Communion. However, we 'made' our First Holy Communion. The difference in terminology was never explained.) The school and the Church were two halves of the same training academy, it was part of the school's function to prepare us for Holy Communion.

For the purposes of training, we first got the theory, being told how bread and wine were turned into the flesh and blood of Jesus Christ. And, no, we were told, we wouldn't be getting the wine. The priest eats the bread and drinks the wine on behalf of the congregation.

'Miss?'

'Miss?'

'Miss?'

'Does that mean we're only getting half a Holy Communion?'

No, she said, it was okay that we didn't get the wine, because the bread somehow included not alone the flesh but also the blood.

14

'Miss?'
'Miss?'
'Miss?'

'If there's blood as well as flesh in the bread why does the priest have to drink the wine as well as eat the bread?'

There was no answer to that, but by and by we concluded that the priest got the wine as a kind of perk of the job.

We received instructions on how to accept the Body of Christ, how we must respect it, how it must not touch our lips as it arrived on our tongues, so we'd have to make sure our tongues were protruding well beyond our lips. Once the Host was placed on your tongue you would have to draw the tongue back into your mouth, using extreme care. It was emphasised that we must on no account chew the Host, nor let our teeth touch it. We must keep it on our tongues until we swallowed it. It seemed like a fairly tricky business.

After the theory, the practical training. We were brought to the Church of the Most Precious Blood, where we knelt and opened our mouths and altar boys placed squares of ice cream wafer on our tongues.

We were instructed in how to make a Good Confession. The opening line was invariable: 'Bless me, Father, for I have sinned.'

Once we had made our First Holy Communion the second line in the Confession ritual would be: 'It's been a week since my last Confession.' It was assumed that we would receive the Sacraments weekly, Confession on Saturday and Communion on Sunday. It seemed to be assumed that we would sin between Confessions. It seemed, somehow, to be expected.

After the preamble, you told your sins. They broke down into mortals and venials. The former, which in legal parlance might be called felonies, qualified you for a one-way ticket to Hell, should you die with one staining your soul. Venials were misdemeanours. They got you a singeing in Purgatory, a postponement of your entry to Heaven, but unless you had a bagful of them, and were impertinently unrepentant, they didn't damn you for all eternity.

15

You examined your conscience and confessed your sins. Then the priest would give you Penance and you had to leave the Confession Box and kneel nearby until you had done your Penance. Then, soul cleansed, you prepared to cleanse your mouth for the receipt of the Body of Christ. From midnight that night you fasted until after you received Communion next day. Nothing must pass your lips, except water.

Instructions over, the day of the First Confession approached. In the week or two beforehand I tossed and turned in bed, full of doubt and fear and guilt.

No sin.

Not a sausage. Zilch. Nada. Nothing to declare. Much to my embarrassment, despite careful examination of conscience, I rated zero on the iniquity scale. Bit of a cock-up on the moral transgression front.

It was a problem. 'Bless me, Father', I would have to say, 'for I have sinned', and I hadn't.

It wasn't that I was a holy joe. I wasn't disputing my capacity to sink to the lower depths of moral squalor with the rest of the seven-year-olds of Dublin. I had, after all, been born with a soul disfigured by original sin, a wicked, morally warped baby, as all Christian babies are reckoned to be, needing the cleansing waters of baptism.

But since then I hadn't done anything that might remotely qualify as a sin. Not in the past week, not in the past year, not ever. And as the big day came nearer I was wishing I had. I searched my conscience, as the instructors had ordered, and poked into corners of my memory in the hope of finding a genuine sin. Nothing doing.

I briefly considered going out and committing a few sins, just so I would have something to tell in Confession. But that seemed like it might be against the spirit of the occasion.

Perhaps my very belief that I had not sinned was itself a sin of some kind, probably pride. But I could hardly start off my First Confession by claiming that the only sin I had ever committed was the sin of believing that I had not sinned.

16

The day came. I joined the line outside the Confession Box and waited, inching along the pew as each penitent before me told his sins and emerged forgiven. I didn't know if I would have the courage to go through with the plan that had finally suggested itself to me. I had considered and discarded the idea of simply saying, 'Bless me, Father, I haven't committed any sins up to now, but I'd like to be forgiven so I can make my First Holy Communion.' That would surely cause the priest to erupt in anger, for I would be appearing to reject what seemed to be a common understanding among the elders and priests of my tribe: that a boy could not reach the age of seven without committing a sin.

I furiously searched my conscience one last time in the hope that there might be some sin I had committed that I had overlooked. Nothing. My soul seemed a pale, featureless expanse, unstained by sin of a mortal or even a venial kind. I went into the box, knelt and waited, trembling, as the priest dealt with the penitent in the cubicle on the far side of the Confession Box. Finally, the panel slid back and the dark figure loomed behind the wire.

'Yes, my child.'

Deep breath.

'Bless me, Father, for I have sinned', I lied, committing my first ever sin.

'I told two lies', I lied. 'And I was disobedient to my mammy three times.'

I had carefully worked out the number of sins to which I would own up in order to make a credible Confession. Two lies seemed like something a seven-year-old might have on his conscience. I didn't want to rack it any higher than that, for fear I'd get a couple of Decades of the Rosary to say, as my Penance. The bit about being disobedient to my mother wasn't cut and dried, neither fact nor fiction. I reckoned I'd probably given cheek at some point, or failed to immediately carry out chores as instructed, though I couldn't recall specific instances.

Not only could I not recall committing sins; when I ran through the Ten Commandments I couldn't truly see myself breaking any of them, even had I wanted to, apart from lying (Eighth Command-ment) and being disobedient (Fourth).

Theft was out of the question, I'd no idea how to do it, I hadn't the nerve.

I didn't, as far as I knew, covet anything (unless it was a Chuck Connors *Rifleman* rifle, and I don't think either Chuck or his rifle had as yet made an impression on me).

I certainly hadn't killed anyone.

I hadn't worked or in any other way failed to keep holy the Sabbath Day.

I hadn't taken the name of the Lord in vain, as I never swore.

Of all the sins on offer, the one that held even less attraction than dragging a big tarpaulin over Mr Kavanagh's wife was that prohibited by the First Commandment: adoring false gods. That seemed a totally ridiculous Commandment. I couldn't imagine anyone actually seeking out another deity in preference to the one we were born to worship. I wouldn't have known where to start looking for another god, let alone how to adore one. Where the fun was in adoring a false god, or any god, was beyond me. It had been made clear to us that adoring God was something we had to do, a duty, a chore, and failing to do a proper amount of adoring would result in Eternal Damnation in the fires of Hell. One adored because one was under severe psychological pressure to do so. Searching out a strange god to voluntarily adore seemed a rather perverse thing to consider doing. So, false gods were out.

And I hadn't yet, as far as I knew, committed adultery, whatever it was.

So, the Fourth and the Eighth it was, being disobedient and telling lies. Having settled on two lies, I decided I'd been disobedient three times. Twice wouldn't do, as I'd admitted to two lies and that would have been too much of a coincidence. Once seemed unlikely. So, three times it was.

The priest gave me absolution and a few Hail Marys to say and that was it. I left the church feeling the almost physical presence of the State of Grace which I knew enveloped me. I looked forward

18

with joy to my First Holy Communion. The fact that the very act of making up sins had for the first time sullied my soul was brushed aside without a thought. This wasn't a Bad Confession, this was just doing my best to fit in.

* * *

We all got new suits for the occasion, albeit suits with short trousers. Shirt and a tie. A rosette on the suit lapel, complete with First Holy Communion medal. A short, basic haircut. These days kids get their hair styled, and they have names for the styles, so you might get something called a Blade One or a Blade Two. Back then, you got it cut. Everyone had more or less the same cut. And the cut didn't have a name, your hair was just shorter than it was when you went into the barber shop. Our local barber was called Ernie, and in his premises over a shop most of the male heads in Cabra West were trimmed. The place had a smell of Brylcream. Ernie had a partner, Joe, the two of them working elbow to elbow, clippers and scissors clicking all day long. You queued on a bench along one wall, and if an adult came into the barber shop the queue didn't matter, it was understood that the adult would be done first. When it was your turn, Ernie or Joe would put a short plank across the arms of the chair and you'd sit up on that and Ernie or Joe would work away; neither was the most gentle of men. He took a section of your hair in his hands and everything that stuck up above his fingers was cut off. At home, I moved on from Brylcream to Tru-Gel, mainly because the smell wasn't as pervasive. Why we needed that stuff to hold in place hair that was hardly long enough to move is beyond me even now.

Scrubbed and groomed, socks pulled up, hair trimmed, we marched in line to our pews in the Church of the Most Precious Blood and when the time came we took our turns kneeling at the altar rail and awaited our First Communion. The priest and the altar boy moved slowly along the altar rail. The altar boy placed the silver plate level with our chins to catch the Host should there be a mishap, and the priest placed the Communion wafer on our tongues. We rose, turned, began the walk back to our seats. Uncomfortable, worried, at risk of chewing Jesus.

Don't chew, they had warned us. Don't let it touch your teeth. Take it on your tongue. Swallow it.

That was all very well in theory. But how to manipulate the tongue so as to get the wafer to slide backwards and down the throat was something that puzzled us, something that later we would talk about amongst ourselves.

Meanwhile, cheeks bulging with the effort to show respect to the Host, trying to get our tongues to curl up so that the wafer would fall towards the back of our throats, fearful that at any second it might slip sideways and come into contact with our teeth, we walked back to our pews in dread, fixed expressions of piety trying to disguise the contortions behind our lips.

We knelt and said our prayers of thanksgiving and slyly watched the veterans, adults who could take and swallow the Host with casual ease, as they made their confident ways back to their pews. Someday, we thought, someday we too will have the knack.

I left the church, the Host eventually having made its way down my throat, feeling myself at the centre of a great white glow. Jesus was inside me. Jesus who had given his life that we all might see the Kingdom of Heaven. I used a pencil to write and sign a promise to Jesus, on the back of a souvenir certificate which attested that I had made my First Holy Communion, that I would henceforth receive Holy Communion 'every Sunday of my life'. The feeling was so good, the high I was getting from my State of Grace was so intense, that my promise was made with all the sincerity my seven-year-old heart could muster. I really wanted to feel this good again and again, into the distant future. My mother and my aunt gave me a card, signed and dated, to commemorate the event. Inside the card was printed the words of one of those hymns, those Classic Religious Anthems of Ireland:

O Sacrament Most Holy
O Sacrament Divine
All Praise and Thanksgiving
Be every moment Thine.

And printed underneath:

In remembrance of the
happiest day of your Life.

As we chattered, as parents came and hugged us, as we had our photos taken, I felt part of a pure goodness beyond my experience, filling me up, filling the whole world with light and grace.

Then it was time for the money. Jesus and holiness were all well and good, but this was the first time in our lives that we were as a right entitled to be given money. We were taken around to relatives and friends and neighbours, so they might admire our suits and our haircuts and our manners. And so that they could slip us a few bob. In chatter amongst ourselves at school, when we discussed impending events, it was not the State of Grace that enthused us but the sure and certain knowledge that the grownups would be coughing up some hard cash.

'Ah, isn't he lovely!'

'He's a credit to you.'

At the end of the day I was wealthy, the possessor of great riches, the pockets of my jacket heavy with shillings and half-crowns and two-bobs and sixpences. No brass, all silver. Oh, there must have been at least a pound.

*　　*　　*

And then it was time, a week later, to return to Confession. Now that we were into the cycle, we were expected to renew our State of Grace, to erase in Confession the sins we were undoubtedly committing, and to obey our promise to receive the

21

Sacraments weekly. And I went and I again confessed my two lies and three instances of disobedience. And the next week it was the same, and the week after that and the week after that. There were times when, out of fear that a priest might notice the repetition, I varied the menu of sins: one lie and two disobediences. Two and one, one and three, three and four, and on and on and on and on. And I made occasional efforts to think up some more exotic sins but I never could.

A theologian might well declare these to be Bad Confessions, but back then I was sincerely resolved to try my damnedest to fit in, to be a sinner so that I could be forgiven and redeemed and made holy again. I was doing the best I could to live up to the Church's expectations of me.

Two

You dipped a rolled-up piece of blotting paper in the bottle of black-blue ink, keeping a small area dry so you could hold it without messing up your hands too much. You took your wooden ruler, held it vertically in one hand, used the other hand, the one with the inky blotting paper, to bend back the top of the ruler and you let go—*schwock!*—the inky missile bounced off the back of a classmate's head, if your aim was true.

You did it carefully, one eye aiming the inky missile, the other peeled for Mr McAuliffe, master of Room 4, St Finbar's National School, Cabra West.

There were teachers in the convent school, and girls continued to have teachers, but at St Finbar's boys' school there were masters. The term was quite appropriate. They were, for four or five years, the masters of our school lives, with the power of knowledge, the power of pain.

When we arrived at St Finbar's we were sorted into the various classes, according to some pattern beyond our knowledge. Friendships made in convent school were casually ended as friends were allocated to different classes. Rumours spread about the masters to whom we were assigned. One in particular was regarded (quite rightly, as it turned out) as a dour, sour individual, handy with the cane. I was happy to be assigned elsewhere until I asked around about the guy who would be my master, Mr McAuliffe.

'Who did you say?'

'McAuliffe.'

'Oh, boy.'

'Why? What? What's wrong with him?'

'Oh, boy!'

'No messing, did you hear anything about him?'

'Oh boy!'

'Ah, come on, what about him?'

'He has a cane with a nail in it.'

'*What?*'

'A cane with a nail in the top. Lashes it into your hand, he does, tears the hand off you, it does', someone's big brother assured everyone.

Someone's big brother was a liar. Mr McAuliffe was as kind and thoughtful as anyone could be who was assigned the role of 'master'. Tall, thin, red-faced, white hair swept back, not a smiler but a pleasant man. Still, the story of the nail in the cane made us wary of him until the evidence proved he wasn't a brute. Maybe it was his smoking that proved his humanity. Whenever on a break from the classroom he lit up, and he smoked the cigarette down to the last quarter of an inch, two fingers and a thumb grasping the tiny butt as he audibly sucked the last molecule of nicotine out of it.

In Room 4 he taught us English, Irish, arithmetic, history, geography, religion. There was just him and us, for five years. There were no parent–teacher meetings, no parent was ever invited up for a pleasant chat about junior's progress. No career guidance. Just come to school, do your time, get out. In financing our education, the state was fulfilling a statutory obligation. It was a perfunctory exercise, with a limited curriculum, the slimmest facilities, and teachers treated as serfs by the Department of Education, given over in bondage to the manager of the schools, the parish priest. The education system hadn't changed much in the thirty-five years or so since the state had achieved independence.

St Finbar's was newly built, along with Cabra West, but even as late as 1963 half of the national schools in the country dated from the nineteenth century.

Some kids, bored or angry at being beaten, or just generally rebellious, mitched from school from time to time. They were always caught, they were always beaten. They hung around the neighbourhood for the length of the school day, having to keep out of sight, confined to out-of-the-way places, as bored as if they had gone to school. For some it was an adventure to be tried once, for others a recurring rebellion, a hopeless kick back against a system that was doing them no good at all. Some of us never mitched, reckoning it was a mug's game.

There were others who mitched not only from school but from family life. They occasionally ran away from home, lived rough. They went 'on gur'. We regarded the kids who went on gur as adventurers, far more daring than the rest of us could ever be; confident, swaggering pirates who had thrown off the chains of childhood and did what they wanted. Looking back, just about each and every one of those kids must have been running from some desperate circumstance.

St Finbar's was E-shaped, and for some reason I became convinced that the E was one of seven buildings, each in the shape of a letter, which had been built across the country for the guidance of foreign aeroplane pilots. The buildings, when seen from above, spelled out I-R-E-L-A-N-D and Finbar's was the E in Ireland. It took a while for this strange belief to wither away.

*   *   *

We bought our textbooks and our mothers used brown paper to fashion covers for them. Back then, there was lots of brown paper around. Today, you want brown paper, you have to go to a stationery shop and they'll probably sell you designer brown paper with a tastefully subtle patented pattern. Our first book was titled, oddly enough, *My First Book*.

> Tom Mary Billy
> Run. Run. Run.
> Run, Tom.
> Run, Mary.
> Run, Billy.
> Run. Run. Run.

25

And like that.

Tom, Mary and Billy and their dog, Spot, jumped on a No. 44 bus and went to visit their Granny on her farm in the country, where Spot chased a pig.

> Tom said, 'No, Spot, no.'
> Mary said, 'No, Spot, no.'
> Billy said, 'No, Spot, no.'
> No. No. No.

Then Tom and Mary and Billy went home and knelt by their beds and asked God to bless Father and Mother and Granny. And that was the end of the book.

The careful implantation, in all circumstances, of the idea of an all-powerful God, watching and besetting us, while we were awake and while we were asleep, demanding total obedience, was—looking back—a pretty lousy thing to do. The methodical creation of a sense of guilt, from the earliest age, was a routine part of school business. The warning that God was some kind of super-master, a mega-grownup, with power to wrench out our souls and consign them forever to a burning pit, was reinforced at every opportunity.

> Through my fault
> Through my fault
> Through my most grievous fault.

Reading Time, another early textbook, had a bit about how 'God sees us. He sees us all the time. He sees into our minds . . .' We were repeatedly told and we totally accepted that our every thought was being monitored by the great bugging agency in the sky. It was an unsettling belief that not alone could you be caught by grownups if you did anything wrong but that God, the ultimate grownup, was constantly scanning the inside of your head and you could be rumbled if you even thought of doing anything wrong.

Oddly enough, *Reading Time* had one page which today would surely have some of our more traditional brethren picketing the Department of Education. It was a poem titled 'Robin and Richard'.

> Robin and Richard
> Were two pretty men.
> They lay in bed
> Till the clock struck ten.

Guilt and deference were drummed into us. The sin of 'impudence' would not be tolerated. It was for our own good, it would mould us into obedient citizens with automatic respect for every whim of authority. It was no accident that the word our culture chose to describe an awkward, troublesome child was 'bold'. If you answered back or were tardy in obeying an instruction you were bold. Why, of all the words that could have been used, did bold come to mean everything we should not be? The word bold means confident, assertive, adventurous, courageous. Bold also means to stand out against a plain background. Smug, self-satisfied Ireland did not want confident children, assertive or adventurous children. And fading into the background, where you were barely seen and never heard, was a cardinal virtue.

* * *

When things got boring we used a pencil to fill in the centre of every O, every A and B and D and P and Q and R. We drew moustaches and glasses and beards on the pictures in our schoolbooks. I wrote my name and beneath that my house number and street, then Cabra West, Dublin, Ireland, The World, The Solar System, The Galaxy, The Universe. And at the centre of the universe, the centre of everything, me.

There was no official uniform but most of us dressed similarly, anyway. Short trousers, usually corduroy, held up with a belt, the same type we all wore, with a buckle in the shape of a horizontal S.

Or, sometimes, braces, which made your shirt ride up and you had to keep shoving it down into your trousers. We wore short trousers until we were twelve or thirteen, our thighs red and chilled to soreness in the winter. (All year round our knees displayed, like a soldier's medals, the scabbed and gashed wounds earned in our daily play. 'Musha', my aunt Eileen would say, cuddling me after the latest disaster, 'you're unfortunate'.) Socks pulled well up over our calves; pullover, jacket, cap. A white shirt and a tie. These were essentials of the unofficial uniform. The white shirt would be Rinso-bright, however frayed and darned the collar and cuffs might be. A properly knotted tie was a sign of respectability. As soon as I quit school I stopped wearing a tie and today I avoid wearing one except on occasions when doing so is unavoidable. I have one white shirt, purchased about three years ago, just in case. It's still in the cellophane. They'll probably bury me in it.

We sat in Room 4 and Mr McAuliffe called the roll and we answered 'Anseo' when our names were called and we put up our hands and said 'Will cad agum dull amok?' when we needed to go to the toilet. We sat at ink-stained wooden desks, slanted desk-lids with a groove near the top where you placed your pen. There was a hole in the desktop designed to accommodate an inkwell, with a little sliding brass cover, but mostly the inkwells were missing and those that remained were never used. We had to bring our own bottles of ink to school. That way our parents, not the state, got to pay for school supplies in our free primary education.

No Biros then, so we wrote with nibbed pens, using the blotting paper to dry our copybooks. You wrote a few words, then the ink ran out. The writing got paler with every word, then darker again after you dipped your nib in the ink. We wrote in the Standard Exercise Book, the one with the red cover, printed by Browne & Nolan Ltd (Belfast - Dublin - Cork).

Every evening we brought home what is now called homework but then was called our exercise—known as ecker. As in: Did you get much ecker? Yes, we got a lot of goddamn ecker. Afternoons, evenings spent scribbling away our play time.

In class, we got what was called Dictation. Mr McAuliffe would read out a line and we would copy it down. I have a copybook from primary school. We gravely, carefully, with only the occasional waver or blot, wrote things like:

He made up his mind that the little baby boys should die. He called a servant and told him to take the babies and throw them into the river.

Throwing baby boys into the river? It lies alone on the page, out of context, no indication of what came before or after. I cannot imagine what the lines are from or what in the name of Christ was going on in that scene. It sounds a little too personal to be Herod. We were ten when we wrote those lines.

'Neither a borrower nor a lender be', we carefully wrote in our painstaking hand. That, and the red sky at night being the sailors' delight, and the stubborn horse that you could take to water but you couldn't make drink, and the observation that March comes in like a lion but goes out like a lamb, and the horticultural notation that April showers bring sweet May flowers. We also wrote of Fiach McHugh, the March Hare and the Dormouse, and we committed to writing the reminder, should we ever need it, that it is too late to sharpen one's sword when the drum beats for battle. And, from 8 November 1960:

Pearse was also a man of action. When he saw that a thing needed to be done he set to work and he did it. He founded his school as an example of what an Irish school ought to be.

We learned our times tables (six ones are six, six twos are twelve, six threes are eighteen) and nearly forty years on if I need to know that six nines are fifty-four I can almost feel that piece of information sliding out of the groove into which Mr McAuliffe inserted it all that time ago and clicking into place in my consciousness. The colours of the spectrum, Richard of York Gave

Battle in Vain (red, yellow, green, blue, violet). Bits of verse planted then ('I see His face upon the rose') are scattered around dimly lit corners of memory. The 'Old Woman of the Roads' was our poetry ('Oh, to have a little house, to own the hearth and stool and all') and although it didn't connect with the lives we were living it became imbedded in us. Even today, heaving myself out of an armchair, or setting out on an errand, a rhyme from Room 4 often comes silently and unbidden to mind: 'Off we go with a hop, hop hop, all the way to the toyman's shop.'

Mr McAuliffe marked our efforts, in writing, arithmetic and so on, out of ten. If you got seven and a half or more marks out of ten you got a stroke beside your name on the chart pinned to the wall near the door. When you had ten strokes Mr McAuliffe gave you sixpence. The sixpences came out of his own pocket. There weren't all that many of them, perhaps, but in those days sixpence was sixpence. Another subsidy to the state.

It was a nice thing to do and we loved him for it. He was, as far as we knew, the only teacher in the school who did that. It wasn't just the money that we wanted, it was the recognition. We longed for that crucial seven and a half marks and the stroke that followed. And as the strokes beside our names accumulated so did our excitement. One problem was that the brightest of us earned sixpences maybe a couple of times a year, while the thicker ones never got more than one or two strokes next to their names in their entire school career.

One time, one of the class psychopaths, a decent-but-wild kid, a somewhat educationally challenged individual, earned the coveted tenth stroke and got his sixpence. It had taken him an age. His face was fixed in a wondrous smile; he just about glowed, he was so happy. Some of us feared him, but we shared his delight, clapped him on the back and cheered his achievement. He and we knew it was a special moment. I lost track of him, but he was a certainty to eventually be lagged by the cops, and if he ended up with a semi-permanent residence in Mountjoy none of us would find it hard to believe. That day, however, we all were genuinely delighted at his joy in his triumph. That was one reason Mr McAuliffe was a good teacher, that he could manage that small miracle. Maybe, who knows, the hard chaw found out that day that he wasn't a born loser and maybe he broke from the path he seemed destined to follow. Probably not.

As he handed over the sixpence Mr McAuliffe always made the same joke: 'Don't spend it all in the one shop', and we always laughed, because we thought it was very funny. We thought he made it up himself.

*   *   *

M r McAuliffe, kind man, gentle man, hefted the bamboo cane and brought it slashing down on my outstretched palm. The pain shot through my right hand, stinging, eye-watering. I held my arm outstretched, waiting, trying to keep my face expressionless. Mr McAuliffe slowly raised the cane again, lowered it gently to my palm. Touched the palm, once, twice, like a golfer teeing up a ball. Then he raised the cane again.

My hand reddened and burning, my arm involuntarily shied away from the bamboo. The palm was still outstretched, but hovering below the required 90 degree angle. Mr McAuliffe aborted the slash, lowered the cane. He put the tip of the cane beneath my hand, tapped the underside, urging my hand up, up, up, up, up, up with each tap, then—as my hand reached the required height and angle—he whipped his arm up above his shoulder and as quickly brought the cane slashing down again across my palm. The sting this time was worse and I made a fist and flexed my fingers. Then, I held my palm out again, brought it directly up to the regulation height and angle, held it there. Let's get this over with.

The cane slashed down through the air a third time, connected with my taut palm and I didn't cry.

My hand throbbed with a pain so strong, so embedded, that it seemed it would never fully leave. I put the hand into my left armpit, turned and made my way back down to my desk. Every classmate's eye was on me, just as my eyes would be locked on the face of Johnny or Riggs or Bonnet or anyone else taking the bamboo slash. It was important not to cry. If possible, make a face, wink, curl your lip, but only when you're turned away from Mr McAuliffe, to show how it didn't bother you at all. Sometimes you couldn't help it, and your hand stayed jammed into your armpit and without wanting to you rocked back and forth in your seat, and there might be tears in your eyes but you prayed—Jesus, help me, don't let me, don't let me cry.

You could not, on the other hand, pretend that the violence hadn't hurt you, hadn't chastened you. On occasion a hard chaw would swagger back to his seat, his every movement a *fuck you* to the master, and if that was too blatant he got called back up. It was Johnny I remember getting that treatment after his body language told the whole class that the beating had been no big deal. Tough Johnny, a smiling little bastard who was great fun if he liked you, but if he didn't he'd smile at you right up to the time he kicked you in what at that age passed for your balls. I got on with him most of the time, with the occasional yard battle in which we took opposite sides.

'Come back here.'

And Johnny swaggered back up, like he was just curious and didn't know what was coming.

'Hold out your hand.'

Sure, no bother, was written on Johnny's face.

Slash, slash.

Then, Johnny turning back, a bit of a smile on a face that was redder now but still magnificently contemptuous of it all. There was a less blatant but still discernible swagger as he made his way back to his desk. You had to admire Johnny.

It was called 'slapping', a trivialising euphemism for violence. Our own trivialising name for it was biffing. When you got biffed it was never a token slap. The master prepared each slashing assault with all the concentration that a Croke Park hurler applied to belting what was likely to be the last free in an All-Ireland final, ten seconds left in the match, score even.

32

Sometimes as the cane came slashing down your nerve failed and you pulled your hand back. The master looked like an eejit, slashing at empty air. That could get you an extra slap. Sometimes you flinched and pulled your hand back but not far enough and you took the slash on the tips of your fingers. That hurt bad, and the master might decide it wasn't a full slap and you'd get an extra one, across the centre of your palm, to make up for the fingertip slash. Sometimes the master's aim was bad and he got you on the heel of your hand. A slash there and you could have a visible mark, a raised line, that stung for hours.

Mr McAuliffe was a straight-across-the-palm man, nothing fancy. He tried to avoid hitting your fingers. Some masters, we believed, aimed for the heel of the hand. Another liked to approach the job with the tips of your fingers pointed towards him. That way, the cane always hit at least one finger and also stung the centre of your palm.

Some kids couldn't take it. They flinched every time, jerked their hands away, faces red, mouths straining against crying. A master would take such a kid's hand in his own, by the wrist, hold the hand out, stretch it right out, and with the other hand raise the cane and slash, slash. The kid almost always shed a tear or two, probably from the humiliation as much as the pain. Sometimes, for something really bad, you got slashed first on one hand and then the other, and you went back to your seat, both hands tucked into your armpits and no one would blame you at all if a tear ran down your cheek.

Mr McAuliffe was a nice man, but he did his duty. And his duty was to hit us with a bamboo cane when he felt we needed some violence to keep us in line. He didn't take pleasure in it, but he didn't duck his duty, either.

There were, it was said, shops where masters bought canes. Some parents bought them too (not in my home). Presumably they were imported. Bamboo grown in some tropical clime (they should have told us about this in our geography lessons), brought from some primitive land to our civilised one. Did they have factories where they put the bend in the top of the cane, to make a handle, before they sold them to the Irish education system, or was that done here? And somewhere there was a factory that produced leather straps—the weapon of choice for some masters—which were specifically designed and manufactured for beating children in national school. These weapons were manufactured, tested, distributed throughout Ireland. Masters went to wherever they bought them, picked them up, tried them out on the imaginary palms of imaginary children. *No, that doesn't feel right, the balance is a bit off. What about this one?* Did they lash the cane or leather down onto the shop counter? Maybe they lashed it into their own palms? *Yes, that feels more like it.*

The leather weapons had stitching all around the edge. Carefully made, custom-designed instruments of pain, it being a condition of employment that teachers be prepared to use them on the children in their charge. I remember seeing the leathers, but I wasn't beaten with them, just bamboo canes. There was a master at Finbar's who liked throwing a leather. He'd roll it up, then suddenly fling it at his victim. He had perfected his teaching skills to the extent that the leather would uncoil while travelling through the air, its tip stinging the victim on impact.

Hitting kids was not only legally tolerated but encouraged by state policy. Come to think of it, the masters must have had lessons themselves, in teacher training school, to instruct them on how and in what circumstances they should hit us. It didn't happen just in the 1950s or 1960s; it went on through the 1970s and it was February 1982 before the state-sanctioned beating of kids in our classrooms was officially ended.

How could they stomach it? They were, if they were like Mr McAuliffe, kind people, teachers who liked kids, who liked imparting knowledge. How could they come in, day after day, and hit kids? Beyond all the theory about imposing discipline and it being for the greater good, and all that nonsense, how could they stomach it day after day, the cane whistling through the air as it slashed down onto a small outstretched palm, the crack as the cane connected? Did it not make their stomachs turn?

Suffer the little children, said the priests. The whole thing was under the control of the parish priest, and endorsed by the state. In the pulpit, and in the daily classroom religious lesson, we were treated to this love-your-neighbour stuff, gentle Jesus meek and mild, turn the other cheek, do unto others as you would have them do unto you. And it never occurred to them that such holy joe preaching might be slightly compromised by the fact that they were as a matter of routine supervising the daily beating of children.

We were beaten for giving cheek, for disobeying orders and on occasion for getting answers wrong, for showing you were not paying attention. Sometimes a single slap, sometimes two or three. I can't remember anything more than that. There were stories, but they were probably just that, stories of terrible beatings. I never saw anyone bleed, I never saw prolonged beatings, I never saw Mr McAuliffe or any teacher take any pleasure in it.

Among the things we were beaten for was doing badly in our Irish language lessons. Getting something wrong through not paying attention was the usual crime. Not often, and not only for screwing up with Irish. But Irish was a special case. We could see where learning to read English mattered, and adding up and multiplying and knowing where rivers and mountains were and what happened to Wolfe Tone, but the Irish language was a dead loss, everyone knew that. It was hard to maintain attention. We resented being immersed in the mysteries of the *Fada* and the *Boolcha*, a language known by few and spoken by hardly anyone except for those stone-age types in the Gaeltacht. They translated prayers into Gaelic and maybe they thought that made us doubly holy. Prayers we learned by rote meant little, remaining mere words we memorised but didn't necessarily understand ('fruit of thy womb'). The same prayers in Gaelic were wholly meaningless, a succession of sounds: *Innamonanahar, agus an vic, agus an spirit nave, amen.*

They translated our names into Gaelic, and maybe they thought that made us more Irish. In official documents they translated me

35

into Eoin Ó Ciarragáin and maybe it made them feel better that I had to write that name on the front of my schoolbooks and exercise jotters, but no one ever called me by that name, before or since. Officially, Eoin Ó Ciarragáin attended school, answered *anseo* to roll call, learned his lessons and sat the Primary Certificate exam, and Gene Kerrigan didn't exist.

The British made the Irish language a liability. To prosper or even survive, adaptation to the ways of the colonial power was advisable. Our ancestors chose to adapt. After independence, intent on reviving the language, the new state tried the type of coercion they had seen work for the British. And they decided it would be the kids who would bear the burden of the revival. The adults could shrug it off, bemoan their lack of fluency in the first national language, and blame the British.

They sought to beat it into us. Without making a big thing about it, they held us to be less than properly Irish. There was Real Ireland, a Gaelic-speaking, GAA-playing, predominantly rural, genuflecting nation, respectful of the old gunmen who presided over the state. And there was the rest of us, who in one aspect or another, or in several, didn't quite measure up. We may have been born and lived on the oul sod but we weren't fully Irish-Irish, Real Irish. We were not native speakers. We were not—not quite—natives. To us, GAA games were games, not badges of national pride. We weren't great soccer fans but we made a hero of Stanley Matthews and when the Manchester United plane crashed at Munich we mourned Busby's Babes, not least because one of them, Liam Whelan, was a northsider. We read English comics, we listened as much to English radio as to Radio Éireann. It wasn't that we were Anglophiles, we just preferred the bright to the grey, the exciting to the dull. Faraway America dazzled; England, though never dazzling, outshone our grey surroundings.

When we bothered to think about them, we thought the oul fellas in the long overcoats, the heroes of the fight for national independence, were a howl. Our culture was not that of the Real Irish. We lived on mean streets, unromantic concrete jungles to those who cherished the rural idyll; a warm and enriching home to we who knew every crack on the pavement between our street and the chipper. Above all, there was the Irish language. For them it was a large part of what made us Irish; for us it was nothing more than a nuisance. A pointless, dead, garbled mouthful. A pain in the arse. Or, more precisely, a pain in the outstretched palm.

The Real Irish, the native Irish, saw themselves as the custodians of ancient traditions, an ethos that encompassed a language, games, a religion and a set of attitudes. They sought strenuously to protect and advance those traditions, and if they looked with less than respect on those of us who didn't hold those traditions so dear, that is understandable.

They withheld state jobs from those who couldn't prove their fluency in the 'first official language'. Early on, they tried forcing us to learn it by teaching every subject through Irish for the first two years of national school. The brains behind that mad scheme was a Jesuit, Father Timothy Corcoran, Professor of Education at University College Dublin. Father Tim, when not screwing up the educational prospects of the kids, campaigned through the loony right journal *Catholic Bulletin* for increased censorship, as though there wasn't enough. To protect the Real Ireland culture, alien influences had to be filtered out.

(Okay, deep breath: these are just some of the alien influences from which the priest-ridden censorship board, the cutting edge of Real Ireland, on one occasion or other saved our culture: Marcel Proust, George Orwell, Maxim Gorky, Honoré de Balzac, André Gide, Jean-Paul Sartre, Noel Coward, Norman Mailer, Margaret Mead, Bertrand Russell, James Baldwin, Graham Greene, Robert Graves, Thomas Mann, John Steinbeck, Sinclair Lewis, John O'Hara, H.G. Wells, John Dos Passos, Raymond Chandler, Aldous Huxley, Ernest Hemingway, William Faulkner, Arthur Koestler, Muriel Spark, Dylan Thomas, Georges Simenon, Joseph Heller, Iris Murdoch, John Updike and Thomas Wolfe.

And among the homegrown chancers whose work had to be from time to time banned for fear it might arouse unIrish tendencies:

James Joyce, Samuel Beckett, Frank O'Connor, Liam O'Flaherty, Sean O'Faolain, Sean O'Casey, Austin Clarke, Kate O'Brien, George Bernard Shaw, Walter Macken, John McGahern, Brendan Behan, Brian Moore.)

The influence of the Catholic Church in secondary education meant a concentration on Latin. Squeezed between the dead Latin and the dying Gaelic, students had little time for other languages. A statistic: in the 1962–63 Leaving Cert exam, in a period in which we were applying to enter the EEC, in which official policy was to open the economy and the culture to wider European influences, 21 per cent of boys took French and 88 per cent took Latin.

In the 1920s, and for decades after, the smug, ruthless and not very bright men of substance made inculcating their religious 'ethos' and the Irish language in schoolchildren the principal aims of primary education. To the latter end, they scaled back on other subjects to the point where in the 1940s an Irish National Teachers' Organisation report established that the island of saints and scholars was turning out educationally subnormal kids.

By the 1950s they were still trying to beat it into us, and they hadn't a clue why fewer and fewer retained any love for the old tongue. The ailing language died in the minds of many of us, arguments for its revival obliterated by the stinging pain in our hands. Most adults didn't bother to speak it; it was obviously of little interest to them. And those who did speak it seemed to do so in loud voices in public places, as though making a point. The job of reviving the oul tongue was to rest on the reddened palms of the kids. If someone had carefully designed a way of finishing off what the British started they'd surely have come up with something pretty much along those lines.

It didn't seem to occur to anyone until later that adults using weapons to beat children mightn't be a good thing. It certainly didn't occur to us. In our smalltime world, inflicted pain was the price of screwing up or stepping out of line, that was just the way it was. Mr McAuliffe didn't hit us more often than the average observer of that time might have considered necessary. It didn't change our view of him. He was still a nice man, a man who liked children. Hitting us was just something that adults were supposed to do. And there was none of that this-hurts-me-more-than-it-hurts-you crap. No, this was hurting just one of us.

*   *   *

We got brawn on Mondays. Aware that nutritional standards in many homes were low, the state provided national school kids with a sandwich and a small bottle of milk for lunch. Monday's contribution to our diet was a brawn sandwich, Tuesday was cheese. Wednesday was a currant bun—the favourite. Thursday was brawn again and Friday was a jam sandwich, because it was a sin to eat meat on a Friday. It wasn't brawn but that's what we called it. It was some kind of cheap spiced beef, square slices, salty and tasty when eaten, soft and mushy when rubbed in someone's face out in the yard.

We drank the milk, we ate the food if we were in the humour. There always seemed to be enough kids, especially on the two brawn days, who weren't hungry or who preferred to use their sandwiches as weapons in our mock fights. No one ever used a currant bun as ammunition. It would have been like throwing jewellery at the enemy.

At home, food was never too fancy. Dinner was in the afternoon, in the evening you had your tea. Tea might be as little as a cup of tea or a glass of milk and a jam or cheese sandwich. The tea was kept in a tea caddy, in our house a blackened metal box which my mother's Uncle Thomas brought home from India, where he went as a soldier in the British army. The tea was kept warm by plonking a tea cosy over the teapot. Dinner was mostly meat, vegetables and potatoes (there was no such thing as a meal without potatoes), cooked in the most straightforward way. (Well, maybe not the vegetables. The vegetables were by tradition cooked to the point of exhaustion.) Food seldom got more exotic than stew or coddle. There was stuff that would make a cardiac specialist blanch. Bread and butter sprinkled with sugar. Beyond the fry-ups, the tangled rounds of black and white pudding, the sheets of ribs, the Hafner sausages and rashers, there was fried bread: bread dipped in dripping, fried on the pan, sopping with artery-choking cholesterol. My Uncle Larry loved it. He lived into his eighties.

Some families used butter, some used margarine, and the choice had nothing to do with cholesterol. Butter was real, margarine was the cheap imitation. To buy marg was to admit to a certain level of poverty. We used butter.

Cream floated to the top of the milk bottle and before you opened the bottle you had to shake it, to dilute the cream. They've refined things long since, but on the rare occasion I open a bottle rather than a carton of milk I still find myself shaking it to disturb the non-existent cream. Few families had fridges and milk was never cold, except when you took it in from the front step on a winter morning. Butter was never hard.

If you stayed home from school, not feeling the best, you maybe got a treat: bread and milk. The bread softened in hot milk, with sugar stirred in. What that didn't cure would be taken care of by Milk of Magnesia or Syrup of Figs. If you needed a pick-me-up you might get an egg flip, a raw egg in cold milk, stirred energetically and swallowed quickly. It was almost worth feeling unwell to get to enjoy an egg flip. Today, I would no more swallow a raw egg than I would ski naked on two slices of fried bread across an acre of limp cabbage.

At school, when we were finished rubbing brawn in one another's faces we drew our swords. Our foot-long wooden rulers doubled as swords, our schoolbags as shields. You could use your schoolbag as a weapon, too. Holding it by a strap and flailing around with it. When the metal bit on the end of the other strap connected with a knuckle or a cheek it produced a satisfying yelp of pain.

The schoolbags were all the same, rectangular leather-effect bags, mini briefcases, with straps for around our shoulders. Schoolkids today carry multicolour schoolbags, each different, each chosen as a tiny element of self-expression. Some are decorated with colourful emblems of allegiance to football clubs and pop groups. Some of them look like the kind of thing you'd wear on your back if you were going up Everest. One schoolbag that was briefly popular had printed on it a half-decomposed face, bloodshot eyes, one eye dangling from its socket, attached to the bag by a bit of string that was supposed to be some kind of gristle connecting the eye to the face. To those of us reared in the monochrome 1950s, such garish artefacts are products of the Enlightenment.

As well as schoolbags and rulers, compasses were sometimes used as weapons. The compass had a sharp point. I never wielded one, nor did any of my pals. There were enough borderline psychopaths, kids with a dangerous lack of imagination, to do that. The willingness to use a compass point as a weapon was one of the defining lines. Those guys you stayed away from as much as possible. Without anyone discussing it, we separated into the run-of-the-mill kids, and those who would go one or more crazy steps further than made sense to the rest of us. It made sense to them to win a fight by kicking someone in the head. It made sense to them to use a sharp, pointed object if they wanted to frighten someone. It didn't occur to them to think of what the point of a compass could do to flesh, imagining the possible consequences was beyond them. We all got a few jabs, only very occasionally was a compass waved in the real.

Fighting was either in the real or in the cod. Sometimes a fight would start, the stretching of young limbs, the frisking of young males testing their strength. And the question would be asked: 'Is this in the real or in the cod?'

Almost always it was in the cod. Which meant no drawing blood, all punches pulled, no gouging, no serious kicking. If it was in the real no one ever had to say it, there was no decent interval in which the question could be posed. It was just up and at him, slash and kick and gouge and do your best to kill.

'Are you looking at me?'

'No.'

'Are you calling me a liar?'

There was no way out, if the headcase wanted a fight.

'Don't come down this road again, right? Or I'll do you, right?'

Bewildered, you asked, 'Why?'

'Cos, that's why.'

The half-hour break in the middle of the school day, when all the classes emptied out into the schoolyard, was the appointed time for most of the less serious battles. The masters took turns playing camp guard, but one adult overseeing a couple of hundred kids was never going to keep the peace. Day after day, scores were settled, serial battles recommenced, and if we didn't have a reason for a scrap we made one up. We fought like uncoordinated windmills, our fists lashing out until something connected. The best tactic was to grab your opponent and overbalance the two of you, hoping you landed on top, knocking the wind out of him. We'd heard of uppercuts but wouldn't know a left hook from a right cross. There were two punches with which we were familiar. The rabbit punch, a vicious blow delivered in a chopping motion to the back of the neck, the side of the hand acting like a blade. It's a deadly punch (as far as we knew, rightly or wrongly, it was the manner in which professional rabbit killers despatched rabbits) and we used it casually on one another. The other punch was known as a deadener. You formed a fist, the middle knuckle slightly raised, and you punched your victim high up on the outside of the arm, aiming for a nerve which, when struck hard, virtually paralysed the arm. Sometimes the knuckle didn't reach the nerve, but it still hurt.

I can't remember why Gerry and I were scheduled to fight. We had insulted one another, perhaps, or maybe it was just our turn. We were part of the same gang, Joe Murphy's outfit. The gang had its scraps with outsiders, and internally we had all at various times had a go at one another. No one ever got seriously hurt, no one ever held a grudge. It was just fighting in the cod.

The one certain thing was that Gerry was going to get a hiding. Not because I was particularly good at fighting—I wasn't—but because Gerry was spectacularly bad. Gerry was so bad, such an awkward, uncoordinated fighter, that he really should have known better than to ever get into a scrap. But to be known for chickening out was more painful than any number of bruises, so Gerry faced up to his responsibilities and took his share of punching and gouging and Gerry always lost.

We found a quiet corner of the yard, during the midday break, and squared up, our mutual friends forming a loose ring. I had recently read a story, in the *Rover*, I think, or maybe the *Wizard*, in which the hero had adopted a fighting technique which stunned his opponent. He kept his guard loose, let the opponent come forward and forward again, the hero taking whatever the opponent could dish out. Then, when the opponent had grown over-confident and exposed his chin, the hero delivered one devastating uppercut and it was all over.

I had decided that this was a fine, noble and stylish way to fight. As the fight got going, Gerry hung back, dancing and weaving, knowing that as soon as we joined battle he was going to get his usual thumping. To his surprise, I offered him my chin, enticing him forward. As if scenting a trap, he tentatively advanced. I dropped my guard, let him see more of my chin. He hit me. I was delighted. Things were going according to plan.

He hit me again. That's it, Gerry, come forward, sucker, see how easy it is. He hit me again. I was by now almost sniggering at the success of my strategy. The poor fool didn't know what he was walking himself into. He hit me again, and my nose felt like it had been pushed right back into my face. Gerry was by now just about as confident as I needed him to be in order to deliver the killer punch. Time to put him down. He hit me again. My arms were heavy and weren't moving as fast as my mind was urging them. My knockout punch was an aimless swipe. He hit me again. By now Gerry couldn't believe his good fortune. All his caution and fear were discarded, he was up on his toes, coming forward, throwing punches, as I tried to figure what had gone wrong with the script. The rest of the fight we need not linger over. As I licked my wounds, and the rest of the gang marvelled at how Gerry had

43

actually won a fight, I considered trying to explain to them that it wasn't that I was a lousier fighter than Gerry, it was just that I had this plan, you see, I'd read about it in a comic book, and . . . and I decided that I didn't need to look stupid as well as a crappy fighter, so I kept my mouth shut.

Most of the fighting was on that level, only a few got into serious blood sports. While playing our games, we had to beware the school's borderline psychopaths, for whom violence was always in the real. Their favourite game during the midday break was throwing kids into the Dungeon. This was a dirty, smelly area down five or six steps, at the back of the school hall. You might be trotting past, your mind elsewhere, and you were suddenly grabbed and pushed, your feet trying desperately to find purchase on the tarmacadam and then you were at the top of the steps, a final push and you were flying through the air, landing awkwardly, maybe falling over into the dirt, maybe twisting an ankle. There was an open shore down in the Dungeon and it was hard not to end up with one foot or the other down the shore, your shoe and sock soaked in dark, foul, smelly water. If you got captured at the beginning of the midday break you spent the whole half-hour down in the Dungeon. Any attempt to escape up the steps and into the open was met with a boot in the chest or the face. You and the other three or four captives shamefacedly ignoring one another, waiting for the bell to ring and hoping that if the psychopaths delivered a farewell shower of spit into the Dungeon the gollier wouldn't get you in the face.

If it's in the real, violence is never cutesy or dramatic, as it is in fiction. Back then, you were threatened, by a look or a word, and you backed down or it happened. If you heard someone giving a warning, that if you don't do this or do that they'd beat you up, that's when you knew they were all mouth.

When fighting in the real was on the agenda you ended up face to face for a few seconds, chin to chin. You had a choice to make and it went like this: do I hit him first?

Hit him and there was no going back. If you hit him the chances were he was more used to this than you and he'd take the thump and he'd hit you back and you'd better be prepared to take pain, real pain, real punches and kicks and tearing of flesh. And you had to know that if it was one of the borderline psychopaths, one of the thickos who thrived on this kind of thing, you were going to end up splattered. If you were the kind of kid who had to think this out you were already in trouble. Because the psychopaths never had to think about it.

If you were head to head for a few seconds and either you didn't back down, show deference, or you didn't hit him, he hit you. Just like that: smack. Maybe a loaf in the face. (A loaf was a head. Rhyming slang. Loaf of bread—Head. So, a loaf in the face is a forehead smacking you full-force in the nose, the eye.) And sometimes that was it, it was all over. One fierce, damaging blow to the face, a bloody nose or lip, your teeth cutting the inside of your mouth, and that was the end of it, you were crying and he was giving you a final contemptuous kick in the arse and that was that.

When violence is in the real, all weapons being equal, victory goes to the thickest, the least sensitive. That applies now that we're adults just as it did when we were kids. The least sensitive is least able to imagine—and therefore fear—the consequences of violence, least likely to wince and draw back when inflicting pain. Least likely to consider the effects, on himself or his opponent, of a loaf in the face. Lacking the fear that makes the rest of us pause, he is more likely to lash out first, delivering the first damaging, possibly disabling, blow. While you hesitate, while you wonder if you can talk or threaten your way out of trouble, he hits you.

Violence is seductive, and if you're a big, thick borderline psychopath, it can be a form of self-expression. It can be something you're good at, something that earns you a kind of respect. In Chazz Palminteri's A Bronx Tale, the kid asks his father: is it better to be loved or feared? We all know the right answer to that one. But if respect and love are thin on the ground, it's hard to blame some of the borderline psychopaths opting for fear as a tribute to their strength. And every day in school they learned the lesson, from

45

listening to the swish of a bamboo cane, that violence is part of what we are, violence is how we solve things.

Violence is seductive. Inver Road, one afternoon, a pal and I bopping along, doing nothing in particular. From a garden a couple of kids we know to see, maybe a year or so younger, insult us. It's strictly in the cod. They want a chase, a mock fight. They run, split up, my pal goes after one, I go after another, he catches his, I catch mine and we wrestle them to the ground and the way it should go now is: I say, 'Okay?', and he says, 'Okay.' 'Give up?' And he gives up.

My pal is delivering his demand: 'Okay?', and the captured quarry shows obeisance. 'Okay.'

'Give up?'

'Give up.'

I apply the same demand to my captured quarry.

'Okay?'

And he makes a face.

'Okay?'

A face, a giggle. He isn't obeying the rules.

I thump him high up on the arm. A deadener.

'Okay?'

He hesitates, about to say 'Okay', then he makes an insulting noise with his tongue and giggles again.

I hit him high up on the arm. His expression tightens, he isn't giving in.

I hit him high up on the arm. No give.

Hit him again. No give.

Hit him again, same place, same spot, where it must be aching by now, where there must by now be a cluster of bruises. No give.

And we are locked into this fucking awful demand and response thing and he isn't playing the game and there is almost pleading in my voice when I say it again, 'Okay?', and he spits. I hit him high up on the arm again and his face is red, joke's over, and he's fucked if he's going to give in now, and what am I to do, let him go and watch him skip away making ya-ya noises?

High up on the arm. Nothing.

Again. By now, hating his obstinacy, hating him for trapping me in this thing.

'Okay?'

'Bollocks.'

Thump. 'Okay?'

Red face, tight lips, silence.

High up on the arm, same place, hard. No response.

Another one and he'll give. Smack.

Nothing but bitter silence.

Another one.

And he cries. His face crumples and his eyes scrunch up and the tears come out and he howls and I say something like 'Yes!' And my pal is standing behind me and he says, 'Ah Jesus.' And I stand up, feeling like shit. The kid lying there, crying, holding his arm. I walk away with my pal and the kid sobs after me, 'Fucker', and he's right and it feels far worse than the time I got a thumping from one of the borderline psychopaths.

I never, ever did anything like that again, I'd never done it before. I can still feel the shame. What if my pal had urged me on? What if we'd been away from streets and houses and the potential intervention of grownups? What if the kid remained obstinate? What if?

*　*　*

In June 1963 we did the exams for our Primary School Certificate. They were minimal exams. I still have my Primary Cert, an English version on one side, and the Irish version on the other, testifying that Eoin Ó Ciarragáin passed his Primary Cert exam and received certificate number 1350. Near the bottom of the certificate there is a note on 'the subjects of the prescribed programme of instruction for the sixth standard in national schools'. These were:

Obligatory subjects: Irish, English, Mathematics, History, Geography, Music, Needlework (Girls).

Optional subjects: Drawing, Physical Training, Rural Science or Nature Study, Cookery (Girls), Laundry Work (Girls) or Domestic Economy (Girls), Manual Instruction (Boys).

We did none of the optional subjects. Although we got minimal instruction in history and geography, mostly we learned the basics of English, Irish and arithmetic. The claim that we had been instructed in music was pure fiction. Although religion took up two and a half hours a week of our school time it wasn't mentioned on the Primary Certificate, nor was it a subject in the exam. It wasn't mentioned because there was no need to mention it, it was as much a part of our schooling as the classroom furniture.

* * *

Hold on: maybe we did learn something about music. A memory hovers, just out of reach. The Feis Ceoil. I don't know what the Feis was (is, it's still going), except that it was part of the Real Ireland's culture, a place where kids went and took turns singing and playing music and someone won and the rest lost and I know I was there once. I waited my turn and then I stood up in front of everyone and sang a song in Irish and I don't know who won but it wasn't me. Then I went home. And that was that.

I have no idea what I sang or why, what the process was that resulted in me going to the Feis Ceoil, but it must have had something to do with school. I remember learning how to sing hymns—one side of the room starts and the other waits a few bars, then joins in—but have no memory of where this happened or under whose tutelage. There wasn't a lot of extracurricular activity at St Finbar's. Maybe we were taken to the Feis as some kind of treat. Doesn't seem likely.

We had, in the entirety of my schooling, one single school outing. It was an aspect of schooling that may well have developed in later years, but for the kids from Room 4 that was it. Today, kids regularly get to visit here and there almost as a matter of routine;

they go to see how farms work, they go to the zoo, they go to factories. Our one and only day out was to the Regal cinema, in town, to which we travelled in a special bus. We got off two by two and were marched up into the darkness, where we took our seats and watched a Spanish film, with subtitles, about a young boy who was raised by monks and who shared his meagre food with a little statue of Jesus and the statue accepted and ate the bread. The film was called *The Miracle of Marcelino*, and at the end the camera panned slowly upwards towards a glowing light as the saint-like Marcelino died and went to heaven, a great example to us all. We were very moved by it and for a while I wanted to die and go to heaven so that everyone would admire me.

It was in black and white. But then, in the Catholic Ireland of the 1950s, wasn't everything?

*   *   *

Here's how important the Primary Certificate was. The year I did the exam, 1963, around 54,000 of us left primary education. Roughly 10 per cent failed the exam, and 10 per cent were noted as absent on the day of the exam. Did this mean that about 80 per cent of us passed? It did not. About 53 per cent of that year's school leavers simply vanished from the records. The education we were getting was so loosely controlled, was held in such low regard by the authorities, that thousands simply drifted out of the system without any attention being paid to their going. Less than 30 per cent of national school leavers came out with a Primary Cert, the lowest certificate of education.

The education setup over which the network of parish priests and bishops had presided since the nineteenth century didn't care very much about such matters. The families of kids from the appropriate class would have sufficient resources to pay for a secondary education (clerically controlled) and those destined to run the country, the professions, business and the civil service, would go on to university. For the rest of us, minimal education standards would suffice for the emigration boat or the grinding, dead-end jobs for which we were destined.

What mattered to the parish priests and the patrons of the schools, the bishops, was the two and a half hours a week of religious instruction designed to instil in us the guilt, fear and loyalty which would for the rest of our lives tether us to the Church. The parish priests weren't too fussy about ensuring that the schools they ran kept us up to the minimal Primary Cert standard. Neither were the politicians or the Department of Education. And when half the pupils vanished from the records before the Primary Cert exam, well, at least their immortal souls would be washed in the tide of the waters flowing from the Saviour's side.

Primary Cert exam over, we went into our summer break and I didn't return in the autumn. There was no big ending, no goodbyes, we just split up as usual for the summer and some of us never went back. Years later, I went to Finbar's for a charity concert (starring Dickie Rock, a local who never turned down a request to help out the old parish). The school seemed so small, far smaller than I remembered. It loomed so large in my memory and now I realised you could walk from one end of it to the other in less time than it took Dickie to sing a couple of verses of the one about the candy store on the corner and the chapel on the hill. (We from Cabra West, when Dickie's record hit the charts, knew that he was singing about the distance from Prenderville's shop to the Church of the Most Precious Blood.)

These are the best years of your life, the adults told us. We laughed derisively, our hands red from the cane, our heads stuffed with bits of Irish, our evenings ruined by ecker, the niggling knowledge that the threatened confrontation with that gobshite from Ventry Road could not be put off much longer. To an extent, the grownups were, of course, right. Our childhood years were years of simplicity, when pure happiness could come instantly and unalloyed; from a small surprise, from a momentary triumph in a game; from a private moment when a tricky juggling move or a one-hand-assisted leap over a fence was mastered; in the hour before dawn on Christmas morning, when you felt overwhelmed by the riches at the foot of your bed. For those of us with stable home lives they were safe years, when you knew that just about any problem could be offloaded onto a grownup (except the confrontation with the gobshite from Ventry Road; stuff like that you had to handle yourself, bringing parents into it only made things worse). We weren't then aware of the bigger picture, of the determination of the forces working relentlessly to instil into us their stagnant 'ethos'. We weren't conscious of the moulding process, of the limitations hemming us in, the insistence on guilt and deference. Such things were as taken-for-granted as the lino beneath our feet.

Time gives our childhood a glow. Grown up ourselves, and enmeshed in the million pressures, demands and compromises of adulthood, we now find it easy to agree with what the grownups then said about those being the best years of our lives. Perspective, though, also lets us see the darker shadows surrounding the glow, and allows us see something of what was going on inside those shadows. There were other childhoods, threads of which were linked to ours. The hard chaws, swaggering through the schoolyard, or contemptuously going AWOL, on gur, living rough and coming home inevitably, to take a hiding. Heroes to our innocent eyes, urban Huckleberry Finns. In truth, desperate children being not raised but dragged up in shitty circumstances. Their lives were bordered by drink, violence, neglect. It happened at every level in society, but on the closeknit Corporation estates you knew whose father was waiting impatiently for the pub to open on Sunday morning; you knew which kids had the run of the streets; you knew whose health was neglected because his parents were too poor to buy treatment or too ignorant to seek it out, and the state had no role in such matters.

Kids learn from adults the limits of acceptable behaviour. The borderline psychopaths didn't learn about violence from watching *Reservoir Dogs*. They didn't learn about it from television or video nasties or any of the other handy excuses we have today. The lessons about the role of violence in establishing one's place in the world were written on the smacked child's face, his bruised legs, his reddened arse. And, courtesy of the state, on his stinging palms at school. On the fringe of our world there were the industrial schools, the factories of discipline. We didn't know the detail but we knew about them and we knew they were places of brutality and the adults mentioned them as places where the bold boys went. (Bold boys ended up in Artane school; big bold boys, real hard chaws, ended up in the Mountjoy prison we passed in the bus every time we were brought into town. The bold went to Artane or Mountjoy, the mad to Grangegorman.) All this was part of the scenery. The other stuff—the kids being pawed and raped, by their biological fathers and by fathers of the cloth, the secret sicknesses that wouldn't be talked about for decades, the abuse of orphans, the secret arrangements to export bastard kids—all that was as alien to us as the dark side of the moon, we who were living through the best years of our lives.

* * *

I saw Mr McAuliffe once after leaving school, a few years later, in a bookie shop in Sackville Place, where I went to put on a bet for my mother. He was standing there studying form, sucking hard on a tiny butt of a cigarette. I thought of saying something to him, but how would he remember one pupil from so many? And, somehow, it felt as if catching him here, in a gambling den, might have been embarrassing for him. So, I turned away, did my business and left. I've often wished I said hello.

Leaving school, most of us had little sense of purpose, no real sense of choice. We would take what turned up. The notion of choosing or planning a career just never occurred to us. We knew our place. And so did everyone else. The middle classes accepted— then as now—that their offspring would by right go to university, no matter how thick they were, and choose a course in life. Education has hugely improved, but the structure and aim remain the same: to filter out the superfluous, to grade the rest.

At Mass in the Church of the Most Precious Blood one Sunday, standing along the wall on the right-hand side of the church, every pew crammed, every bit of standing space at the back of the church packed, I listened to a priest ask for prayers for children of the parish sitting an exam the following week. Let us pray, he said, that each and every one of them passes the exam. It occurred to me that he was kidding himself. The function of exams is not to have pupils pass them but to have them fail, to weed out a percentage. Only so many pupils are needed at the next stage of education. If everyone passed they'd simply raise the height of the hurdle, to ensure that there was the required percentage of failures.

I can see the church, the packed pews, I could go back today and point out exactly where I was standing when this occurred to me. I can't remember which had the greater effect, the realisation of how the education system works or the realisation that the priest's prayers were meaningless.

The function of the education system, now as then, is to equip kids for their role in life—politics, the professions, the civil service, business, trades or the shit-shovelling levels at which work is poorly paid and provides little personal satisfaction. The multi-tiered education system is designed to service the supply of labour to the various levels of society. There is some crossover from one social class to another, but it is random, accidental and doesn't affect the structural inequality. Kids from St Finbar's today have little better chance of a third-level education—and all that goes with it, the contacts, the networking, the choice of career—than they did then.

The middle classes live with this by convincing themselves that there is something inherent, perhaps even genetic, in the way in which the various classes find their own levels.

In 1963 no less than 45 per cent of those doing their first-year university exams failed. The universities had the job of educating the progeny of the middle classes to a standard sufficient for filling the clerical, banking, civil service and professional positions in a moribund society. The students, as the exam results show, weren't the brightest, but they had access to higher education by virtue of their family resources and had gone on to secondary school and then third level, steered onto the path to a comfortable career. The middle classes had—and have—it sewn up. The offspring of manual workers got 2 per cent of university places.

Come to think of it, if you work out the dates, many of those sons of the middle classes who hobbled over the low academic hurdles of the time must over the past twenty years or so have been filling the higher reaches of the professions and of public administration. It explains a lot.

For the rest of us, the thing to do when you escaped national school was get a job, any job, and the miracle was that there were some jobs to be got. Whatever job you managed to get determined the shape and content of your working life. Most of my generation in my neighbourhood seemed to manage to stay in Ireland, though kids coming onto the labour market before us and after us weren't so lucky. The economic changes were having an effect, factories were opening up behind Bannow Road, where the Batchelors Foods factory had for years been a source of employment. Some would emigrate for a while, then return as things picked up and there were jobs to be had. Almost every family had big brothers who had emigrated, usually to Britain, a few years earlier and had put down roots and never came back. Up to then, emigration had been as natural as leaving school at fourteen, it was part of our heritage.

I spent four months or so in Tech, waiting to turn fourteen and for a job to turn up, then I dropped out and went to work at the Cabra Grand cinema, where my Uncle Larry was chief projectionist. Technical school was a wonderland of educational possibilities compared with national school, where Mr McAuliffe taught us everything ('and still they gazed and still their wonder grew, that one small head could carry all he knew'). At Tech there were different teachers for each subject. Some teachers took two subjects, some one. There was neat stuff such as woodwork and metalwork and science. Mr Hingerty taught woodwork, and since his name was Hingerty and he had a habit of drumming a ruler on the bench and since the Beatles were all over the pop charts just then and their drummer was Ringo Starr, Mr Hingerty was known as Hingo. He was cool, knowledgeable, amiable.

'What's the name of the British royal family?' I can't remember which teacher asked it or why, but no hands went up. No one in the class had a clue. I knew. Windsor, that was their name. And I was about to put my hand up and something made me pause, some lack of confidence that made me doubt that I would be the one kid in the whole class to have the answer. 'Windsor', said the teacher, my hand stalled halfway up, my heart plunging. Over thirty years later I hear the name Windsor and I feel a tiny—really small, believe me, it's hardly worth mentioning, no big deal, it's not like it means anything anymore, I swear—twinge of regret somewhere deep down.

One sneering, superior, nasty little louser taught us both Irish and English. His pretensions were pathetic. He told us of how, when he recently bought a car, he insisted that the garage remove its sticker from the back window. 'I won't be labelled', he intoned, with all the gravity of Spartacus giving cheek to the Roman Empire. He loved teaching Irish, hated English but had to teach it. He said things like: 'Sentences are made up of individual words, each carefully placed alongside the next, like pearls on a string.' Only people who can't write for nuts think up nonsense like that. Amongst ourselves, we rendered him a figure of fun by mocking the tuft of hair that stood out from each side of his balding head, like wings.

For religious instruction we had the nice priest.

* * *

The nice priest. Young. Idealistic. He'd thought it through and he was part of an awakening Ireland, an Ireland that rejected the old authoritarianism. He wanted to help, he wanted to be part of the solution. Not for him the role of the sterile priest of old, riding shotgun on a subservient laity. This was the end of 1963, the young priest set off on his mission of enlightenment around the same time as the Second Vatican Council opened. This was a new-style priest, one of a type that would blossom throughout the 1960s and 1970s. In historical terms, the Catholic Church was adapting to a changing audience, allowing its younger agents to express themselves in a way that might better match the mood of the times. In personal terms, this young priest was a fresh, open mind, a soul yearning to help us enhance our spirituality within a changing, questioning society.

He couldn't have been long out of the moulding process. We were, I think, his first class. He wasn't there to hand down meaningless pieties to be learned by rote. He talked to us. He wanted to get us talking in the vernacular of the day about eternal truths. He didn't try to put us on edge by frowning that too-familiar priestly frown. He smiled a lot. It seemed no matter what happened he smiled. Outside, he wore an anorak over his suit and collar. In class, he didn't sit or stand behind his desk, he came forward, mingled with us, sat on top of an empty desk halfway down the classroom, his feet on the seat, a pamphlet or textbook open in front of him, to be used or discarded as he thought best, depending on how the lesson went. His sleeves rolled up. Smiling, open to dialogue. He wanted to be our friend.

We ate him alive.

We treated him like shit. We laughed and we talked and we ignored him. He smiled. He said things like, 'Come on now, lads.'

'Ah, lads', he appealed, as we continued talking as though he wasn't there.

It must have been hell for him. He wanted nothing but good for us, he wanted to approach us on our terms, he respected us. And we laughed in his face. Every now and then he put on a stern expression and told us to sit down, to pay attention, but before long he was saying things like, 'Ah, please, lads, come on, now . . .'

What was he going to do? He couldn't hit us. He wasn't going to report us to the Head, the whole roomful of us. That wouldn't be a friendly thing to do and he wanted to be our friend. And—

looking back on it now—it wouldn't have reflected very well on him.

So he took it, and when I quit Tech after a few months he was still taking it and I don't know how that all ended. Not badly, I hope.

He offered friendship, we smelled weakness. All our lives men in collars, women in wimples, they were authority, they told us what to do and we couldn't imagine them taking no for an answer. This young priest, he wasn't just a victim of a bullying class of brats, he was a victim of every priest who had made us feel small and vulnerable, who had treated us as low-ranking soldiers in the army of God. Who had treated us without respect.

Now we had a priest who didn't enforce the authority which came with his position. We mistook love for vulnerability and we seized him by the throat. He came to us with his arms open and he didn't think it mattered that he was wearing the uniform of dominance. Whatever his good intentions, he really shouldn't have expected us, the longterm subjects of spiritual martial law, to respond positively to this new democracy.

I think of him every now and then and wonder did our rejection make him change, did it turn him into a harsh priest of the old type. He was little more than a kid doing his best. I hope we didn't damage him.

*   *   *

Flicking through some of the schoolbooks of the day, those which randomly survived the years and the moves and the clearouts. Nothing too special. There's a rather boring geography book. *A General Geography, For Senior Standards.* Published by Browne & Nolan Ltd. It covers the whole world, starting from The Earth as a Globe and working through Ireland, Britain, Europe and the US to Africa and Australasia. It's full of Extent and Population statistics, lists of mountains and rivers, lots of stuff about climate and mineral wealth. There's a picture of the Leaning Tower of Pisa and there's a paragraph about the River Po, which we all thought was very funny, because a po was what was kept under your bed when you were very young, for you to piss in during the night. There are terse stipulations, facts and figures about Religion and Education and Industry and Agriculture, and other exciting stuff.

It tells us there are 'close on two million Europeans' in South Africa, but it doesn't tell us how many blacks. Black people were, like Protestants, unfortunates who deserved our charity. We had two boxes on our windowsill at national school: one for donations to Little Willie, a polio charity; the other for donations to help the Black Babies in far-off Africa. In our *General Geography*, under Peoples, we were told, with the confidence appropriate to a superior race which sent missionaries out to save the Black Babies for Jesus:

The present populations of Australia and New Zealand are of European stock, chiefly English, Scottish and Irish. The native inhabitants of Australia, many of whom are still in the country, are of a very low order of intelligence, but those of New Zealand, the Maori, are highly intelligent.

* * *

At Tech, they didn't hit us. Violence was reserved for national school. And one day I did something or didn't do something and it was time to show me who was boss and the teacher told me to stand up. He was a confident type, a seasoned pro, none of the let's-be-friends crack about him. He began to needle me, to mock me. With his adult skills, his facility with words, his ability to wield sarcasm, he could twist me and turn me on the spot, and he did.

I remember nothing of the detail of that incident except one aching wish that filled my mind. I was humiliated, red-faced, willing him to end it, please let me sit down, pick on someone else. I hadn't the necessary verbal skills to protect myself, my ego, my pride, from the relentless, contemptuous assault. And I remember wishing with all my heart that it was like it used to be in national school. That I could just hold out my hand and take the pain and let it be over. When you're determined to hurt a kid, you don't have to have a cane to do it.

Three

Woke up this morning, Monday 25 November, to the news that Michael O'Hehir died yesterday. Radio, TV and the newspapers are full of tributes and there is a warmth to them that goes beyond the usual routine expressions of sympathy. They're calling him 'the voice of sport', but he was very much more than that. Michael was part of the aural scenery in that other country where we grew up. The unmistakeable voice, a verbal Gatling gun grinding out at ferocious speed an unceasing stream of adjectives and nouns from radios across the land.

Michael O'Hehir was a summer Sunday. Families sitting out the back, catching some sun, several radios in the neighbourhood blaring out through open windows Michael's commentary on the GAA game of the day. The newspapers would print little diagrams in the shape of a playing field, with the names of the players of each team printed in the position in which they would play that day. I would sit near the radio with the diagram in front of me, imagining the scene as O'Hehir told of the ball going from one player to another, and me trying to visualise from the diagram an approximation of where on the pitch the action might be.

It never mattered much whether it was hurling or football. It was the thrill of the event that we enjoyed. Even those of us who developed little love for either game loved the event. And it was his central role as the link between the event and the rest of us, in every corner of the land, that made Michael O'Hehir more than a sports commentator. His sense of enjoyment of the games elevated him above the petty concerns of the Real Irelanders. He was the best-loved voice in the country. Gay Byrne might become more central, more influential, but many were wary of Gaybo for one reason or another. Some thought him an agent of the devil whose mission it was to disrupt a cosy Catholic Ireland. Others saw him as a Catholic loyalist, a moderniser helping the Church survive in an era of drastic change, an apologist for the Christian Brothers. He was too left wing, too right wing, too this or too that. Michael O'Hehir, though, never put anyone's nose out of joint. If something nasty happened on the pitch he would draw a euphemism over it and find something nice to talk about while a defender's teeth were being removed from a forward's inner thigh. Even those who came to dislike this covering up for the unhealthy aspects of the game saw Michael not as a deceiver but as a gentle man who wanted to see the world as a gentle place.

I saw him once, way, way back, in my late teens, back in the days of the CIE buses with open platforms at the rear. I was standing on the platform of a 22, waiting to get off when the bus reached the stop in Dame Street. He was in a car stopped at the lights at the bottom of Church Lane, whether driving or in the passenger seat I can't remember. As the bus moved past I caught his eye, recognised him, and instinctively nodded, as though I had come across a friend or neighbour. Just as instinctively, he nodded back.

Years later, in 1985, Michael O'Hehir had a stroke and was taken to the Mater hospital. I had good reason to know the place. Eileen, my aunt, who with my mother had raised me, had just died in there, of the second of two strokes. Sister Joan, a wonderful nurse, helped Eileen through her terrible weeks in the Mater and gently dealt with we whose lives were drenched in fear of what was about to happen. On the morning Eileen died the inevitable priest was assigned to comfort my mother and me, sitting on a bench at the end of a corridor. He was a nice young man, younger than me, and it seemed just slightly embarrassing to be calling him Father. He genuinely wanted to help us in our pain, but he seemed uncomfortable with our grief and I had to assure him that we were okay. Eileen had been five weeks in hospital and we had been hoping for the best but prepared for the worst. We had made a mantra of that phrase: hope for the best, prepare for the worst.

After a while the priest wished us well and left, probably hoping that he had been of help and aware that his technique needed some work. His compassion was genuine, not professional, and the awkwardness came through. I ended up, roles reversed, worrying that the occasion might have upset him.

Shortly after that Michael O'Hehir had his stroke and was taken to the Mater. I read about his plight and although I knew nothing about them I felt I knew what his family were going through. In the weeks before Eileen's second stroke I had read up on the treatment of stroke survivors, the constant care they need, the fear that if they aren't sufficiently exercised each day their limbs might curl up. It seemed like a dreadful regime for both the patient and the carers but that wouldn't have mattered if only Eileen survived. We would help her recover, however long it took. We constantly asked the doctors when they would let her home, she hated being in hospital, and one day a doctor said he was thinking more of the hospice than home, and a few days later she was gone.

Michael O'Hehir survived and I remember silently cheering him on and envying his family for getting to take him home. And he lived on for eleven years. Not a great quality of life, and maybe Michael himself was not to be envied. But they had him for another eleven years.

* * *

Beechinor's, the local newsagents, with a post office in at the back, and me standing there doing my Michael O'Hehir imitation. I was maybe six or seven, had never seen a Gaelic match of any kind, hadn't a clue what Michael O'Hehir was chattering on about, but his voice was so much a part of our lives that I could do a reasonable impression of the non-stop outpouring of words. I was talking gibberish, a rush of meaningless sound all strung together. To me it sounded just like O'Hehir. The shoppers, mostly housewives, smiled indulgently. Eileen, my aunt, smiled proudly.

Years later, as an older schoolboy, I got a chance to go to Croke

Park (or Croe Park, as it was always known, we never pronounced the 'k'). At St Finbar's we had some small experience of hurling but for some of us the prospect of wading into a throng of bowsies wielding lengths of wood with metal bands wrapped around them wasn't the most appealing thing on offer. My involvement was peripheral, and I retain but one memory of a prematch briefing in which the grownup in charge gave us some advice, demonstrating how to use the hurley to hook away the ball, frustrating our opponents. 'If you can't get the ball', he added, bleakly, 'get the man.'

Figuring that in another room somewhere another adult was giving our opponents similar advice, and being very much attached to my shins, I decided in or around that time that I could live a fairly productive life without partaking in the great national game.

One summer, perhaps because of Mr McAuliffe's GAA connections, some of us in the school got a shot at selling programmes outside the weekly matches, on commission. You arrived at Croke Park before noon, with your schoolbag. At the GAA offices you queued up and eventually one of the officials took your name and gave you a bundle of programmes and you stuffed them into your schoolbag and off you went, to stand outside the grounds, bawling the availability of 'official programmes'. The sales tempo increased as the minor match kicked off, the crowds swelled and the queues grew longer. When the punters stopped coming you went to the office and paid in the money and got your commission. Then you got to go up into the stand and crouch down on the steps and watch the remainder of the match.

The GAA was a huge presence within the community, a centre of culture for many. For some of us, it was a big, strange culchie outfit, one of the pillars that kept in place the strict Ireland in which you were expected to be grateful for the received truths handed down to you. We who were distanced from the Gaelic world, the Real Ireland, were considered something less than truly Irish—and we knew it. To be indifferent—as we were—to the first official language and to the native game was to be doubly unIrish.

We didn't dislike the GAA, no more than we disliked the Catholic Church, or the Irish language fanatics. They were all just there, looming, insistent, not so much demanding but assuming allegiance. The culchie GAA men, the Gaeilgeoirí, the parish priests, the Real Irish, there was a sameness about them, a sameness of arrogant presumption, a parochial sameness they shared with the old men in dark suits who ran the country. They shared grim, fervent ideas about the narrow little world in which we were to be moulded. And how that world should be policed, through fear, through pain, through guilt. And they ruthlessly sought to make their dreams come true.

The Catholic Church denounced dancing, usually meaning foreign dances where people wriggled and swayed a bit more than was good for the immortal soul. (The bishops approved of Irish dancing as it was energetic and would wear out the dancers, hopefully making them too tired to do anything else. 'Irish dances', the hierarchy announced in 1925, 'do not make for degenerates.') The GAA, too, slagged off foreign dances, concerned not so much for the souls of its members as for their Irishness. The GAA expelled any member who dared play or even attend soccer or rugby or hockey or cricket games. The ban was enforced, and not just for small-fry members. In 1938 the President of Ireland, Douglas Hyde, got the bum's rush from his position as patron of the GAA because he had the impudence to attend, in his official capacity, a soccer match at Dalymount Park. The ban would be carried into the 1970s, at which time it would be laughed out of existence.

(The Real Irish were very proud of themselves for having installed a Protestant as the first President. But Hyde caused some embarrassment to our great leader Eamon de Valera. When Hyde died his funeral services were held in Christ Church Cathedral and Dev, aware of the Catholic bishops' ruling that condemned to eternal damnation all Catholics who attended non-Catholic services, waited outside until the service was over and the funeral continued.)

For those of us from St Finbar's who got the gig selling match programmes at Croker, the GAA was an opportunity to make a little money, and to engage in semi-adult activity, to take a step away from childhood. For the first time, I was meeting culchies galore, masses of them, red-faced men in caps and overcoats, men in boots, men with thick culchie accents. To my great surprise, and somewhat disconcerting for my prejudiced view of our culchie brethren, it was the culchies who were most generous with tips. 'Cape de change, bhoy', they'd cheerfully say, while my fellow Dubliners waited grimly for every last penny to be counted out.

It was my first experience of work, my first earned income, a toe inside the world of the grownups. Your arms tired as you held up the programmes, your voice became hoarse as you shouted your wares, but at the end of the afternoon there would be money in your pocket. One Sunday, after a few weeks at this, I flogged every one of my allotted programmes and with my fellow sellers went to the office where we awaited the financial calculations and the determination of our commission. The official on the other side of the table, his dark oily hair brushed over in a quiff, glanced at the ledger in front of him and told me that according to the records I had been given several dozen more programmes than I knew I had received. The money I was due to pay in was more than the total I had accumulated over the afternoon's selling, including commission and tips. I would have to hand it all up, I would get nothing.

I stood there, the blood draining from my face. All that work for nothing. The commission amounted to a few shillings but it meant more to me than the bare value of the coins. It was earned income, a bonus to clink in my pocket, the wherewithal to buy extra comics and sweets, money for going to the pictures. I blurted that there must be some mistake and the GAA official looked me in the eye and replied that there had been no mistake, hand over the money, and that was that.

I handed it over, all of it. No choice. But, if I'd really been given all those extra programmes, if I'd sold them all, I'd have the extra money. Why wasn't he demanding it all, why wasn't he accusing me of holding back the extra money?

No cheek, now, be off with you.

The routine of going up into the stands to watch what was left of the game had lost its appeal. I walked out of Croke Park that day and I've never been back. Without bus fare, I walked home, feet dragging, temper rising. At home in my room I kicked my schoolbag from one wall to the other, I swore and screamed and cried at the sheer unfairness of it. I had behaved properly, I had been honest, I had lived up to my side of the contract. If there was a mistake it wasn't mine. My mother tried to comfort me, told me to put it out of my mind, to hell with them, the lousers. 'Bad cess to them.' But the anger burned. I think I believed then, as I stood whitefaced in front of the official, what I believe now. There was no mistake. The GAA man was stealing my money and there was nothing I could do about it. You are a kid, they are big people. They run things. For the first time, I'd come up against brazen lying, blatant thieving, and what was most shocking, far more so than the loss of the commission, was the realisation of my impotence. Welcome to the world of the grownups.

* * *

'Bad cess to them.' It was a dire but innocent curse cast by members of a generation that didn't indulge so easily in the colourful language that we use today. It was part of the sayings and euphemisms and beliefs that had been passed down through the years.

The euphemism *feck* was widespread. It had two meanings. You could tell someone to feck off; or a thief might feck something from a shop. We kids used *flip* as a euphemism acceptable even in adult company. Flip it. Blow it. In extremis, damn it. Until we graduated—strictly amongst ourselves—to the real thing. Then, no activity seemed complete without the word. You didn't just get tired of something; you moaned, 'Fuck this for a game of cowboys.'

Janey was the respectable way of saying Jesus or—the Dublin pronunciation—Jayzus. A totally harmless expletive was derived from this, acceptable even to nuns, let alone parents: *Janey Mac*.

Cess, when you look it up, is not what you probably thought it is. It has nothing to do with cesspits. It could be from the Latin for *cease*, and the wish for bad cess might therefore be for a bad end to one's tormentor. Cess might be related to the cess which is a variant of *sess*, which was a tax or levy for which one was assessed; so, wishing someone bad cess might be wishing on them a heavy tax.

That generation, though receiving a minimal education, seemed on average to have greater facility with words—better handwriting, even—than we do and to use language more precisely. A word such as *accoutrements*, meaning bags and baggage, was commonplace. Today, we'd settle for 'I'm picking up my *stuff*.' If someone used the word perambulate or wherewithal in everyday conversation (and someone might), there was no need to explain it. If someone asks us today about the excitement in the pub last night we'll tell them about the *row*. Back then, the word *commotion* very much more accurately conveyed what went on.

There seemed to be sayings for every occasion. Never cast a clout 'til May is out. If you can't do a good turn, we were warned, don't do anything at all.

If you dropped a knife, 'That's a man to the house.' If you dropped a fork it was a woman coming to the house. Sure enough, the insurance man would come collecting, or the milk man, or someone down and out, trying to sell holy pictures. And my mother would nod, the fallen knife's prediction vindicated: 'A man to the house', she'd murmur.

Why wouldn't we believe in Santa, in magic? Adults believed in all sorts of magic; reading palms, reading the stars. Among visitors to our house was an old friend of my mother's, Nana. One of my first memories is of that old woman holding me up in the air and smiling at me. She'd visit, coo at me, have her tea and a bit of cake, then she'd solemnly take my mother's cup and then my aunt's cup and read the future as written in the tea leaves.

There were all sorts of half-believed notions about black cats crossing your path, about blackbirds and about walking under ladders or breaking mirrors (seven years' bad luck). If you spilled salt accidently you had to deliberately throw some more over your shoulder, to avert bad luck. The belief that vinegar thins your blood was probably peculiar to my mother.

As a young child, in a temper, I once or twice lashed out at my mother. She didn't slap me. I was rarely slapped at home, and then just a tap on the lower leg. My mother, when threatened by my puny fists, raised a warning finger: 'Ah, now', she said, invoking a rarely used but powerful saying: 'The hand that strikes the mother is the hand that'll stick up out of the grave.' More proof of the readiness of the child's mind to accept the existence of magic and to give credence to the word of an adult, no matter how outrageous the words being said. The image of my hand forcing its way up out of my coffin and through the clay, to stick up into the clear air above my grave, revealing my shame to the world, was sufficiently shocking to ensure that I henceforth kept my little fists to myself.

* * *

It's probably the best time of year to be writing about childhood. It's 8 December now, the Feast of the Immaculate Conception of the Blessed Virgin Mary, a Holy Day of Obligation. Christmas is coming up fast. Christmas does things to our sense of time, interweaving our childhood and adulthood. We help create magic for the children and in doing so stir memories of our own childhood. And through our enjoyment of our children's pleasure we get echoes of how our parents must have felt making magic for us, and of what we meant to them.

Despite the hustling, the fraught shopping, the commercial manipulation, Christmas is for some of us the season around which the year revolves. In a way, it is the magic around which our lives revolve. We learned that there existed a magic man who lived at the North Pole, whose whole existence was devoted to making children happy. He could in one magic night visit the home of every child in the world; he could come down a chimney or through a wall. Whatever the commercial hustle which now envelopes Christmas, that magic remains unsullied at the heart of it all.

From early November there is an air of preparation, like a massive army is arranging itself for a big push. The kids maimed and blinded by Hallowe'en bangers and fireworks haven't yet been discharged from hospital when the forward units of the Christmas army start softening us up with a few well-placed rounds of advertising. Have you booked somewhere for your Christmas party? Are you alone for Christmas and would you like to pay us to let you share Christmas in our hotel? Chocolates, lingerie, perfume, driving lessons, jewellery, electric power saws, we got it, you need it, someone expects a seasonal bouquet, a basque or a set of aluminium wheel rims, sign here for a Happy Christmas.

But the moaners who decry the hustling miss the point. Of course it's overcommercialised. So is the production and distribution of food, so is the provision of housing. Television is over-commercialised, and books and art and children's play centres and newspapers and music and clothes and religion and sport and flowers and bingo. We live in a hustling society, market-driven, in which things are organised according to whether someone can squeeze a buck out of the transaction. People starve because they don't have the money to make it worth our while to feed them with the food which we have to pay a fortune to store until it goes rotten, in order to artificially jack up the prices charged to those who can afford to pay. So, there's not much point whinging about the lack of purity in the Christmas celebrations, the commercialisation of a completely artificial season out of which we somehow manage to extract some magic.

It was ever thus. Christmas started with a bunch of unwashed pagans terrified that the Sun God had taken away the life-giving golden ball in the sky. In the depths of winter they sought to placate the Sun God, and by kissing his ass persuade him to bring back the golden ball. Invariably, he did. The earth turned (not that the dopey pagans knew that), and by and by the sun shone, things flowered, and all was well with the world. The pagans celebrated not out of some pure regard for the time of year but in the belief that dancing up and down would help make their crops grow. A purely commercial motive.

Christians appropriated the winter celebration and falsified the calendar to arrange Jesus's birth on the appropriate day. The Saint Nicholas that became Santa Claus is an accumulation of legends. The image Santa acquired, fat and hairy, came from the drawings of Thomas Nast, a cartoonist with the American magazine *Harper's Weekly*, a hundred years ago. Some years later, Santa acquired his jolly red-dominated persona when he posed for an advert for Coca-Cola. By and by, the retail business made Christmas the centrepiece of its annual marketing strategy.

And with all that, the magic still comes through. It's about making ourselves feel good by making others feel better. The reds and the greens and the snow that usually doesn't fall, the tree and the decorations and the turkey and the carols, bind together our memories and our wishes, put on hold our knowledge and our fears, and invite us to be as cheerful and helpful and hopeful and as downright happy as we can be, for a while.

There is something appropriate about even the blatant hustling for a buck. It adds a steely edge to the Christmas sentiment. The magic still exists, for the children, in the story of Baby Jesus and the story of Santa. For the rest of us, there's no such thing as a free Christmas. Money saved, money borrowed, difficulties set aside for the moment, reality will have to wait for January. Christmas comes brightly wrapped, with a price tag, Santa's on a zero-hour contract. If it seems like today it's more commercial than when we were kids that's because there's more money around, more things to sell us, the market has expanded, become more inventive in its pursuit of a buck. But there never was a time when they gave away free turkeys. There was scrimping and saving back then, money carefully put aside month upon month in the Christmas Club in the local shop. There was the Diddley, a pre-credit-union form of local financial management, whereby someone in the neighbourhood or the workplace would take on the running of the Diddley, collecting weekly amounts from friends and neighbours, the accumulated money being doled out when appropriate.

We kids didn't notice much of that back then. The financial pressures which must have troubled the minds of the grownups had nothing to do with us, we didn't notice much of anything beyond our small, hopeful, expectant world. Which is, of course, the way it should be.

Four

If you look at a map of Cabra West you will have no doubt about the location of the Catholic church. The estate, built by Dublin Corporation at the beginning of the 1940s, is laid out in a geometric shape designed around a space allocated for the church. The church is the centre of the web of streets, holding the whole design together. The Catholic Church, as an idea, was so integrated into the lives of our parents' generation that it seemed entirely appropriate that the physical representation of the Church was the central element in the layout of a whole community.

Cabra West got a bit of a tough reputation at one point, but nothing serious and it soon settled into a quiet, respectable working-class community. The neighbourhood was briefly known as the Wild West, and some of us found a bit of glamour in the fact that the old Irish name for the area, Cabragh, meant Badlands. Old Cabra, East Cabra, the slightly posher bit, had been there since the 1930s. Cabra West went up in the 1940s, as the city spread out. Culchies were leaving the land, settling in the cities. A couple of thousand Dubliners made homeless by the German bombing of the North Strand were housed in Cabra West. People were leaving the overcrowded inner-city tenements for the new estates. I was one year old when my family arrived in Cabra from a southside flats complex, in 1950, and the place was by then on its way to being settled.

The speed and extent of social change in the past thirty years obscure the length and depth of the stagnancy that preceded it. The Cabra West of 1950 was new, part of an expanding Dublin, but within an Ireland that had changed little in the three decades of independence. A hundred years earlier, much of Ireland was little more than a mud hut society. There were great houses, fine buildings, a small class of people doing well amidst brutal conditions for the many. In the mud hut society homes literally were made from mud, little more than one big room, where families gathered around a fire in the middle of the mud floor, the smoke drifting up through a hole in the roof. The image of the pig in the parlour was close enough to the truth, except there was no parlour for the pig, he had to make do with the one big room everyone else shared. Animals were brought indoors for warmth. An 1841 census showed that 40 per cent of houses in Ireland were mud cabins consisting of one room. Another 37 per cent were superior mud houses, with more than one room.

In the years between the Famine and Independence there were shifts of wealth and power within Irish society, the consolidation of a new Catholic middle class, a new landed class. There were improvements, there was some prosperity, but for the bulk of the labouring classes, rural and urban, life was still a few steps up from primitive. There were no mud huts in the cities, but there were overcrowded tenements where families lived in crushing poverty, slaughtered by disease. Employers held wages down ruthlessly, defeating trade union efforts to organise. Lousy wages meant poor diet, low resistance to disease, the elimination by illness of whole families. Efforts to relieve the deadly conditions were undermined by corrupt officials and slum landlords who bought and sold influence in Dublin Corporation. Demolition of dangerous buildings cost a fortune, as officials took backhanders and overcompensated the landlords.

With independence, new classes of commercial clerks, state employees, lawyers, doctors, merchants and shopkeepers replaced the old gentry. Their relative wealth and the build-up of commuter railways, trams, buses and ownership of private cars enabled them to move out to the suburbs, leaving the overcrowded inner city to the poor.

Among the labouring classes independence brought little improvement. In Dublin in 1911 there were 8,743 households of

73

four or more persons living in one room. By 1936 that figure had risen to 9,117. One of the families living in a one-room household in the 1920s was my grandfather's. Hugh Kerrigan was born in 1879, thirty years after the Famine. He was fourteen when he enlisted in the British army, 3rd Battalion Leinster Regiment, a child called to the colours. He learned the cornet and played in a military band. The family proudly remembered that he played in front of Queen Victoria. His brother Thomas too joined the army. In one of the few photographs I have of my grandfather he sits as a boy at his father's knee, his father wearing an army uniform.

Hugh Kerrigan married Frances McDonnell and together they had six children. Because the army life had him moving from barracks to barracks their children were born in various places. My mother, Bridie, was born in Navan in 1910.

Hugh Kerrigan left the army in January 1916, three months before the Easter Rising. He had served for twenty-two years and was a month short of his thirty-seventh birthday. To support his family, he went back to working for the army, as a civilian packer and loader with the Transport Department, at the Royal Barracks, Kilmainham, in 1919. That would, presumably, have made him a legitimate target for the IRA during the War of Independence.

In June 1922 his daughter Eileen, the last of his six children, was born. Eileen's birth was difficult and it left her mother an invalid.

With his wife immobilised, Hugh cheerfully took on the job of looking after the household in St Augustine Street. In December 1922, six months after Eileen was born, Hugh Kerrigan was discharged from his post when the last of the British army finally packed up and departed. His discharge paper, Army Form C 330, is dated 7 December, eleven days before the last contingent of British troops pulled out (the Civil War had been under way for six months). The form notes that Hugh was being discharged due 'to reduction of Staff, owing to change of Government'. He supported his family on a British army pension of 27 old pence a day, or £41 a year.

Hugh did the housework, with the help of the teenage children. Frances was confined to bed until she died fifteen years after giving birth to her last child. Pleasures were simple, and usually free. Hugh would regularly visit a friend, an old mate, and the two would talk about current events, and by and by his friend would walk Hugh home and the two would stand outside the front door, chatting away, and after a while Hugh would walk his friend home, the two still deep in conversation. The radio was the main form of entertainment. Hugh listened to the radio with a musician's ear, mocking his children's fondness for the popular singers of the day. 'Ann Shelton? Sounds more like Ann Shoutin', if you ask me.' He had a gentle sense of humour and would rib Frances about her 12 July birthday: 'Sure, yer only an oul Orangewoman.' They remained very much, and very obviously, in love until parted by death.

Frances died in 1937, aged fifty-five, Hugh died in 1945, aged sixty-six. Despite his British army background he was an unqualified admirer of de Valera. He heartily approved when Dev responded strongly to Winston Churchill's insulting attack on Irish neutrality during the Second World War. Two months before he died Hugh sat in the Iveagh Buildings flat in which he then lived with the two of his children who had not married, Bridie and Eileen, and listened with obvious pride to Dev's eloquent speech on the radio.

We may from our vantage point look back at the de Valera generation as a tight-minded, chest-beating lot, steeped in petty nationalism, and there's truth in that. But the widespread feeling of pride in nationhood was relatively new and deeply felt, after an age of national and religious subordination within the empire. That pride brought with it a lot of dodgy baggage. There was a lack of confidence and a kind of arrogance, which led to a reckless insistence on crudely protecting the iconographic national treasures—the language, the games, the religion—no matter who got hurt. But that national pride grew from a feeling of real achievement and was felt even by an old veteran of the British army who had been reared to see his country as a mere province of a vast and inhospitable empire, who had served that empire from boyhood, and who had as he entered middle age seen his country emerge as a free state.

Although Dublin Corporation's new housing estates had spread out around the city, the harsh tenement life continued for many Dubliners right up to the 1950s and beyond. Overall, Irish life remained grim. The 1961 census found that 43 per cent of private dwellings lacked piped water, 35 per cent had no indoor toilets. As late as 1963 the government had to mount an inquiry to find out why houses in Dublin kept falling down. Into the early 1950s, tuberculosis was ravaging the country. It hit every class, but mostly the poor. Crammed together in bad housing, whole families were wiped out. Just as in the early part of the century, working-class living conditions and malnutrition aided the spread of disease. Doctors, with no room to treat those who got TB, had to send them home, knowing that over the months to come the rest of the family would come down with the disease. You feared TB, you feared infecting your loved ones, you feared people knowing you had the disease, you feared the isolation and rejection that would follow. My aunt Eileen got it, and when she went for checkups she stayed on the bus until the stop after the hospital, so people wouldn't see her getting off at the TB stop. At home, ten years after her TB was cured, there was still a cup which she put aside for her sole use, for fear of infecting me or my mother.

The politicians weren't up to dealing with the crisis. Anyway, it was mostly the underclass that was being laid waste. Then Noël Browne became Minister for Health, an eventuality of pure political chance. He rifled the Department of Health for every spare pound, built sanatoria, opened thousands of TB beds, limiting the spread of the disease while preparing to treat the victims. The drugs which eventually tamed TB were coming on the market. However, without Browne's ruthless compassion, many more would have died while the machinery of state got into gear. Eileen was one of the first into St Mary's sanatorium in the Phoenix Park. A quietly committed Catholic, through the years she would never hear a word said against Noël Browne, however the bishops rubbished him. He saved my life, she said, and she knew whose side he was on. 'I'd love to write a book', Eileen said from time to time, speaking about times, places and things left unrecorded.

Eileen was the first in her ward to undergo a radical operation designed to stem the disease. The operation involved removing a number of ribs and a lung. A doctor anxious to demonstrate that it was no big deal assured her that she would indeed be able to smoke after the procedure. And, after the operation, when she woke up from the anaesthetic, the doctor went along with her to the ward. He gave her a cigarette and lit it for her, so the others in the ward could see the operation was nothing to worry about.

As the city spread, and the new Corporation estates of Cabra West and Drimnagh and Crumlin were opened up, expectations remained low. The new estates were very much better than the dreadful tenements, but it was accepted that for many life remained limited. Work hard, long hours, if you were lucky enough to have a job. Pay the rent, buy your daily bread, enjoy the regular escape to the exotic delights of the cinema, a pint or two and a daily newspaper, and that was as good as it got.

The evening newspaper was purchased primarily for 'the deaths', the obituary columns, which were methodically combed through each evening, with the occasional discovery of the passing of a friend or neighbour from the old parish. Keeping an eye on 'the deaths' informed you not only of who died, but of who they had married, where they moved to and how many children they had. There was the *Press*, the *Herald* and the *Mail*. The street sellers developed a chant, urging passersby to buy the final edition of the papers: 'Evening Press, Hedellaw-Mail, fie-nell'. The *Mail* didn't last long and the chant became 'Hedellaw-Press'.

I lingered over the comic strips, Mandrake the Magician, Jeff Cobb and Jiggs and Maggie. The Mutt and Jeff strip was reputed to contain coded tips for major horse races. It didn't seem at all unlikely that an American comic strip, produced to a formula over decades and syndicated around the world, should contain tips for horse races at Punchestown or Aintree. My mother, who followed

77

the horses with the keenness of a professional gambler, keeping track of the form of the horses, the trainers and the jockeys, firmly believed in Mutt and Jeff and spent many an evening hour trying to decipher the tips.

Holidays, if you went anywhere, meant a day's outing to Bray or Dollymount. You brought your own sandwiches. In Dollymount you found a spot among the sand dunes and you spread towels on the ground and for a special treat you might get a packet of Tayto crisps with your sandwiches. The cheese and onion flavour came ready-salted, but there used to be plain Tayto and that came with a little twist of paper inside the packet, holding a pinch of salt, and you unwound the paper and shook the salt over your crisps. There never was anything that tasted so lovely as tomato sandwiches that had been wrapped in greaseproof paper since leaving home.

Later, there were the times when my Uncle Larry would take me, along with his sons, out to Ireland's Eye, the island off Howth. The journey out was an adventure in itself, in a motor-powered boat run by local fishermen. As soon as we cleared Howth harbour the choppy sea had the boat pitching this way and that while we held firm to rails and stanchions and looked fearlessly out at the horizon, short-trousered but grizzled sailors in search of a new world. And, for us, Ireland's Eye was indeed a new world. Rocks to climb and ruins to explore. Whole flocks of seagulls to holler at, a beach to run down, a picnic in the sand. There was a strange area covered with what looked like grass, but it was cushioned and we could throw ourselves backwards onto it and it was like bouncing on a bed.

One evening I went fishing off Howth with Uncle Larry in a little boat, half a dozen of us, everyone years older than I was. I used a handline and caught a few cod. A shoal of fish quite conveniently placed itself directly underneath us and you could almost reach down and scoop them into the boat. I can remember what those moments felt and smelled like, the quiet, the laughter, the grunts of satisfaction as a fish was landed, the texture of everything I touched that evening almost forty years ago, the gentle movement of the boat, the feel of the wind. I can remember every word of a joke my cousin told.

Bray was the special place, a train ride away, in a train made up of small compartments, each window secured in place by a leather strap. Bray, with its chip shops and the amusements, the bumper cars and slot machines, the beach and the esplanade, the deck chairs, the band on the bandstand, the kiosks selling sweets and ice cream and buckets and spades and little propellors on a stick to hold up and watch the breeze make them spin, the chair lift up Bray Head, and at the top of Bray Head, the crucifix overlooking it all. The vacuum flask had not yet become commonplace. You brought cups and tea, a teapot, and you bought one of those little triangular cartons of milk. There were houses near the seafront with handwritten signs announcing that you could buy boiling water there. We bought boiling water, we went down to the beach, my mother made the tea, and we had a picnic.

If it wasn't Bray or Dollymount for the day it was Dún Laoghaire for the afternoon. You walked up and down the pier and you watched the mailboat, which didn't do very much. Dún Laoghaire, to be honest, was a bit of a drippy place for a kid. Much better was the CIE Mystery Tour. You bought a ticket and got on the bus and it took you to a mystery destination. It was usually the tiny village of Ashford, in Wicklow. It got so that it was almost always Ashford. Getting onto the bus, my mother would nod to the driver: 'Ashford again?' and he'd smile inscrutably and she'd say, 'Big mystery, is it?' And, sure enough, before long we'd be speeding down the familiar road. When you got to Ashford you looked at the scenery and went for walks and had your tea in a café and on the way home in the dark there was usually a sing-song and someone went down the aisle with a cap, collecting tips for the driver.

* * *

Among the few family photos that were taken back then, and the fewer that survive, is one taken outside a pub in Ashford, when Auntie Kathleen and Uncle Paddy were home from England on holidays. Kathleen took the picture. I'm in short trousers and the socks and sandals that kids wore in the summer. My mother has her arm around my shoulders, Paddy and Eileen stand beside us, the four of us in front of the CIE Mystery Tour Bus. Kathleen and Paddy were two of the countless thousands who left the smug republic in search of something better. Kathleen was one of my mother's four sisters, the eldest of Hugh and Frances's children. She emigrated to England in the 1930s and there she met Paddy from Limerick. Paddy was a welder. His trade kept him out of the army during the Second World War and in the London blitz he helped cut free from the wreckage and rubble the victims of the previous night's bombing. Decades later he still couldn't talk about what he had seen.

Kathleen and Paddy remained emotionally attached to home, but there was no going back. They kept in touch, Kathleen and my mother exchanging regular letters that told of all the developments in the wider family. Kathleen was the source of many a welcome parcel of goodies, arriving by post: magazines and comics and Kathleen's old clothes passed on.

For years our Christmas Day celebrations were linked with those of my Uncle Larry's family. We'd spend much of Christmas evening together. One Christmas, we all did our party pieces into the microphone of Uncle Larry's new reel-to-reel tape recorder and he sent the tape to Kathleen. Kathleen immediately went out and bought a tape recorder and played the tape over and over and over, the sounds of her sisters' children, the sound of her sisters laughing uncontrollably as they sang Gilbert and Sullivan's 'Three Little Maids', the sound of Larry singing 'Kilmainham Hotel', the sounds of home. It was probably the last of the big family Christmases, before Larry's family grew up. His wife Mary died shortly afterwards. There were no more Christmas tapes. Years later when I visited Kathleen in London she laughed as she quoted something from the tape as though she had listened to it just the day before, which may well have been the case.

In the 1950s and 1960s, when times were good for them, Kathleen and Paddy came home on holidays and stayed in our house in Cabra West. They always had gifts of exotic goods not to be found in grim Ireland. Spangles, packets of glassy sweets, were an especially treasured item (we had something similar here, called Charms, but they hadn't the glamour of Spangles). Kathleen and Paddy were, to our eyes, wealthy people. In reality, by English standards they were comfortable working class, living on a tradesman's wages. Kathleen developed a soft English accent. Paddy never lost his Limerick accent. They were attached to their roots, but England had long become home, in terms of work Ireland simply had nothing comparable to offer. And there was far more to life in England in those days than there was here. So they stayed, but they returned on holiday as often as they could manage.

Then came the telegram. My mother and Eileen trembled when it arrived. They began to mourn before they knew why they must mourn, for when you received a telegram it meant someone was dead. They stared at the unopened telegram, knowing they had lost someone, hoping it was not anyone close and knowing it must be, mentally enduring the possibilities, unable to resist holding at bay for a few agonising seconds the certain knowledge of who it was that had gone. Eileen opened the telegram and read it aloud, her voice fading as she said Kathleen's name. We all took the boat to Holyhead and the train to Euston Station. We took the underground and then the train. At a tube station, Eileen hesitated at the top of a steep escalator, reluctant to step onto it. I went ahead of her, Uncle Larry stood behind her, holding her hand. There were no escalators in Ireland.

When Paddy opened his front door he saw my mother. 'Bridie . . .' There was nothing to say, the enormity of his loss left him shaking his head. Kathleen had died of a heart attack, in her sleep, lying beside him. He found Rennies indigestion tablets in the pockets of her housecoat. She had mistaken the symptoms of the impending attack.

Now my mother wrote to Paddy the newsy letters she had written

81

to Kathleen, and he wrote back. He came over once on holiday, but it wasn't the same for him without his beloved Kath. Nothing was the same for him. He was lost, childlike. Then, weeks passed without a return letter from Paddy and my mother wondered if he had become so bereft that he couldn't pen a few words. I was in London for work reasons and I phoned around, locating Paddy's local Catholic church, finally finding a priest who knew him. He told me that Paddy had died a couple of months earlier, alone at home. His body hadn't been found for some days.

They had no children, just each other. A paddy and his missus, two of the countless thousands separated from their roots, their deaths little noticed in their adopted country, causing deep aching loss back in the homeland that was no longer theirs.

* * *

The reason there are photos from that trip to Ashford was that Paddy had a camera. We seldom had our pictures taken, except a couple of years on the trot we had mugshots taken at school. Personal cameras were rare enough to make it worthwhile for street photographers to work the pavements of the city centre, taking snaps and handing out little numbered cards. If you wanted a copy of the picture you went to an office in town, put in your order and collected the snaps a week or so later. Uncle Larry took pictures at Christmas and on outings. We had an old box camera but it broke. When it worked it took weeks before you used up a roll and then you left it into a chemist shop and went back a week or two later to collect the pictures.

If it was the chemist shop of the legendary Mr Mushatt, in Francis Street, near Hugh Kerrigan's family home, it cost a shilling to have a film developed (big money), six pence for a postcard-size print, and five shillings and sixpence for a lifesize print. For an extra ninepence, Mr Mushatt could also arrange to have a black and white print coloured.

It seems like even the memories of those times, as well as the photographs, are in black and white. Some of the older women in shawls. The men in hats and overcoats, the women too. Working-class women mostly wore scarves. (A woman dare not enter a Catholic church without covering her head with a hat or scarf. In an emergency she could put a handkerchief on her head. A man, however, had to bare his head. What theological genius came up with those holy rules?) Bikes everywhere. Horses and carts, men driving the horses, cracking makeshift whips and howling something like, 'Giddy-yap!', like they were Walter Brennan trying to coax the stagecoach into Deadwood before the injuns caught up. Most women out and about in the neighbourhood were carrying shopping bags. Women ran the house and they went to the shops every day. No freezers, no fridges. You went to the local shops and you bought exactly what you needed for that day, which if you were lucky was precisely what you could afford. People spent what they earned, putting the barest minimum, little or nothing in many cases, aside.

Various rites of passage (First Communion, Confirmation, marriage, death) required careful saving or worse. There were money-lenders covertly at work, charging very high rates of interest. When RTÉ's *Seven Days* programme exposed this racket in the late 1960s a corner house not far from the Church of the Most Precious Blood was featured. Within days the garden wall was daubed with abusive graffiti.

In or around that time, the local credit union was formed, rationalising and maximising the finances of the neighbourhood. In the years before that, pawn shops were for some a necessary element in budgeting. Grocers' shops and newsagents had tick. When you had established your creditworthiness you might be allowed run up a tab and pay it off when you could. Put it on tick, put it on the slate. Pawn shops and the tick were for some of us things to be avoided. Pay as you go, owe nothing to no one.

Some things had to be bought on HP, hire purchase, the never-never. Furniture mostly, perhaps from Cavendish's in Grafton Street, from Todd Burns in Mary Street, from Black's or from some place in Capel Street. Those who could afford to pay cash got things cheapest. Those who had to pay by the week, as they earned it, paid a lot of interest over the odds. Families went methodically about furnishing a home on the HP, and there was pride and satisfaction and a sense of achievement when, after years, the final payment was made.

There was no sense of deprivation. This was a way of life. I knew we weren't rich. And we had a roof over our heads, food to eat, coal, toys at Christmas, a radio to listen to and a newspaper each evening, which meant we weren't poor, because poor people had nothing. So, we weren't rich and we weren't poor, I concluded, so we must be what was meant by the term middle class.

Nothing was discarded while it could possibly be of the slightest use. A sweeping brush would be baldy before anyone would think of replacing it. You bought a scissors or a bread knife or a screw driver and it lasted years and no matter how blunt or nicked or bent it became it would never occur to you to buy a new one until the old one was lost or the handle fell off and you'd tried and failed to stick it back on. Trousers were patched, socks were darned at the heel and at the toe, jumpers had repairs knitted into the elbows. Bicycle tubes were patched until the patches had patches. The steel wool pads used for scouring pots and pans turned rusty and almost disintegrated before they were thrown away. An umbrella would have to be little more than bare spokes before it was discarded (and then, denuded of the spokes, it became my Bat Masterson cane).

Nothing went to waste. Yesterday's cinders were added to today's coal, to enhance the glow. Cheap, glorified coal dust, called slack, was dampened and packed tight onto a blazing fire, eventually warming to a red hot glow that lasted for hours. There was a vase, there was a drawer, where stuff accumulated. The vase was clogged with cards of wool, lengths of elastic, lengths of string, bits of pencils, tacks and drawing pins, safety pins, little packets of sewing needles, buttons, leaflets with prayers to the Virgin Mary or Saint Thérèse of Lisieux. There were knitting needles in the drawer, and old combs, a small spanner, a couple of bobbins that belonged to nothing else in the house, a small tin of vaseline, two of those tins of shoe polish with the gadget on the side for prising the lid off, old Dublin Corporation rent receipts, a tweezers that was never used except when you got a splinter in your finger, a flashlamp bulb, the back of a packet of Players cigarettes with a recipe for barm brack on the inside, written in pencil. Reels of thread lingered at the back of the drawer for years, because there was a few inches of thread left and as sure as you threw it out you'd need that exact shade within twenty-four hours. At the bottom of the vase there were always a few electrical fuses, and you could never tell if they were in working order. A rolled-up length of bandage.

'Lift your feet when you're walking.' The reprimand was a constant, as we dawdled and dragged the soles of our shoes on the pavement. It had nothing to do with posture. Drag your feet and you ruin your shoes. Shoes were repaired back then, over and over, not disposed of and replaced. Repairs cost money.

There was hard, shiny toilet paper in the school toilets. At home we used yesterday's newspaper, a practice quite common in the 1950s.

The shortages of the Second World War period, the Emergency, were not long over. On a shelf in a press in our house there were a couple of ration books. And two boxes containing gas masks, souvenirs of a dangerous time barely past, one that to us kids seemed like distant history.

(The Second World War was known in Ireland as the Emergency, as a state of emergency was declared on the war's outbreak in 1939. The war ended in 1945. In 1947 de Valera told the Dáil that after careful consideration the government had decided that it shouldn't end the state of emergency just yet. 'World conditions', he said, 'are still far from settled.' Twenty-nine years later, in 1976, after an IRA atrocity, the government of the day decided to declare a state of emergency and bring in repressive laws. It was somewhat embarrassed to realise that in order to declare a state of emergency it would first have to repeal the state of emergency declared in 1939.

85

We were unaware, in those best years of our lives, that we were growing up within an official state of emergency.)

We were sent to the Corporation rent office, a couple of streets away, where the house rent had to be paid every week. We were sent to the shops to buy the groceries, the money wrapped up in a note that listed the goods required, the little package tucked inside a glove. We didn't call them groceries, we didn't go on errands, like the English kids did in *Just William* and in the comics. We called them messages. I'm going to get the messages. (Some shops delivered your messages, via a teenager riding a messenger bike, a special bicycle constructed to hold a wide, deep basket in front of the handlebars.)

You went to get the messages, carrying a shopping bag or a string bag, and if you came across a priest you saluted him and when you went past the Church of the Most Precious Blood you made the Sign of the Cross. You didn't have to remember to do it, you did it as automatically as you said, each night as you went to bed, 'Goodnight and God bless you.'

* * *

You make your way as a kid, unaware of where exactly you fit into the big picture, unaware that there is a big picture. It is as well that we knew little of the context within which we were growing up, as it was in truth a sorry little setup. The revolutionaries of the 1920s were trying vainly, sincerely, for want of anything else to do, to fashion the country in their own image. Self-sufficiency was the order of the day. Once the Brits were gone, the whole thing was like kids building themselves a treehouse, pulling up the ladder and imagining they could spend the rest of their frugal, parochial, smug, self-satisfied lives there. The economy, like the literate mind, was to be starved of stimulating (or, depending which foot you dug with, perverting) outside influences. As prospects became more grim, the rhetoric became more inflated.

'We are a great mother country', said Taoiseach John A. Costello, declaring a republic in 1949. 'We are making a big noise in the world and we will make a bigger noise still.' They had the sensibilities of county councillors, but they saw themselves as statesmen on the world stage.

And they had no doubt about their preeminence within the state. Listen to Alexis Fitzgerald, leading member of the comfortable classes, philosopher of the elite, adviser to the cabinets of John A. Costello (his father-in-law) in the 1950s and Garret FitzGerald (his buddy) in the 1980s. A high emigration rate, he wrote, 'releases social tensions which would otherwise explode and makes possible a stability of manners and customs'. And: 'While we should so cultivate our resources that as many Irishmen as possible can live their lives in Ireland this should not be done in a manner or to the extent of imperiling the imponderable values and liberties of our traditional society.' The traditional values he had in mind were those of a comfortable class surviving within a stagnant culture, a culture of guilt, praying for its own salvation, while the labouring classes shovelled shit or took the boat to England.

Alexis and his chums weren't up to the job of running a country. The economy turned in ever-decreasing circles, the emigrant ships were full. From Cabra West alone, over 2,000 people took the boat. By the mid-1950s there seemed little point to it all, beyond allowing Mr Costello and his fellow statesmen feel that they were making 'a big noise in the world'.

Through it all, the politicians, the comfortable classes and the bishops marched shoulder to shoulder, scratching one another's backs. Despite Northern unionist beliefs, the bishops did not run the state; they and the politicians and civil servants and the Real Irish were partners in a joint enterprise. There was no conspiracy between the Catholic Church and the state, there didn't need to be. They were of one mind, just like the Unionist leaders and the Orange Order and the RUC.

During those best years of our lives all sorts of codology was accepted without question: women teachers or women civil servants who got married had to give up their jobs. It was called the marriage bar. The notion of parents having any say in educational matters would have been a cause of disbelieving mirth, had anyone had a mind so anarchistic as to think of and express such a thought. Few were of such a mind.

The Pope's *Ne Temore* decree ensured that Protestants who married Catholics had to raise their children as Catholics. On the other side of the border, de Valera's loyalist counterparts were building an equally bigoted statelet.

In 1955 the state cooperated with Archbishop McQuaid's unsuccessful attempt to stop a football team from communist Yugoslavia playing in Dublin. Two years later producer Alan Simpson was arrested for staging a Tennessee Williams play. In 1958 the embryonic Dublin Theatre Festival was cancelled after McQuaid objected to plays by O'Casey and Beckett. In 1965 John McGahern lost his teaching job as a result of the direct intervention of Archbishop McQuaid when a novel McGahern wrote was banned. All of this was in the years after the bishops' clash with Noël Browne revealed the extent of the politicians' partnership with the hierarchy. Hysterical in their antipathy to any expansion of the role of the state, the bishops described Browne's free health scheme for mothers and their new-born babies as 'a ready-made instrument for future totalitarian aggression'. These were known as the Good Old Days; alternatively, the Rare Oul Times.

It couldn't last. The fantasy Ireland of the de Valera generation was too estranged from the real world. As the economy seized up, Seán Lemass took over from de Valera and there was a decision to ditch the self-sufficiency of the treehouse political culture and open up the economy to international capital. And that required a relaxation of the cultural Stalinism and reform of the stagnant education system. The changes would take some time to work themselves through. We hadn't a notion that any of this was going on, being too busy enjoying the best years of our lives.

* * *

In Cabra West we were now about to become part of what an advertising slogan would call 'The Go-Ahead Ireland of Today'. Some got ahead more easily than others. We had in our house just one electric socket and that was enough through the years, into the 1970s. There wasn't much call for sockets. There were no appliances. There were no lamps to plug in, the lighting for each room came from a single bulb hanging from the centre of the ceiling. In some rooms the bulbs even had shades. You might plug in a two-bar electric fire in the depths of winter, but mostly the lone socket was used for the radio. And later the television.

Wallpapering. Wet, cold, lumpy paste. The awful job of trimming the edges of the wallpaper before hanging it. Around ten years old, I was helping—more likely hindering—my cousin Larry, my Uncle Larry's son, who was papering the parlour for us. 'Do you like the new paper?' my mother asked. She and Eileen had spent an afternoon carefully choosing it. 'Ah, lovely stuff', said Larry, 'Just the job.' I looked at the pale green flowery pattern and answered honestly: 'No, not really.' When my mother had gone Larry continued making long sweeps with a cloth, smoothing a length of wallpaper onto the wall, and quietly talked to me about people's feelings and how honesty is all very well but there's nothing wrong with saying the paper is lovely if to do otherwise might be hurtful. First lesson in doing your best not to be a pain in the ass.

At intervals of years, Corporation painters would blitz the estate, painting the front doors a dark shade of brown over a light shade of brown. Then, while the top coat was still wet, they'd run metal combs down the surface, with the odd twirl and flourish, producing a wood grain effect. We'd sit and watch, entranced at these skills. Fussy people bought covers for their front doors, lengths of cloth that stretched from the top of the door to the bottom, protecting the paint from the heat of the sun.

There were about 15,000 people living in the estate. Two rows of shops (one to the left of the Catholic church, one to the right), two pubs (Kennedy's and the Oasis, one to the left of the church, one to the right), two playgrounds (one in front of our house, the other on the border with Old Cabra), a couple of green spaces (compounds, they were called) and the Bogies. The Bogies was a large green area accommodating several football fields and a pavilion. We had many a battle there and when we were younger we dare not venture towards the most distant part of the Bogies; for that, our parents warned us, was where the Bogeymen lived. In the wake of the 1979 Papal visit, during which Pope John Paul II stayed at the Papal Nuncio's home, on the far side of the Bogies, the field was officially renamed John Paul II Park. It's still the Bogies.

A Corporation house, upstairs and down, totalled about 640 square feet. Ours had two bedrooms, a front parlour and a 16 by 10 foot back room that was a combined living room, dining room and kitchen. Up against the wall at one end of that room, the kitchen consisted of a gas stove, a wooden drainer atop a small press, and a sink. No work surface, unless you counted the drainer. At the other end of the room was the fireplace and fireside chairs; in the middle the dining table and chairs, the sideboard and the sofa. Having one room serve several functions made sense, especially in the winter, when only that one room was heated.

The house had sufficient room for two adults and a child. Some houses had two bedrooms and a box room. Families of two children, four, six, eight and more were raised in such houses.

There were no washing machines. Water was boiled and poured into a basin and clothes were mercilessly pounded and scrubbed and rolled and squeezed and rinsed and squeezed again (some families put the wet clothes through a mangle) and then left on the line to dry, and then they had to be left aside for another day or two to be 'aired'. (There doesn't seem to be, these days, the same obsession with 'airing' clothes. And you can put clothes away without protecting them with smelly mothballs. How come you never see mothballs anymore? Have moths changed their habits, don't they eat holes in clothes anymore?)

At one stage, as financial circumstances improved, some firm began promoting washing machines around the neighbourhood, offering free trials for a week. The cute thing to do was take a washing machine on trial and over the next few days wash every stitch of clothing in the house, and every stitch of clothing belonging to your relatives and neighbours and friends, and their relatives and neighbours and friends, and at the end of the week tell the salesman 'That's a powerful machine right enough, but I don't think we'd get the hang of it at all, at all, but sure, we'll think about it.'

The grandly named parlour was for us the ground floor room at the front of the house that wasn't used, except for dumping stuff you couldn't find room for elsewhere.

Carpets were uncommon, lino was the universal floorcovering. In the coldest days of winter you crouched near the fireplace, everyone having retreated to the one room where the cooking, the eating, the reading was done, where the radio or the television was, and that room became bearably warm. A coat was laid along the bottom of the door, to keep out draughts. If nature called, you tried to ignore it until it would be ignored no more, then you made the shivering dash up the stairs to the icy bathroom, did your business and scarpered back down to the refuge.

At bedtime there was the ritual of the hot water bottles, of filling them to a certain point, of patting them with a towel to expel the steam, of wiping the hot water from around the inside of the neck, bringing them up to warm the beds a half-hour before bedtime. In bed you created a cocoon of warmth. In the depths of winter overcoats would be used on top of the blankets, to increase insulation. Next morning, leaving the cocoon to get dressed was misery itself.

(We were just, at that stage, moving out of the utter prohibition on throwing coats on beds. That prohibition had something to do with fear of the migration of fleas from outer wear to bedclothes. Fleas and nits were a matter of some concern and every home had a fine-tooth comb. At the first sign of an itchy head an adult, armed with that comb, would go on safari through the kid's hair in search of livestock. The reasoning behind the prohibition on opening umbrellas indoors is lost in the mists of time.)

There was some sort of pipe arrangement which was supposed to provide hot water if you had a fire blazing long enough, but it never worked. For baths, you boiled water in saucepans on the stove, and you very, very carefully carried the steaming water upstairs to the bathroom, making countless trips before the bath was filled to a serviceable height.

* * *

There was a tin church at first, to be going on with, and in 1953 the Church of the Most Precious Blood was raised, at great expense, and we were all brought by the hand to stand and watch the opening celebrations. John Charles McQuaid himself, Archbishop of Dublin, was there to do the honours. McQuaid was an imperious type, used to having his way. He combined a genuine commitment to charitable works with an unbending resolve to preserve the Catholic Church's political, cultural and social position in the smug little republic. It was not long since his triumph of forcing a coalition government to abandon plans to provide a free health service for mothers and children, but we kids didn't know anything about that.

High above the altar of the new church were chiselled the gold-painted words that I would stare up at year after year, Sunday after Sunday, throughout my childhood. *Redemisti Nos, Domini, In Sanguine Tuo.* I hadn't a clue what it meant, still don't, though I would guess that it had something to do with being redeemed in blood (of course, when we're dealing with the subject in hand that's a fairly safe guess). Although I never knew what it meant and I haven't been near the Church of the Most Precious Blood since my mother's funeral eight years ago, I bet I've got the Latin spelling right.

The Church of the Most Precious Blood was one of thirty-four new Catholic churches built in Dublin between 1940 and 1965, in a determined and successful effort to maintain the Church's central position in the life of the community, as the population left the land, as the inner-city tenements emptied and the city spread out. John Charles McQuaid himself oversaw the strategic adaptation to the changing circumstances. In the nineteenth century a church-building programme had established a physical presence in rural areas, consolidating Catholic communities around the churches and sinking the institution's roots deep. Now, as society changed, the same strategy was working. All we knew was we were getting a big solid church to replace the little tin one. To the hierarchy, the bricks and mortar constituted an investment in the future.

Huge churches, dominant in style and location, were central to the growing urban parishes. Mass-going was becoming the hinge on which Catholicism swung, to an extent not known before. Surprisingly, perhaps, there was a low rate of turnout for Mass in the old rural society before cars became common. It shouldn't be surprising, as people had to trudge long distances to churches and home again. Now, in the 1950s, in the Dublin estates, where communities congregated around sturdy churches, relays of Masses, from 7.30 a.m. right through Sunday morning to 12.30 p.m., each filling the churches from wall to wall, were needed to cope with the demand. 'Faith of our fathers' holy faith', we chorused with full hearts, 'We will be true to thee 'til death.' These, for the Catholic Church in Ireland, were the good old, never better, days; and better than they would ever be again.

Five

The city centre, three miles to the south-east of Cabra West, was seen as something apart from us, it was 'town', a place to visit, for shopping or for movies. Although some would lament the decline of the city centre, the loss of sedate little eateries, the end of the alleged 'rare oul times', such things meant little to us. There was no tradition of eating out. You might go to Caffola's, in town, but very rarely and usually just for an ice cream or for chips. Even those with money to spend on eating out didn't have a great choice. Jammet's, the city's only decent French restaurant, is legendary more for the fact that it existed than for its food or social significance. Only when the likes of Captain America's, Thunderbirds, and eventually (and far more significantly) McDonald's (garish, grease-ridden, anti-union, but cheerful and affordable) came to town did the centre of Dublin open up and the habit of eating out become widespread. As the economy began to move and we all had more to spend, middle-class exclusivity didn't generate as much cash flow as the mass sales of the new retail outlets, so Jammet's gave way to the fast-food restaurants. Bourgeois gentility had to make way for youth and the working class. There are those who bemoan the alleged decline of once-proud streets. Plastic signs, fast-food joints and Pound Shops are pointed to as evidence of cultural vandalism. But these by-products of the mass market were an inevitable part of an opening up of the city centre. Genuine concern for aesthetic values is in some quarters mixed with ill-concealed annoyance that the city also belongs to the hoi polloi for whom cheap food and a Pound Shop are not a sign of cultural disintegration. There are periodic efforts to re-gentrify areas within the centre city, some well-meant and some mere snobbery.

Despite the culchie-versus-jackeen playacting, Ireland is small and quite homogenous. There is a cultural overlap between country and city. In the new urban estates in the 1950s that was even more noticeable. Many of the families new to Cabra West kept chickens in the back gardens. Many turned their back gardens into vegetable plots, with rows of cabbages blossoming. There were common spaces, officially designated allotments where people grew vegetables. Nearby on the Navan Road, there was a piggery which produced an astonishing smell. On our way to the Phoenix Park we'd fill our lungs with the petrol-fume-drenched air of the main road and run through the piggery smell that was so thick we could almost see it. Cabra West was subjected to daily cattle drives, with herds of smelly cows being driven down our streets from the Liffey Junction railway halt to the cattle market at Hanlon's Corner. The cattle were tended by cowboys on bicycles, men with overcoats and hats, furiously pedalling this way and that, whacking the cattle with their sticks and shouting at them, the bewildered beasts leaving heaps of shit on the road as souvenirs of their passage.

There were fields to the north of Cabra West, and a wide green space between us and Finglas. A walk away was the Royal Canal, and countryside in which to go picking blackberries.

The smell of burning turf was as pervasive in the new urban gathering as in any rural outpost. On the edge of Cabra West nearest to town there was a turf depot, from which turf was distributed to old age pensioners. Local entrepreneurs charged a few pence to carry the turf, on old prams or homemade carts, from the depot to the customers.

The estate was serviced by visiting coal lorries, or a coalman driving a horse and cart, the driver shouting the 'Co-well!' announcement that he was doing his rounds. We didn't keep coal in the bath, but we kept it under the stairs, in a little nook which also housed the gas meter.

The bread man left his turnovers and loaves on windowsills, the milkman left his bottles at the doorstep and one evening a week they came knocking for their money. The visitor whose persistence was greatest was the insurance man. Insurance was almost a matter of religion. However tight things might be the insurance had to be paid. There had to be money put by for when you died, for the funeral. It was a matter of honour with the old people. From the 1920s or 1930s, families signed up, and each addition to the family was added to the policy at perhaps a penny a week. The years went by, the premium increased to real money, each week the insurance man came to the door and collected the cash. Companies merged, were taken over, years more went by, policies were amalgamated, decades went by, and every week the insurance man came, cheerfully taking the money and entering the payment in his own book and the family's insurance book. And when one death followed another and I was tying up loose ends I cashed in the last of our family's policies, some of them stretching back to the 1920s, and there was hardly enough to pay for the brass handles on a coffin.

The visitor most welcome was the gasman. The gas meter was fed shillings to keep the gas flowing, and the box containing the accumulated money was emptied at regular intervals by the gasman. He made his rounds from house to house, where he unlocked the box, sat at the table and emptied the money onto a newspaper. Then, the fingers of one hand whizzing in a blur, he skimmed the coins into the open palm of the other hand, counting and stacking the shillings like poker chips. Then he checked the meter, calculated the odds, and there was usually a shilling or two left over, a rebate, after the rest was bagged and scooped into his leather satchel. If there was more than a couple of shillings rebate I usually got one of them, so the gasman's whizzing fingers were watched with intense interest.

The gas meter was the target for the regular break-ins which occurred. There was little else worth stealing in such houses, but the cost of a broken window was more than most families could afford. The family also, of course, had to make up the amount stolen from the meter. It took months to pay back the money, in instalments. The gardaí would come, dust the place for fingerprints

96

and go away, never to be heard from again. Eventually, to remove the temptation, the gas company took out the money box and we used the same shilling over and over and the charges were calculated from the meter, and by and by the use of coins was ended.

We knew who the thieves were, the chief culprit being Macker, a pinch-faced little gurrier with the morals of a rat, his parents drunkards. Every now and then he was caught doing something stupid and did a bit in Mountjoy.

Those were the days, as we are often reminded, in which you could leave your front door open. Yes, you could. But that was because there was almost always someone in the house, with families of six and eight kids, with the mother working fulltime at home. The houses were small, so it wasn't like someone could be burgling the west wing while you were wetting the tea in the kitchen. And, pre-video, pre-CD player, pre- any jewellery worth stealing, there wasn't much apart from the gas meter to entice a burglar.

We didn't know much about serious crime but we did know, for instance, that the lane around the back of the shops was not a good place to go, because the wilder elements often gathered there. And it was in the lane, one night, that a young woman from up the street was raped. We didn't know what rape was, but we heard about her being attacked and we knew that the young woman was thereafter considered in the neighbourhood to be less than respectable. In the culture of the time, the rape was considered disgusting, the rapist was declared to be a bowsie, but it was generally held that no respectable girl would have had any business being up that lane with a youngfella in the first place.

Two or three brothers from a Carnlough Road family had a dreadful reputation for cruelty. It was said that they killed cats by hanging them. I have no idea if this was true, but back then we all believed it. The same family became one of the most respected and prosperous in the neighbourhood, but some of us still wonder about the cats.

Most people were quiet, industrious, family-centred. Way across the other side of the Corporation playground was what was known as the Hooley House, home of a family whose house seemed each weekend for a few years to be the site of one long, relentless party, music and singing and the clinking of bottles way into the night. Up the street was the home of a pair who most nights could be heard making their drunken way home from the pub, singing, canoodling. At least once a week the lovey-dovey stuff would mutate into a row and the cops would be called. She was known as Garda-He-Hit-Me.

Few homes didn't have a picture of the Sacred Heart, with Saint Anthony (the man to talk to if you lost something) or Saint Thérèse or the Child of Prague or some other holy image as a backup. We had Saint Martin de Porres, a family favourite since the days he was merely a Blessed. The statue of the pious seventeenth-century black man, his hands crossed on his chest, was for years in a place of prominence, his eyes looking thoughtfully up at our ceiling. We got the monthly magazine devoted to him and we prayed he'd be made a saint and eventually he was and we felt a quiet pride that our guy had got the promotion.

On the landing at the top of the stairs, on a windowsill, year after year after year, stood a luminous statue of the Blessed Virgin, a prize that I won in convent school, having triumphed in some class competition. It glowed in the dark, and it stood on the windowsill for so long that eventually the glow faded and died. Thinking about it now, I have a small sense of dread, wondering what substance made it glow and what it did to us while it was lighting up the Blessed Virgin.

In our hallway, as in most hallways of the time, there was hung on the wall a small plastic Holy Water font, regularly restocked with blessed water brought home from Knock or Lourdes by a friend or relative. The routine was to dip your fingers in the font and bless yourself before leaving the house, a spiritual precaution in case you didn't make it home again.

They announced one day that Father Burke was being made a cannon. As we made our way home from school we kicked around this interesting but odd piece of news. The old man was going to be a cannon. We knew this didn't make sense, but the image was a pleasing one and we pretended to believe that the parish priest was going to be turned into some class of an artillery piece.

Father Burke was head honcho in the school and in the parish. The masters controlled us, the Head Master kept an eye on the masters, and the whole shebang was overseen by Father Burke, Parish Priest and school manager.

We soon learned it was a canon they were making of Father Burke, whatever a canon was. I didn't know then and don't know now, except for having some vague notion that a canon is something like a major in the officer class of the Catholic Church. More clout than a sergeant or a lieutenant, but certainly not as important as a senior officer such as a bishop or a cardinal. It was somewhere in between, and Father Burke had been promoted to that position, and was henceforth to be known as Canon Burke.

In pictures I've seen since back then he wears a kind smile, and he must have been as complex as the rest of us, but in memory Canon Burke is a hard, simple, unsmiling man, always with a bone to pick. He was an authority figure and he lived up to that, whatever his personal feelings. He was around seventy. He had a little sliver of skin sticking out of the corner of one eye, which you saw up close if you went to him in Confession. And if you went to him in Confession you usually didn't go back. Other priests might wave Absolution as soon as you'd told them your sins, but Father Burke always had something to say, a ticking off for this sin or that. Probably he was trying to put a personal element into the sacrament, but that's not how we saw it. And where other priests gave Hail Marys for Penance he gave whole Rosaries. On Saturday, as most of the parish turned up for Confession, the lines outside most Confession Boxes were long. Outside Father Burke's Confession Box the lines were short, with only masochists or those in a hurry willing to brave his sternness.

He organised a boy scout group and presided over the setting up of bands and clubs and charity collections but to us he was a man with whom it was better to avoid eye contact.

He would regularly come into the school, to visit classes. He would ask questions. Had anyone missed Sodality? Had anyone missed Mass? Had anyone missed Confession? It never occurred to us to keep our mouths shut. We believed he would know, just by looking at us. And we put our hands up, admitted missing this sacrament or that holy event. We were always asked for explanations, being made to stand up amid our classmates to be questioned. All part of the inculcation of guilt.

I put my hand up, he turned to me. 'You', an invitation to own up. I missed Confession, I told him, my face red, my mouth dry.

'Why?'

Because I had been up the canal with my friends, fishing for pinkeens, and hadn't noticed the time and when I got home I had to have my tea and it was too late to go out again. Fixing me with a glare of intense, damning disapproval, Father Burke uttered two withering words. 'Very convenient.' He spaced the words out. *Very . . . convenient.* And made me feel like I had personally played a part in hammering one of the nails into Jesus's hands. He nodded to another boy whose arm had gone up in reluctant admission. I stood there, hardly daring to sit down without formal dismissal, until it was obvious that he had flushed me from his mind and I was free to sink into my seat and my shame.

We didn't like him but he certainly, in his own way, cared a lot for us. He sought and was granted an unusual request, that he be buried in the church grounds, buried in the centre of the community he served and presided over. He died in 1966. On his memorial card, circulated to parishioners that they might pray for his soul, there was a plea that Jesus 'remember Thy Priest, departed, for the sake of the souls he has saved and the crimes he has prevented'. A couple of weeks after the funeral there was a break-in at a local shop and hundreds of cigarettes were stolen. Some of them were later found underneath the flowers on Canon Burke's grave, stashed there by some smartass thief who found the hiding place very . . . convenient.

Priests loomed large in our lives. They oversaw the running of the school, they held court in the church, they visited our homes. One of the first things we learned in convent school was that when we came across a priest in the street we must salute him. If you were wearing a school cap you had to lift it a few inches off your head for a second or two, as a sign of respect.

If Canon Burke represented authority, to the kids of the parish, Father Farrell was fun. His Masses were packed, his Confession queues were long. No sermons at Mass, just stories. He swayed back and forth in the pulpit as he lashed out the Biblical tales and we sat there open-mouthed. He favoured the follier-upper format, stopping the stories at crucial points: 'And so they rolled back the stone from Jesus's tomb and they gathered around and they strained to look inside and suddenly . . .' And then he would chant his catch-phrase: 'And what will happen next!' And the church bubbled with chatter as we briefly considered this latest development and Father Farrell jumped down from the pulpit and ran back to the altar to continue the Mass. And we all turned up the following week for the next instalment.

There were always children around Father Farrell, always laughing, always happy to be in his presence, to receive his nod of approval. He would drive around the parish, his arm out the open window of his car as he came to a stop, slapping his palm on the roof of the car and calling, 'Hi, gang!' and the kids would drop whatever they were doing and descend on the car for the pleasure of a minute or two in his company.

Father Farrell shared a house with Father Kavanagh. And Father Kavanagh's Masses were the best-attended on Sundays, even more crowded than those of Father Farrell. The popularity stemmed not from his holiness, his wit or the grace of his sermons. He said Mass in half the time the average priest would take. Fifteen minutes, tops, and you were on your way home. He was known as Flash Kavanagh. When he died suddenly in 1960 the parish was shocked and thousands of us turned out for his funeral.

Today, we wouldn't see things with the innocence of those days. Father Farrell, a priest who went out of his way to make himself likeable to kids; today, someone would smell a rat. There would be quiet words in this ear or that. Father Farrell would be taken aside, caution would be urged on him, he would maybe be transferred. I know in my bones that Father Farrell was a fine, decent man, an innocent man who loved kids, whose only wish for them was joy in life. But, the way things have gone, it wouldn't happen today.

And Canon Burke got a nickname from his perpetual fundraising and his ability to put the touch on people for a donation. He was known as the Toucher. Imagine it today: you've got a new parish priest, folks, and he's known as the Toucher. And his curate's nickname is Flash.

* * *

The Catholic Church permeated every pocket of our lives, but we knew little or nothing about religion. We were members of the One, Holy, Catholic and Apostolic Church, and that was most of what we needed to know. It never dawned on us that these terms had specific theological meanings, excluding from the realm of the truly Holy those Churches without a traceable chain of succession stretching down from the Apostles to Archbishop John Charles McQuaid himself.

Looking back, my own drilling in Catholic beliefs was relatively unsectarian. The Apostolic stuff could have been (and elsewhere, perhaps, was) used to slag off the Protestants. With us, it was understood that no one could be saved from eternal damnation unless they belonged to our Church, but it was said entirely in sorrow, not at all in triumph. There are stories of rabid Catholic teachers and priests and brothers denigrating Protestants but such things didn't happen in Mr McAuliffe's class. There was no need for it. Catholicism was so dominant in our world that Protestantism was no competition. We knew they existed, we knew they were out there, somewhere, the Proddies. Some of the older folk might occasionally make a remark about the Proddy-woddies. We'd heard of them but it went without saying that there were none of them in our neighbourhood.

We were Us, they were Them. They were un-Us. It wasn't that there was anything wrong with Proddies, they just weren't what we were. We certainly didn't hate them, we mostly felt sorry for them in that they had lost the true faith. How they had done so, how they differed from us, we didn't know. We knew nothing of the differences between Methodists and Presbyterians and Baptists and Unitarians and whatever else they were. To us they were all just Proddies. We gathered that they weren't as respectful as we were of Jesus's mother, which seemed a bit begrudging but hardly something worth starting a whole other religion over. Later, there was something about Henry VIII wanting a divorce, and the Pope wouldn't let him so he started his own religion. Beyond that, we hadn't a clue. We didn't understand our own faith's tenets, much less anyone else's. We didn't have to, we were the One, Holy, Catholic and Apostolic Church. We may not have known or cared what Apostolic was, but we were One, we were Holy, we were Catholic, and our spiritual supremacy was taken for granted. We clung to our Church with the blind loyalty of a football fan clinging to his team.

Saturday evening, back then. Out playing, Lord knows what game, with the friend of a friend. We just bumped into each other and since our mutual friend wasn't in the vicinity we mooched around. I'd known this kid, played with him in the company of others, on occasion for a couple of years. We'd never before played without others and we got on well, we had fun doing nothing much in particular. It was getting late and I had a spiritual chore to perform and so I said I'd be heading off. I was backing away, talking, and he was talking, chattering routine stuff, and it suddenly occurred to me that we might do our spiritual chores together.

'I'm going up to Confession', I said. 'Are you coming?'

Casually, 'I can't', he said, 'I'm a Protestant.'

I laughed. Good joke. I don't know now why I thought it was a good joke, but it seemed so at the time.

'See ya', he said, running off towards home. And I realised he wasn't joking and I hoped I hadn't offended him. I turned and headed off up to the Church of the Most Precious Blood, to make yet another Bad Confession.

It never mattered at all that he was one of Them, and we shared each other's company occasionally after that. We never mentioned it, I can't remember ever raising it with our mutual friends, it had no relevance to our lives. It was just startling for that moment to come across the Other and to find him so familiar, so unstrange.

* * *

Four years or so after First Holy Communion, there was Confirmation. It was another Occasion of Money. Again we got a new suit (still short trousers), new shirt and tie and pullover. I got a new overcoat, too. Again we visited relations and neighbours and showed off our new clobber in the sure and certain knowledge that our pockets would be lined with silver, but we couldn't expect to get as much as we got last time. First Holy Communion was the biggie, moneywise.

We never thought of what it meant, Confirmation. Looking back, it was surely superfluous to mount a special ceremony to Confirm our membership of the Church, given the utter relentlessness with which we had been clasped to its bosom from the moment of our birth. As if we were making a choice. The significance, perhaps, was that up to now we had been marshalled in our membership of the Church by mere rank and file priests and the canon. Now we would be Confirmed in our Catholicity by one of the senior officers of the Church, a bishop.

Our main fear was making a show of ourselves in front of the bishop. We were told he would choose a number of children at random and ask each a question about their faith. To get the answer wrong would be to disgrace the class, the school, the parish, the master, the canon, your parents, yourself. So, we studied our Catechism with fearful concentration. In training sessions, questions were thrown at us and we shook our heads in annoyance if we got a word of the answer wrong.

We were devout Catholics but we knew little of our religion. We knew to pray, we knew the stories about Jesus's birth, Herod and the like, the miracles, the Crucifixion. Of the philosophy of Christianity we knew hardly anything. Everything we learned came from the Catechism, and we memorised it like actors preparing from a script. Some of the simpler formulas were understandable, many meant little, they were just sounds to be memorised.

It was in the early 1940s that the Catholic bishops had set up a committee to attempt to gather into one short book a Catechism that would lay out in simple terms the religious teaching which every Catholic should absorb. The Catechism question and answer format had been around for a long time, invented by the Protestants, no less, around the time of the Reformation. It drilled into the learner a series of simplistic formulas which would be learned parrot fashion. By the 1940s there were various Catholic Catechisms being used and the bishops' committee sought to create a single national Catechism which would unify the formulas being instilled in schoolchildren. Various efforts were prepared and in 1948, with Archbishop McQuaid presiding, the committee circulated to the bishops a draft Catechism, for amendment. Since they were constructing something designed to last through the ages, the bishops took their time. It took another three years before, in February 1951, A Catechism of Catholic Doctrine was published. It was a green-covered 103-page book in which the official teachings of Irish Catholicism were summarised in 443 questions and answers. Its title page was honoured with the splendid imprimatur of Archbishop McQuaid: Joannes Carolus, Archiepiscopus Dublinensis, Hibernia Primas. It was the most important, the most used book in our schoolbags.

Mine was the first and last generation to have those particular questions and answers drilled into it. The Catechism didn't last through the ages. Eleven years after it was published the Second Vatican Council was opened, and parrotry went out of fashion.

Who made the world?
God made the world.

Who is God?
God is our father in Heaven, the Creator and Lord of all things.

By the eighth question and answer we were getting down to business, the inculcation of fear and guilt.

Does God see us?
God sees us, for nothing is hidden from his all-seeing eye.

Does God know all things?
God knows all things, past, present and to come, even our most secret thoughts and actions.

Knowing that the all-seeing eye could read our most secret thoughts, we buckled down to learn this stuff off by heart. Not all of it, just selected portions. It wasn't taught for our enlightenment but in order that sufficient questions and answers would be instilled for us to be eligible for Confirmation, when the bishop gave some of us The Big Test. Who would the bishop pick to answer a question? Would the kid let us down? Please, God, don't let it be me.

It wasn't. No one I knew was fingered to answer a question, maybe the whole thing was made up to frighten us into memorising the Catechism.

The bishop (I can't remember which one, a big man in a pointy hat) passed down the row, touched us on the cheeks, and we were Confirmed in our membership of the One, Holy, Catholic and Apostolic Church. If he asked anyone any questions I didn't see it.

We had, of course, received stage directions for the event, so we knew what to expect, including the bit about how the bishop would slap our cheeks. In our discussions about the impending Confirmation the slap became an open-handed wallop, a smack in the gob, and amongst ourselves we resolved that, Bejazus, if he gives me a clatter he'll get a root up the hole, no kidding.

* * *

What we knew of our religion was enough to satisfy a bishop should he come tapping us on the cheek and asking something like, 'What is Prayer?'

Prayer is a lifting up of the heart and mind to God.

And enough to implant fear and guilt. This was done openly, frankly. Take the Catechism's revelation of the Seven Gifts of the Holy Ghost: 'The seven gifts of the Holy Ghost are: wisdom, understanding, counsel, fortitude, knowledge, piety and the fear of the Lord.'

The gift of fear.

A gift for children. They boasted, our holy men, of their role in giving us, with the help of their Holy Ghost, the gift of fear.

Beyond the fear and the guilt and the responses learned by rote there was little to engage us in our Catholicism. Half our religion could be wrapped up in a single sentence. Obey God or he'll punish you. It was a concept of god that was easy for kids to accept. He's a big guy with rules that don't have to make sense (why can't you chew the Host? It never occurred to us to wonder, it was a rule, you obeyed it). The big guy's rules don't have to make sense—because he's a big guy.

The other half of our Catholicism could be contained in a second sentence. Love God and he'll save you. Trouble was, although we said our prayers and pledged our love not alone to God the Father, but to God the Son and God the Holy Ghost, there was little love involved. To be warned that if you fail to love someone, and failed

107

to display your love by attending Mass each Sunday, you will be cast into eternal agony, will indeed compel an emotion. Whatever that emotion might be, love is hardly the word for it.

Was it really so terrible, we sometimes wondered, for someone to occasionally lie on in bed on Sunday, to just wallow, to miss Mass? Would it truly cause pain to God if one among his millions had a lie-in? And, if it did, and if the lazy sinner died suddenly, was eternal agony a just punishment?

The Church, aware that it was pushing two contradictory motives—fear and love—for obeying its god, created two levels of Confession. The aim was to ensure that penitents showed contrition, bowed the head, for one reason or the other. There were, we were told, two kinds of contrition: there was Perfect Contrition, which required that we sorrow for our sins because we realised we had hurt God. And, for those too selfish to be won over by love, there was Imperfect Contrition, which was when our sorrow derived from fear of what God might do to us in retaliation for our sins. While we should always strive for Perfect Contrition, our Catechism told us, 'To receive Penance worthily, Imperfect Contrition is sufficient.'

Ask for forgiveness. God forgives. God is love. God is good. God is rampant power. Love God, but be afraid.

The religious philosophy, simplistic to the point of brutality, was suspended by a massive web of devotional trappings, singly and in concert designed to tether the sinner not to a religion but to the Church, weaving the Church into the very flesh and sinews of the community. At the centre of everything was the Mass, to be attended at least weekly. Attached to the Mass were other sacraments, Confession and Communion. And Benediction, usually tacked onto the end of the last Mass on Sunday, not compulsory but available to those whose depth of faith, and schedules, permitted attendance. The Forty Hours Adoration. The Exposure of the Eucharist. The Novenas, the Retreats, the First Fridays. The Stations of the Cross. The Shrines and their small candles and the slot where you put your pennies.

There were the annual occasions of prayer and obeisance: Ash Wednesday, Whit, Palm Sunday, Lent (invariably, we gave up sweets for Lent, having no other vices worth giving up), Spy Wednesday, Holy Thursday, Good Friday, Easter Sunday, Ascension Thursday. The Blessing of Throats on Saint Blaize's Day. Feast days. Corpus Christi. Holy Days of Obligation.

There were just plain prayers, reams of them, from the ones everyone knew (Hail Mary, Our Father and Glory Be) to obscure little forms of words that turned up in leaflets and prayer books originating in the last century and to which individuals became attached. You prayed for yourself and your loved ones, you invited others to pray for your 'Intentions'. Everyone had Intentions, a kind of wish list of things, great and small, with which Heaven could help. You prayed to God and his mother and you prayed to the saints, and everyone had their favourites. While Saint Martin was our family favourite, and everyone knew that if you lost something there was no one better to put on the job than Saint Anthony of Padua, I always had a soft spot for Saint Thérèse of Lisieux, the Little Flower.

The processions. The lists of the dead read out at Masses, with the request that the congregation pray for the souls of the faithful departed, through the mercy of God, rest in peace, Amen. (One Sunday at Mass in the Church of the Most Precious Blood one of the names read out on the list was Christopher Lee. To a generation accustomed to Hammer horror movies, this was Dracula himself allegedly gone to his eternal reward. A soft titter was heard, then—we couldn't help it, the idea popping simul-taneously into hundreds of minds—an outright guffaw exploded from the congregation. *Jayzus, he thinks yer man is dead—boy, is he in for a shock!* The man's family must have been mortified.)

The significant junctures of life have ceremonies attached which require the supervision of the institutional Church. Baptism, marriage, funeral. The solemnising of these events, the ritual celebration, reflects a deeply felt human need. And where there has been a death the priest offers comforts which can be found nowhere else. Apart from the pre-death rituals (and has anyone ever come up with a more offputting name than Extreme Unction?) the funeral service meets a profound need. It offers resurrection, it comforts and it takes advantage of deep emotions. Our fear of death is not just about loss of our own life, or even primarily so, but distress at the loss of those we love, and when we are in grief there are few more comforting or powerful ideas than that of resurrection. Life is not meaningless, there will be a reunion. There are funerals where the priest is perfunctory, professional ('To whose aid are we coming this morning?', whispered the priest at Auntie Kathleen's funeral, and ten minutes later he was making a speech about what a wonderful woman she was, as though he knew her and cared about her and we all despised him for his casual insult to a good woman); there are funerals where the priest digs into his own experience and finds the heartfelt words that comfort. This, more than anything else the Church offers, engenders belief and attachment.

At home, an array of accoutrements, devotional aids: the Rosary beads, the prayer book, the holy water font, the crucifixes and holy pictures, the holy statues, the relics of the saints. The Miraculous Medal, the Pioneer pin, the white star you wore when you promised not to say any bad words (and you were warned that if you broke your promise everyone would know because a bit of the white would flake off, cross my heart and hope to die). The Scapulars, two pieces of flannel, with religious images emblazoned, with flannel strings attached so the Scapulars could be worn around the neck or hung in an appropriate place (after we'd been burgled twice my mother hung a pair of Scapulars over the back window, to ward off Macker, the neighbourhood predator; it worked, he never came back). The family Rosary in the evening (the Joyful Mysteries, the Sorrowful Mysteries, and . . . what were the other Mysteries?), with the trimmings that went on and on (Oh, Mary conceived without sin, pray for us who have recourse to thee). The prayer each night before you laid you down to sleep. Grace before meals, a mantra once chanted at a million teatime tables.

Bless us, O Lord, and these Thy gifts
Of which Thy bounty we are about to receive;
Through Christ, our Lord. Amen.

The hymns, the psalms, those anthems of fervour, the organ music, the woman or man with the trained voice singing 'Ave Maria', the vestments, the big candles, the Latin, the holy tabernacle, the incense, all creating an atmosphere of awe. In the Church of the Most Precious Blood we had a magnificent organ we were proud of, imported from Holland, and a blind man, Mr McElroy, who played it. (Mr McElroy made a living selling sweets and cigarettes from a kiosk at the bottom of Carnlough Road. He was known to one and all as The Blind Man.) Our Stations of the Cross were imported from Switzerland.

(Glorious, that was the other one; the five Glorious Mysteries of the Rosary.)

The Sodalities, the Confraternities, the Devotions. The Sodality was one of those regular extracurricular prayer events attended by the truly holy, the extra-devout, and the kids who had little choice. Sodalities were less regimented than Confraternities, but they were more formal than Devotions. Such structured events were used in a consciously manipulative way to recruit particularly devout parishioners, to praise and reward them and put them in positions of authority where they might be envied and emulated.

One of the most enjoyable and engaging rituals was the Mission, for which priests from outside (usually, memory suggests, faintly exotic guys, often with beards, who were home on leave from Africa) came into the parish for two or three weeks and conducted special prayer and sermon events which were intended to reinvigorate the faithful.

Indulgences. The amazing frankness of retail Catholicism. You invested your prayer, with a guaranteed return. 'Sweet heart of Jesus, be Thou my love.' Every time you said that, or countless imprecations like it, it got you 300 days off your punishment in Purgatory. The one-liners were printed for your convenience, in prayer books, in missals, in those little leaflets that accumulated around the house. 'Heart of Jesus, once in agony, pity the dying.' That got you 100 days off your sentence.

The system of indulgences presupposed some kind of heavenly accountancy department which kept track of every verbal ejaculation or silent prayer, identifying the person gaining the indulgence, and updating the file which specified the appropriate amount of parole to be allowed against the Purgatorial sentence. It was a brilliant idea. Say a one-line prayer and it takes the guts of a year off your time in Purgatory. Say it ten times, that's nearly ten years. Say it a hundred times. Some little prayers could be said only once a day. Others gave three-year or even seven-year indulgences. You could go through whole lists of imprecations and ejaculations, each of them with a dividend attached, mouthing them in turn, racking up a huge score. You could bank the indulgences against the day you might find yourself in Purgatory, or you could use them to reduce the amount of time a loved one had to burn in the Purgatorial fires. As a means of getting lots of people to engage in endless, repetitive recitation of one prayerful formula after another, it was inspired.

If you stopped to think, you might wonder why saying, 'Sacred Heart of Jesus, have mercy on us', would get you 300 days off your sentence; while saying, 'May the Scared Heart of Jesus be everywhere loved', was worth just 100 days. But, best not to stop to think.

Some prayers could get you a plenary, or absolute, indulgence, wiping the slate clean at the point of death, but there were conditions. This is from my aunt Eileen's 1947 Irish prayer book, giving the rundown on the time off you'd get for the good behaviour of saying a certain prayer to your Guardian Angel:

Indulgence: 300 days each time. Plenary, once a month, on usual conditions, when recited daily . . . Plenary, at the hour of death, to those who (*a*) have practised this devotion frequently during their life; provided (*b*) that after confession and communion or only with sorrowful heart they pronounce the Holy Name of Jesus (vocally or at least mentally); and (c) that they accept death patiently from the hands of God as an expiation for their sins.

There are stock market manoeuvres which are less regulated.

Prayer was part of everyday language. 'Please God', we said at every opportunity. It is short for, 'If it pleases God.' We said the weather would be fine, please God. The bus would come soon, please God. The horse would be first past the post, please God, and the odds would be reasonable.

Very few could make it to Lourdes in those days, but—luckily enough—Knock was nearer to hand. Or you could climb a rocky hill at Croagh Patrick in your bare feet. Or you could go, as I did around 1960, with my Uncle Larry, to Drogheda and see the head of the martyred Oliver Plunkett. Archbishop Oliver got a dreadful death in 1681, caught up in the Protestant-versus-Catholic intrigues and convicted of treason. His head, preserved in a glass case in Drogheda, was a lesson to us all about how a decent Catholic could end up if he got on the wrong side of the Prods.

In 1979, when the Pope went to Drogheda, a team of men in sashes, Knights or Confraternity men, solemnly carried the gnarled 300-year-old head of Plunkett, in a glass case, to a position of honour. As the ceremonies ended and the Pope departed, the crowd rushed the altar to collect souvenirs. For a moment, as the temporary altar creaked and shook, the head of Oliver Plunkett swayed and—as could be said—but for the grace of God it might have come bouncing down the steps, a macabre end to the occasion. The preservation and veneration of preserved bodies or body parts is one of a number of habits Catholicism shares with its hated foe, Russian communism.

You might not stop—as most of us did—at being a passive consumer of Catholicism, you might find the rituals attractive. You might become an altar boy or a flower girl. In time, you might make your family proud by becoming a priest or a nun or a Christian

113

Brother. There was a prestige involved, and the prestige was reflected in the scorn reserved for the spoiled priest, one who couldn't take it, who dropped out. 'Once a priest, always a priest', the older people intoned, shaking their heads in sorrow. There were those who became priests to make the mammy happy. There were those who felt a deep urge to serve their god. There were those who saw the priesthood as a way of serving their community. There were those for whom the priesthood offered an escape from the emotional traumas of civilian life, of going out alone into the world, of finding a woman and supporting a family. There were those who saw the priesthood as a secure position in a society steeped in unemployment and emigration. There were those, a small percentage, who found that the collar, the trappings of authority, provided a convenient cover for getting close to kids. But that kind of thing never crossed our minds back then.

*   *   *

The extent to which Confraternities and the like were exploitive, condescending outfits designed to manipulate religious faith can be seen from a manual written in the 1930s. It was called *Confraternity Work and Its Problems*, by Father James Cleary, Director of the Holy Family Confraternity in Limerick. In cool, frank language it outlined for other priests the way in which they must organise disciplined Confraternities. There was a military smell to it. Divisions and orderlies, prefects, subprefects, badges of office (usually ribbons, although Father Cleary favoured brass chains). The priest in charge, the Director, controlled the Confraternity with absolute authority. Prefects, the NCOs of the Confraternities, had their simple, deeply felt faith manipulated with pious ruthlessness. Prefects, wrote Father Cleary, must give the Director a regular account of their stewardship: 'it keeps the prefects alert and attentive to their duties; for whenever they become careless they know they will have to face an interview with the Director, which will put them to shame'. Father Cleary was no small man playing with martinet fantasies; he organised the most successful Confraternities in the country.

Prefects who weren't up to the job were ruthlessly dealt with. They would at first get veiled suggestions that they get lost; but what, wrote Father Cleary with brutal frankness, if 'your intended victim refuses to take the hint'? Some might, he knew, 'cling on to their little authority'. Answer: once a year all the prefects must hand back their brass chains. The 'victims' would simply not be reappointed. This 'not only supplies the Director with a means of getting rid of useless prefects, but it has a wonderful effect in keeping all the prefects on their mettle'.

Nice man.

The dismissed 'victims' were of little account, for 'even should they, through vexation, abandon the confraternity, the confraternity will manage pretty well without them'. The new prefects would be solemnly presented with their brass chains and all would return to their seats and sing 'Happy We Who Thus United'.

Membership of these outfits was rewarded. 'It is essential', wrote Father Cleary, 'that arrangements be made to ensure that all the members be provided with the best seats in the church, and that they possess at all times first claim to make their confessions.'

The last thing Confraternity members needed was religious moralising. 'Men come to the confraternity meeting freely', wrote the good Father, 'they come to hear something special, to be entertained; for them moralising would be, generally, out of place.' A shin-kicking, Satan-thumping, blood-pumping sermon was required; none of that 'What do we mean by love?' codology they go on with nowadays.

You had to wait three months after you applied before you were admitted to membership of the Confraternity. It was a tactic designed to get the aspiring parishioner spiritually salivating. Membership, wrote Father Cleary, 'should be looked forward to as a favour to be appreciated and the more difficult—within reasonable limits—its attainment, the more it will be valued'. The ritual was cynically given an air of mystification which the priests did not themselves share. 'The ceremony of consecrating new members should be carried out with as much solemnity as possible', wrote Father Cleary. 'It is surprising that some priests do not at all realise the value of solemnity on such ceremonies, and their power to impress the minds of ordinary lay folk.'

Guilt and fear were, of course, useful weapons. The Director must use his authority to put the frighteners on the rank and file. Before each meeting, wrote Father Cleary, the Director should walk down the church aisle, select a row at random, and ostentatiously look along that row. This 'look into a section will give it a spur; it will affect even the absent, for those who are present will speak of it afterwards, and those who are absent will imagine that their absence has been remarked by the Director'. The Director, and the way he might look at you.

Fear should be stoked by regular expulsions of those not fully meeting their obligations. Expulsion caused shame, and fear of shame was a routine method of keeping people in line. So, wayward members were not allowed resign, as 'the weapon of expulsion is a most potent one . . . giving the other members a salutary lesson as to the serious results of negligence in observing their duties'. Father Cleary boasted that his Confraternity expelled, on average, a hundred members a year. 'Make a virtue of necessity and formally expel them, for the sake at least of the lesson thereby conveyed to the other members.' About a third of those expelled would sheepishly come back to reapply. It was standard practice to refuse them membership and tell them to apply again in a month's time—deliberately increasing anxiety. On applying the second time they would be readmitted. But they wouldn't be allowed wear their Confraternity ribbons for up to three months. They'd have to attend week after week, ribbonless. Finally, having been publicly humiliated, the sinners were allowed wear their ribbons of honour.

Up into the 1950s and 1960s the Limerick Confraternities claimed about 10,000 members, in a city of 50,000 people. Similar outfits proliferated throughout the country.

The Confraternities finally dwindled, not least because other sources of entertainment became available, and people became less easy to impress and intimidate.

*　*　*

There was love in what they did, love of their god and some kind of condescending compassion for our dim selves. And it didn't all go to waste. Some of the saints held up for our admiration were role models with greater depth than many currently on offer. Within the grim message of love-thy-god-or-he'll-squash-thee-like-the-bug-thou-art there were also passed on simple, worthy, timeless values. Love thy neighbour. Do unto others as you would have them do unto you. Be wary of throwing the first stone. Whether such values were adhered to by those passing them on to us is beside the point.

At the heart of religion there is fear—of the unknown, of mortality, an eternity of oblivion, the permanent loss of loved ones, hell, the anger of God; there is also a human need to belong to something bigger, more powerful; there is the need to believe that this is not all there is; there is the urge to do good, to help build a less imperfect world. This is expressed in Christian activism—both liberal and conservative—in charity, in everyday decency; in loving your neighbour and all that goes with that.

Such values, notions of equality and fairness and simple decency, speak to the best in us, just as the emphasis on fear and guilt speaks to all that is timid and backward. How exactly those values shaped us is arguable, but shape us they did, for better and for worse. The 'black baby' culture, and the casual bigotry with which a schoolbook could describe Australian aborigines, might or might not have helped shape the racism which emerged as soon as immigrants became more plentiful in Ireland. At the same time, the compassion we were urged to show to those less well-off and far away might or might not have helped create the notable and consistent positive response to appeals for aid to devastated peoples. The crude nationalism peddled by the Real Irish helped excuse intellectual backwardness and institutionalised sectarianism; but the same nationalism left a legacy of sympathy for faraway anti-colonials in trouble.

The circumstances which led us to patronise the 'black babies' also created the men and women, priests and nuns, volunteers, who went to the godforsaken spots of the globe to bear witness to finer values than accommodation to the local thug or dictator. Some stayed home and stood by the oppressed or spoke out against the complacency of the comfortable classes. The emphasis on spiritual values at least suggested that we strive to see a nobler aspect to life. And that had its own virtue in a world where we would be increasingly assured that the only values worth our attention are those of the market.

Our religious guardians didn't trust us, though, and they didn't trust the values they were promoting. They felt they had to fit us with blinkers of fear and guilt so they could shepherd us quickly across the narrow bridge of life, from birth to Heaven, fearful that we might look to left or right, that a bright colour or a raucous sound might attract our attention and lead us into temptation, over the parapet of the bridge and into the abyss of evil.

Six

U p there, beyond the green space, was Finglas. Over beyond the Bogies was the Navan Road. The Cabra West crowd fought the Finglas crowd for control of the grey, featureless public swimming baths that was halfway between the two estates. I forget who won. I remember watching a skirmish, maybe throwing a stone or two and running away. I didn't care much who controlled the baths. I couldn't swim.

We fought the Navan Road crowd because they were middle-class posh gets and their territory bordered our own. There were occasional battles, then we all retired to our own turf and made aggressive noises. Such fights involved throwing stones, rushing, thumping, kicking, screaming quite a bit and running away. Small beer. It would have been easy for someone to get a serious injury but I don't think anyone ever did.

We made weapons. Sometimes for specific battles scheduled with opponents. Mostly just because we wanted to make them.

The hatchet. You got an empty tin can, something that might have held peas or beans, and you got a length of stick. You sat on the kerb of a street on the bus route. You placed one end of the stick inside the empty can. Then you waited. You were waiting for a bus. And since this was the 22 route you might be waiting quite a while. By and by the doubledecker came along. As it sped by, several tons blazing past maybe two or three feet away, you casually leaned forward, holding the tin can on the end of the stick, and you laid it under a wheel of the bus. The tin can was instantly crushed, moulded to the stick, and you had a hatchet. You rubbed the flattened can on the side of the kerb to grind an edge to your blade.

Discarded ice-pop bags, dried and brittle, made excellent

grenades. You filled them with pebbles, twisted the top of the bag shut. You got within throwing distance of the enemy and you flung the grenade as hard as you could at some surface near to them. The impact ripped apart the brittle ice-pop bag and the pebbles exploded out of the bag like shrapnel. I once scored a memorable hit, throwing a grenade with pinpoint accuracy at a lamppost, hitting it a few feet above the enemies' heads, the shrapnel raining down on them.

The gat was the deadliest weapon, so powerful that there was an unspoken gat treaty which applied to all of us except the borderline psychopaths. A gat was a sling, a catapult if you wanted to get posh about it. You broke from a tree, or found somewhere, a Y-shaped piece of wood, and with chicken wire and strips of rubber cut from a bicycle tyre you turned it into a weapon that would fire a small stone at a speed that a bullet might envy. We made gats for fun, for firing off into the distance, for firing into the canal, for firing into bushes. Every now and then you'd hear of someone losing an eye, but never anyone I knew personally. Even a psychopath, if he was threatening you with a gat, pointed it at your legs. It hurt, but no major organs were lost.

Summer was the season for bows and arrows, because the heat made the tar soft. You cut a notch in one end of a long, narrow piece from the branch of a tree. You attached a string, and bent the piece of wood to form a bow, attaching the other end of the string to a notch in the other end of the piece of wood. You stripped the bark from long, thin, straight pieces of wood, to make arrows. You wound some chicken wire around the head of the arrow. You softened an area of tar on the tarmacadam edge of a pavement and used it to add weight to the arrow head. If you were really good at it, you made a flight from a seagull's feather, but I never got that fancy. (Truth to tell, my bows and arrows were on the wonky side but I could do you an ace hatchet.) You readied your weapons with all the solemnity of a Mohican preparing to drive out the colonisers. You went over to the Bogies and fired your arrow in the air. Bows and arrows were occasionally used in mock fights, but you

120

had to be careful to aim low so that you wouldn't have the bother of finding an adult to take some kid with an arrow in his eye to hospital.

When we weren't making weapons we sometimes played at dying. Over in the Bogies, someone would get to play the ambusher. He would lie down and point a gun—maybe a handgun, maybe a Chuck Connors *Rifleman* rifle, maybe a hurley stick, maybe an imaginary weapon. The others would stand maybe twenty yards away. Then, one by one we would ride towards the ambusher, slapping our imaginary horses, gathering speed. When you got maybe twenty feet from the ambusher he fired. And you instantly reared back, fatally wounded, maybe throwing your arms in the air as you fell off your horse, groaning, falling, rolling, finally lying still. The game was to see who died best. The ambusher was the judge.

A season would change and suddenly everyone was playing conkers, pounding holes in chestnuts and threading old shoelaces through the holes. Long summer evenings and it was Kick the Can or Hide and Seek (we called it Hide and Go Seek) or Relievio. Winter afternoons you gathered on someone's front step until it got too cold and you played jackstones. Sometimes a fashion swept through the neighbourhood and everyone was suddenly playing the same game. Marbles, perhaps; one foot on the kerb, the other on the road, aiming your steelie at Jimmy's marble six feet along the gutter.

Just about any time of year someone was making a trolley. It was a piece of wood, maybe a bit of a door, with a makeshift seat, attached to two axles, the front axle steered by a loop of rope. The wheels were sometimes scavenged from an old pram but usually they were heavy, impressive, steel things full of oiled ball bearings. It never occurred to me back then to wonder where such sophisticated pieces of engineering came from and I still couldn't imagine, but they were all over the place. Once the trolley was made, we would take turns sitting on it or pushing. It reached what I remember as supersonic speeds.

If it rained, kerbsides became rivers in which you could float ice-pop sticks, sometimes racing your stick against a mate's, watching the two sticks rush along, swinging this way and that as you ran to clear pebbles out of their way, and finally the sticks vanished down a shore.

In the winter there were nights when it got icy and someone always had a sack and someone else prised open a shore beside the kerb and the sack was dipped down into the disgusting water (we knew that you got 'fever' from that water if it got into your mouth). The wet sack was smacked against a stretch of icy road or footpath, over and over until all the water was beaten out of it, the water freezing on the road surface until there was an icy slide several feet long. You ran for maybe twenty feet, then you reached the slide and if you didn't slip and fall you slid gracefully, maybe one knee bent, the length of the slide.

If the slide was on the road, cars had to inch across the ice. If the slide was on the pavement old people would snarl at the kids as they crossed the road to a safer pavement. Today, I'm with the oul fellas and oul wans, cursing the inconsiderate kids.

A nice trick was to get one of those triangular milk cartoons and fill it with water. Then you placed it carefully on the footpath and you moved to a safe distance. Eventually some prat would come along, usually a bigshot young guy with a girl on his arm (that type could never resist trying to impress), and he'd casually lash out at the carton, demonstrating his football skills, and with any luck the pair of them would get their legs drenched.

In the evenings, you could tie a thread to the knocker on someone's door, feed the line back down the pavement, behind a wall or hedge, then pull the thread and knock on the door. You could hide behind the hedge or, if you had the nerve, just stand around casually, or pretend to play a game. And someone answered the knock, came out, looked up and down the street, usually didn't see the thread, and went back in. Just as they closed the door you pulled the thread again and they came back out instantly. When they saw no one running away it dawned on them and they reached for the thread. Meanwhile, you were on the far side of the road, mimicking an intense interest in scraping a piece of tar off the footpath. They knew what you were up to and they might let a roar at you, but there was no evidence, was there, missus? Today, there are too many electric bells, the knocker is a relic.

There were more sophisticated things to do. There was, for instance, the mowl. Set into the pavement in front of every house in Cabra West there is a small metal cover. The cover has on it the word Uisce and somewhere underneath there's a tap to allow Dublin Corporation turn off the flow of water to the house. The whole thing is usually clogged with earth, almost to the top, leaving a shallow cup or hole. The word 'hole' became mowl, and the mowl became a street game. You stood with your heel against the open mowl and you threw a coin off the footpath, putting sufficient spin to cause it to roll back and take cover behind the kerb. The other players threw out, then everyone in turn aimed at the mowl and there was an amount of measuring of who was closest to the mowl. If you got your coin into the mowl you got to aim at other players' coins. If you missed the mowl your coin lay there within reach, vulnerable to the next player to hit the mowl. The rules and the skills involved were as complex as those in golf, with great importance attached to the ability to spin the coin, to dictate the direction it would take when it hit the ground. Measurements were reckoned in handspans, the distance from the tip of your thumb to the tip of your little finger, when your fingers were spread wide. Throwing a penny little more than an inch in diameter, to hit another penny six feet away was no mean feat. We played for pennies, sometimes, but mostly in the cod.

We had just pennies to spend but we weren't deprived, as there was little to spend them on. A fizz bag, a lucky bag, or one of those hard, reddish-pink lumps of sugar in which you might find a threepenny bit, or so the legend went. Liquorice that left the whole inside of your mouth black, except it wasn't liquorice, it was a length of coagulated sugar steeped in black dye. Bubble gum (shameful confession: I never could blow bubbles, despite hours of mastication and effort, and to this day cannot do so), sweets in the shape of cigarettes, the legendary bulls' eyes, pink and white slabs of nougat (nugget, we called it), pink and white marshmallows, hard-iced pink and white Clarnico-Murray sweets, Cleeves's toffee, Scot's Clan, broken biscuits, sweetshop shelves laden with big glass jars full of sugary things. Bars of Urney's Regal chocolate. The centrality of family life was so taken for granted that the sharing of a weekly family bag of sweets was a ritual recognisable enough to be exploited in advertisements. Each weekend, newspaper adverts told us that 'It's Saturday—Don't Forget Your Lemon's Pure Sweets', and an illustration showed Dad arriving home with his bag of sweets, while smiling family members gathered round him and licked their lips in anticipation.

Sometimes we kids would pool our buying power (although I can't remember what it was we would collectively buy). To do this was to bunce in. This is not to be confused with bunk in, which was to get in somewhere without paying. This usually meant the cinema, where someone would pay in, then go to a side exit and open the door bolt and let his mates in.

We got pocket money and there was a loose understanding that we would in return do chores. Shelling peas, maybe, or cutting the grass. The worst: holding up wool in my outstretched arms so my aunt Eileen could roll it into a ball. Getting the messages. Setting the table, clearing the table. Setting the fire first thing in the morning, the house freezing. Rolling newspapers into tight, short lengths, putting sticks on top, then coal. Lighting the fire and, when it faltered, holding a double-spread of newspaper in front of the fireplace opening, to create a draught from beneath the grate. On occasion, you watched as one spot of the newspaper grew pale brown, then darker, then it came alight, and you rolled it into a ball to smother the flames.

Making toast, before toasters: you wait until the fire is glowing, you hold a slice of bread on a fork, as close to the red coals as you can bear, holding it there, hoping it will brown before you have to jerk your hand away.

To supplement pocket money you could hunt out old clothes and beg your mother to let you have them. 'I never wear it anymore, Ma, never! It doesn't fit me, I swear, cross me heart!' The ragmen would regularly visit our neighbourhood, usually horse-powered, later they had vans. They had all sorts of cheap nick-nacks they would give us in exchange for old clothes. It was like there was a whole section of the economy based on circulating goods from the poor to the poorer.

When you got new clothes you got 'hansel', a few pence in a pocket of the new garment, to bring you luck.

Older kids had real money and they gambled. They played cards, Brag or Don or Poker. Or they played pitch and toss. The players gathered in circles, and if it was nighttime they stood under a streetlight. The two coins were flicked into the air and the circle widened as the coins hit the ground and everyone bent over and the heads went down to see how the coins had landed. If a garda arrived suddenly on the scene there was a scatter. It was understood that everyone in the area of a certain age was honour bound to warn the players if a cop came in sight. Once, on my way to the shops for the messages, with a pitch and toss school in session on Ventry Road, I spotted a garda coming round the corner from Broombridge Road on a bike (there used to be a garda who regularly cycled around delivering summonses, which were carried in a leather satchel hanging from his shoulder). The thing to do when a copper appeared was yell 'L-O!', which meant Look Out. Some of the more intense pitch and toss schools employed kids to wait at strategic corners and stand L-O. You could also shout 'Rozzer!', indicating more specifically the impending arrival of a member of the constabulary. Or you could yell, to the same effect, 'Bluebottle!', which was the option I chose. The players quickly pocketed their coins and adopted nonchalant poses. One of them gave me a thumbs up, and I felt like I was now a small but important part of the underworld, like I'd just helped John Dillinger case a bank.

The cops were alien to us; not that we who were almost all of us law abiding had much contact with them. They seemed for the most part to be big culchies with red necks, looking with suspicion at us as they plodded or cycled on their way. Lugs Brannigan, a policeman who gained his reputation (and his nickname, due to beaten-and-cauliflowered ears) in boxing circles, was an establishment character, a legend, in a city that took its 'characters' seriously. (Dublin was full of characters, poor spacers such as Bang-Bang, who ran around town pointing a key at people and going, 'Bang! Bang!' Johnny Forty-Coats, a vagrant wrapped in several overcoats, was another. We had our own Cabra West character, Danny from Broombridge Road, who never paid his bus fare: he'd stand up and sing and the conductors, once they got to know him, accepted a song as Danny's fare. A strict and humourless conductor would occasionally demand that Danny pay up in the traditional manner, winning dagger looks from the rest of the passengers as a saddened Danny handed over the few pence. It wasn't the money that mattered to Danny, it was the notion of being able to charm people with his voice.)

'Here's Lugs!', someone would shout, and anyone in the vicinity doing anything that might be interpreted as wrongful, mischievous or bold, scarpered in fear of Lugs Brannigan. More than once I did a runner myself, but it was never the real Lugs, just a normal copper, or whoever shouted the warning was acting the can. Lugs was known for hitting people. He believed that a clip on the ear was the most effective punishment for minor crime. If he caught some youngster he thought was up to no good he gave him a thump. Lugs, a crude and well-meaning copper of the old school, was highly regarded within the community for this carry-on, and his violence was known to and tolerated by his superiors. Kids feared Lugs, and his violent antics were almost certainly exaggerated, but whatever the results of his carry-on it could not be said that he spread amongst the young a respect for the forces of law and order.

Among the other things kids did that they weren't supposed to do was rob orchards. Adults told us this was called 'Boxing the

126

Fox', but we preferred the more blunt term: robbing orchards. Over the wall, dodge from bush to tree, up, grab, fill your pockets, stuff the apples down your jumper, drop to the ground, run. I never much fancied it. Too much work for a few sour apples that ended up being thrown away. And the illegality didn't appeal to me. The nostalgia for their own childhood romps that led adults, even teachers, to cheerfully chuckle an endorsement of 'Boxing the Fox' was disconcerting. Right and wrong, it seemed, didn't matter much if you gave the act a cutesy name. For all we knew, sticking up a bank was okay, as long as you called it Batting the Cat.

The more daring amongst us smoked. The more prosperous kids might be able to afford a Woodbine or two (among adults the choice of the truly hard up), Gold Flake, Craven 'A', Sweet Afton or even Players (and corner shops routinely sold cigarettes in ones and twos to kids who couldn't afford a whole packet), but mostly we made our own. This involved collecting butts from the street, opening them up, extracting what flakes of tobacco might be salvaged and rolling a new cigarette in a piece of paper. It was something that I did just once, to show I wasn't afraid of doing it, but I preferred pretend cigarettes made from rolled-up corrugated cardboard. You lit the end of it, shook it to put out the flame, and there remained a glowing paper ember. You took a few drags on it, making the ember glow brighter until it eventually flickered out. Not a very satisfying smoke, but we felt tough.

'It won't harm your throat', said the advert for Craven 'A'. It said nothing about your lungs.

Like kids everywhere and at every time, we had a world within but separate from the grownup world. 'Where did you go?', your folks would ask when you wandered back from an afternoon of climbing up and jumping off things.

'Out', you said.

'What did you do?'

'Nothing.'

Our little world had its own rules, its dares, its triumphs. Grownups could see the outer shape of our world, but the interior, its depth and texture, was hidden. It was as mundane as an ad hoc game of chasing, where someone was declared to be 'on it' and had to run after everyone else until they touched someone and he in turn became 'on it'. And it was as dangerous as a gamble with a speeding lorry.

It was called scutting, grabbing onto a handhold at the back of a lorry and holding on. The driver might see the kids in his mirror, as they jumped on at a traffic lights or a corner. If he gave a damn, he'd jerk to a stop, jump out and chase them off. Then he'd run back to his cab, dive into his seat and put the boot down, trying to get away before the little gurriers could regain their grip on the back of his lorry. He seldom did. I tried it a couple of times, but it was as frightening as it was exhilarating, and best left to the borderline psychopaths.

Buses were great playthings, back when they had an open platform at the back. You could wait at a bus stop and howl at the bus conductor: 'Any empty busrolls? Ah, go on, mister, any empty rolls?' And if he felt like it he might throw you the remnants of a busroll and you could spend half a day unrolling it and running around with it streaming behind you. (It doesn't, right enough, seem like a terribly exciting way to spend your time, but it's what we did.) You could wait until a bus was moving off from a bus stop and you ran after it, jumped onto the open platform, swung around the bar and hung on until the conductor came back towards you with an angry scowl on his face, at which point you jumped off and hit the ground running, trying to run fast enough so you didn't tumble over with the momentum.

We jumped off things. We got up on walls and railings and trees and ladders and we jumped off and we sometimes got gashed but no one ever seemed to break anything. We ran in and out of traffic in the sure and certain knowledge that we were fast enough to escape any damage. And we were.

Two-thirds of the way down our stairs I would climb over the bannisters and, after waiting a moment to enjoy the anticipatory thrill, at eye level with the cardboard picture of the Sacred Heart pinned over the living room door, my backside pointing at the holy water font nailed to the wall, I'd drop down into the hall. The hall was three foot wide and ten foot long. To me it was a canyon, the bannister a cliff-face.

We jumped through hedges and swung from branches and crawled through back gardens and in our short trousers we got our legs reddened by nettles. We called them stingers, because that's what they did, raising reddish-white blisters. The alleged cure was to rub the welts with dock leaves, which we carefully did, feeling like Indian scouts living off the land, applying ancient remedies to our battle wounds. (The cure for warts—which seemed to be far more widespread then than they are now—was a purple paint of some kind, daubed on the offending part.)

Spitting. Someone might spit a long one, for no reason, and someone else would make a hacking sound and spit a few inches further and before you knew it there was a spitting contest going on. Some guys specialised in long distance spitting at enemies, as a gesture of contempt or challenge. Such a specialist would draw his head back, his arms stretched out behind him, then propel his head forward, the forward movement stopping at the instant the spit passed his lips, creating maximum propulsive spit-speed, the gollier leaving his lips like a shell ejected from a gun barrel. Mostly spitting was casual, a squirt through the barely opened teeth being a way of demonstrating how cool you were. I was a lousy spitter and gave it up after a couple of cool squirts ended up on my shirt front.

We didn't have to sit on a see-saw to chant 'See-saw, maggedy-daw'. Why we went around chanting 'See-saw, maggedy-daw' is a complete mystery to me today, and not one on which I tend to expend much thought, but chant it we did.

Sometimes you just leaned over the metal gate in front of your house or someone else's and you swung back and forth, back and forth, the gate squeaking, until an adult came out and told you to go away. Maybe you made music with your mouth, imitating a trombone or a sax, convinced that the noise you were making was indistinguishable from that made by the real instrument. Or you lay down on the grass somewhere and made a meaningless sound, like maybe *baaaaaa-boooo*, *baaaaaa-boooo*, over and over and over, just because you felt like it, and you kept it up until an adult told you to stop that bloody noise and go somewhere or do something.

If you wanted to be a truly irritating smartass you went to a public phonebox (the one where you had to press Button A to be heard, or press Button B to get your money back) and you rang the operator and you asked what time it was. She would say something like, 'It's eh . . . twenty-five minutes to . . .' And you were in like a shot: 'No, it's ten hairs past my elbow', and you slammed down the phone. One day my friend Frankie and I did that and we almost fell out of the phonebox on the Navan Road, in convulsions of laughter at our daring wit, and there was a plainclothes cop standing on the pavement.

You never mistook a plainclothes cop for anything other than a plainclothes cop.

'What were you doing with that phonebox?'

Other kids smashed glass or kicked the machine until the money fell out. We annoyed the operator, a grownup, and that was in our world a sin as grievous as any act of vandalism. We looked around, seeking an avenue of escape. Through the traffic, maybe, across the road, he wouldn't follow us in and out of the speeding cars— except, there, on the other side of the road, there was another cop. They came in pairs. Just then a van stopped right in front of the other cop and he couldn't see us and, two criminal minds working as one, making an instant decision, we scarpered off across the road, dodging cars, around onto Nephin Road, bent over, arms and legs pumping, and down towards the lane that led into the back of the Bogies. Puffing, panting, flinging ourselves up onto the gate into the Bogies, we looked back to see what kind of a lead we had. No sign of the cops. It was almost insulting. They had us bang to rights and they didn't even bother running after us. We strolled off across the Bogies, casting just the occasional anxious look behind. Relieved to have escaped from the rozzers and now just slightly chuffed to have stumbled into such an outlaw escapade.

Much time was spent just doing nothing much. Taunting someone, to the tune of the Blue Danube: 'Gick-gick, la-la, it's all down your leg, gick-gick, la-la'. It seemed funny at the time. We'd pull out an imaginary gun and point it as a highwayman might: 'Stand on your liver!', we cried, mightily impressed with our own wit. 'Or you'll have none to stand on!'

> Will I tell you a story
> About Johnny McGory?
> Will I begin it?
> That's all that's in it.

Lord knows where this classic wit came from, but we all had it spouted at us, and in turn tried it out on other kids who hadn't yet heard it, and we stood back and waited for the peals of laughter. And they always came.

We made threats that were only half-mocking. 'You keep that up and I'll get my big brother after you.' I was somewhat disadvantaged in this one, as I didn't have a big brother. But the arguments developed. 'My brother's in the army, and he'll get the army after you.' We said such things, straightfaced.

My retaliation: 'My uncle was in the British army.' This was true, my Uncle Joe having joined the British army as his father had before him. He fought Rommel in the desert. As the saying goes, Rommel lost. The fact that my uncle's war ended before I was born mattered little. I felt sure the British army would remember Uncle Joe. 'He was in the war. He'll get the British army after you.' And everyone knew the British army was bigger than the Irish army. Someone came back with: 'My cousin is in the American army!' It was a blatant lie, but there was no way of proving it. 'And he'll get the American army after you!' None of us knowing a power greater than this, the argument ended there.

Everything was either cowboys or soldiers. It being a dozen years or more after the end of the Second World War, we fought the good fight all over again. I could (and still can) draw a reasonable

Stuka dive bomber and a very good Spitfire fighter (and could at once distinguish the latter from a Hurricane). I was knowledgeable about the Lancaster bomber (and built an Airfix model of it) and knew all there was to know about the V1 and the V2 rocket-bombs (and the bravery of the Spitfire pilots who would fly alongside a rocket and use a wingtip to flip it over, making it crash harmlessly). From American movies and British comics we were casually familiar with what happened at such places as Guadalcanal and Iwo Jima. The date 6 June meant—and to us always will immediately signify—D-Day. We knew that in that invasion Sword and Juno were codenames for beaches at Normandy. I had an adaptable hat, courtesy of Santa. A blue cowboy hat. And if the game was soldiers I could turn the hat inside out and it looked a little like an army helmet. Unfortunately, it looked at first a little too much like a German army helmet and that wouldn't do, so I cut off a bit at each side, softening the profile so it looked more like an American GI's helmet. When the game switched back to cowboys, and I turned my hat right side out, it looked a little tatty and misshapen, but that was okay, as I might have just come in from a hard time on a cattle drive.

On a Saturday morning, we might wander down to the Church of the Most Precious Blood, in case there was a wedding. We stood outside and waited for the happy couple and then we started shouting 'Grushie! Grushie!' Eventually, the best man would throw a handful of change in the air and we scrambled and pushed and tugged and punched and dived for the coins, no quarter asked or given.

Our reading matter, through which we gained some knowledge of a wider world, consisted of comics. At first the British ones, the *Dandy* and the *Beano* and the *Beezer* and the *Eagle* and the *Victor* and the *Lion* and the *Tiger* and the *Hurricane* and the *Hotspur*. I preferred the *Rover*, because it told its stories in written prose, not drawn pictures. I was initially attracted to reading stories rather than looking at them not because of a preference for prose over graphics but because such stories were better value. You looked at the panel drawings in the *Lion* and they were great but the story was over in a couple of minutes. In the *Rover* or the *Adventure* or the *Wizard* (all of which eventually amalgamated into one comic, as business dwindled) you had page after page of written stories that would take you days to read. Alf Tupper, the Tough of the Track. Braddock VC. The Will o' the Wisp o' the West. Sexton Blake. Commando Jim. Brython of the Elephants. That the comics assumed in their readers a very English sensibility didn't bother us at all. We happily dug into Lord Snooty and Dennis the Menace, Roy of the Rovers, Desperate Dan, the Bash Street Kids and Beryl the Peril. In our kiddie books, we could connect with the likes of Noddy or Just William while recognising the distance between their Englishness and our own cultural surroundings.

Auntie Kathleen, in London, each week posted home her *Woman* and *Woman's Own* magazines, and for me a copy of the *Eagle*, with cowboy Jeff Arnold and space pilot Dan Dare.

In Beechinor's, the local newsagents, there was a young girl behind the counter who let me have last week's comics for a penny each. Fullprice, they cost sixpence, so instead of being able to afford one comic once a week I could buy half a dozen, as long as I didn't mind reading last week's comics.

When we were flush we might buy one of those small British war comics, *Commando* and the like (they're still selling them and they seem to have changed little in over thirty years), with black and white drawings, in which every story had a German soldier screaming 'Achtung!' as the British tommy came storming in, his Sten gun chattering. 'You vill die, Britischer svinehund!', the Nazi would promise. And there'd be a close-up of the spitting muzzle of the Sten gun and the filthy German would go down screaming, '*Aaaarrrggghhh!!!!*' Those little comics always seemed to tell pretty much the same story.

Then we discovered American comics. *Dell* and then *Marvel*, colourful, exciting, imaginative, full of big cities and exotic villains and superheroes (favourite: The Fantastic Four), showing us a world not limited to the events of the previous twenty years on the battlefields and playing fields of Europe.

The comics had adverts which gave hints of the exotic world out there. In the English comics there were adverts from an outfit called Ellisdons, which sold tricks and jokes and gadgets. You could send off for a plastic shrunken head, a midget Bible, a nose flute or a Seebackroscope, which let you see what was going on behind you. There was a little gadget called a Ventrilo, which was supposed to allow you 'throw your voice'. You could, the advert promised, make it seem like your voice was coming out of a suitcase or from under the bed. 'Fool your teacher', we were urged. It was irresistible, the notion of having a magic skill that would make you superior to the grownups, who would be agog at your abilities and treat you as their equal.

The American comics had panel drawings of a skinny Charles Atlas arriving at the beach and having sand kicked in his face by a big bully while, in the background, bikini-clad girls laughed. He did his Dynamic Training and cultivated muscles and came back to the beach and decked the bully and the girls flocked around him. Now, Charles wanted to teach others his Dynamic Training methods and we too could have a body like Charles's, the advert promised, if we coughed up the dough. It hadn't yet dawned on me why I might want to have bikinied girls swarming around me but I didn't believe Charles's claims, anyway.

The inside back page of such comics often had an advert from some outfit called the Rosecrucians, a religious cult which promised to show us how to straighten out our lives by learning to love God. I wasn't buying, having been well looked after in that department by Canon Burke and his mates. I sent off for the Ventrilo, though, the gadget that promised to allow you 'throw your voice'. It didn't.

Irish comics? You must be joking. You might as well ask if there were Irish movies.

(Well, yes there were 'Irish' movies, but even we knew that they were crap. *Darby O'Gill and the Little People*, that kind of thing. There was a British movie called *Rooney* which my Uncle Larry insisted I see, with John Gregson playing hurling at Croke Park, running down the sideline with the ball glued to his hurley stick. It wasn't up to much, but it showed Dublin more or less as it was, without ladling on the leprechaun sauce, so it was admired.)

One summer, home on holidays, Auntie Kathleen gave me my first real book: *Reach for the Sky*, by Paul Brickhill, a biography of a Second World War hero, legless RAF pilot Douglas Bader. After that it was *Biggles* and *Hornblower* and *Ellery Queen's Mystery Magazine* and Leslie Charteris's *The Saint* (every book in the series), and *Treasure Island* and O. Henry and Arthur C. Clarke's science fiction, and from there to the public library in Phibsboro and Sherlock Holmes and Jack London and anything else between covers. The paperback revolution, the growth of mass sales through Pan and Corgi and Penguin and Hodder & Stoughton, was getting into its stride around then and I came to know every secondhand bookshop in town.

Most Wednesday afternoons my mother and aunt would bring me into town, where they would do their shopping. We went on the CIE bus with the flying snail logo on the side. To Winston's, Pim's, McBirney's, all gone now. Or, Madame Nora's women's clothes shop, near the Happy Ring House. There was an element of spectacle in some shops. In Clerys you could watch the sales assistant write an invoice, take the money, place the money and invoice into a small cylinder which was then attached to the network of wires that linked every counter to a central cashpoint, somewhere high up above us all. The assistant pulled a handle and with a *ssscchhhhhhwoppp!!!* the cylinder was shot at tremendous speed along a wire towards the cashpoint. The receipt and change would moments later come flying back down the wire. It was a little drama in itself.

You could, in winter days when darkness came early, stand in D'Olier Street and watch, high up on a building, an animated lighting advert for a meat company, with two pigs tossing a sausage back and forth, catching it on forks. In its day, this was an entertainment highlight.

Passing down Liffey Street you used any excuse to linger a

135

moment at Alpha Bargains, to look at the knives, the commando daggers and the hunting knives you'd need to survive in the wilderness, the tent which would protect you from the rain, the compass that would point your way back to civilisation. Just looking at the Alpha Bargains window display was like living one of those stories from the *Adventure* or the *Wizard*.

Over at the Monument Creameries, near the Carlton cinema, you could watch the sales assistants wrap butter. With a couple of paddles, a chunk of butter was cut from a huge slab of the stuff, slapped down on a piece of greaseproof paper and weighed, a bit cut off or added on, then it was smacked into a rectangular shape with all the skill of a sculptor knocking off a small masterpiece.

Shopping done, we'd rush to get to the Carlton before the admission price increased at 5 p.m. It was a shilling in before five o'clock. The Carlton was preferred because it always had a double bill (known to us all as the big picture and the little picture), great value for money. Places like the Savoy and the Adelphi usually had just one picture and a load of trimmings, crap like the British newsreel, *Movietone News*, and the *Look at Life* series. Or, worse, an interminable travel film about the delights of Bali. The Royal had a stage show in addition to the film, with Tommy Dando and his Organ (he was known as Tommy Dando and his Organ) rising up like magic from the pit in front of the stage. (One moment from a stage show: big Noel Purcell getting into a phone box; there was an explosion; the door of the phone box opened and out stepped dwarf Mickser Reid. We nearly got sick with the laughing.) As Tommy Dando played, the words of the song were projected on a screen and we all sang along.

The Royal was for special occasions, the Carlton was the weekly entrance gate to the Hollywood dream factory. What we didn't know then was that the Carlton, in order to fit in three double-bill programmes a day, used to mercilessly chop chunks out of the movies. Ten minutes here, twenty minutes there, a nip and a tuck and even the longest movie fitted into the schedule.

When I went with pals to the local cinema, the Cabra Grand,

part of Britain's Rank empire, where the walls were decorated with portraits of minor British stars, and the whole building was saturated with the smell of freshly made popcorn, it was usually to see a western. The hero was called the chap. At school or on the street, you retailed the plot of what you had seen, describing how the chap did this and the chap did that. 'And then, and then . . .' Movies, if they were any good, were about chaps and their achievements. The Grand ran the same movie from Monday to Wednesday, then a new programme from Thursday to Saturday. The Sunday show was made up of any old rubbish, usually prefaced by one of those dire Edgar Lustgarden true crime dramatisations with Superintendent This and Chief Inspector That ploddingly solving a dull crime. After the little picture, a sales girl walked up and down the aisle carrying a tray laden with ice cream tubs and popcorn and Lyons Maid ice-pops. Behind her, on the screen, a giant shell opened up, revealing the Cinema & General Publicity logo, as the adverts started. We talked through the adverts and shut up when the trailers came on.

We talked through the limp bits of the movies, the tedious plot exposition, we jeered during the kissing, we cheered when the chap took on the bad guys. Inevitably he would jump on his horse and chase after the head bad guy and when they came to a clear space with a gentle incline down to one side you knew it was time for the chap to dive off his horse, grab the head bad guy, knock him from his saddle, and the two of them would roll down the gentle incline to a neat space where they'd slug it out.

Weekly serials, *Flash Gordon* and the like, were on their way out of fashion by the time I started going to the pictures. We never used the word serial. The events in one episode were followed up in the next. Therefore, a serial was a follier upper.

Practically everyone in Cabra West was a Three Stooges fan, though I never much liked them. Someone early on, probably someone's big brother, authoritatively mispronounced their name and in our neighbourhood they were forever after known as the Three Stewdees.

Seven

No one ever escaped: they always ex-caped. You never said something was the same: it was the very ex-same. No one drowned, though someone might have drownded. Things seldom got worse, though they often got worser. You would never follow anyone but you might folly them. You didn't swallow your food, you swallied it. There were no ghosts, only go-stez. The playground was the layer. The canal was the naller. A chimney was a chimley. The zoo was the iz-oo. When you went to a cinema you saw a fillum. If something was cool it was rapid or ace; if it was bad it was shite. If it was really bad it was chronic. Girls were young wans; their mothers were oul wans. Girls didn't get embarrassed, they got scarlet. A windbag was a mouth. An aggressive windbag was a mouth almighty. A boot was not an item of footwear but a kick, usually in the hole. You might thump someone but you'd more likely mill them. If things got really serious you might have to claim them, or even burst them. A girl would never threaten to scrape you with her nails: the promise was, cut that out or I'll scrob you. You didn't behave mischievously, you acted the can. You didn't peek at the answers in a schoolmate's jotter, you cogged. You didn't loyally stand by your pal in time of trouble, you'd stick up for him. Money wasn't halfpennies and pennies and sixpences and shillings and half-crowns; it was makes, wings, tanners, bobs and half dollars. A spit was a gollier. Christopher was Christy sometimes, but mostly he was Gitters. Anthony might be Tony but more often he was Anto. Peter was usually Yayters. Murphy was always Spud. Anyone who ran fast, even for a bus, was called Ronnie Delany. Anyone who tried a stylish move at football was dubbed Stanley Matthews.

At Hallowe'en we went knocking on doors and no one used the nancy request, 'Trick or treat'; when the front door opened we chorused: 'Help the Hallowe'en Party', as though we were neophyte politicians canvassing wealthy patrons. That or the blunt demand: 'Any apples or nuts?' (And we knew no such delicacy as peanuts: they were monkey nuts and they came not in foil packets, not salted or roasted, but in their shells.)

Hoops, they don't have them anymore. A denuded bicycle wheel and a piece of stick to hoosh it along with, and you could wander the neighbourhood for hours. A hoop was to us what a horse was to a cowboy. It made the journey easier. Back then there were fewer cars, herds of bikes roamed the city, weaving around the horses and carts. Not enough bikes now, not enough discarded wheels.

A lot of fads eventually made their way here from America. Hoola hoops, a plastic commercial effort, an invention that lasted a brief season. You spun it around your waist and shoved your pelvis back and forth, and no matter how energetically I did it the hoop always immediately dropped down around my ankles. Yo-yos were all the rage for a few weeks, promoted by an American who came to town on tour. He was Billy Panama, Yo-Yo Champion. He appeared on stage at various cinemas, including the Cabra Grand, demonstrating his yo-yo skills, making the yo-yo drop, hang still, then spin back up into his hand. He could Walk the Dog, making the yo-yo walk along the ground in front of him, at the end of the string, or he could Rock the Baby, which didn't look anything like a baby rocking. We tried the tricks, found them impossible and concluded that life was too short to get excited about yo-yos. Billy didn't impress us. What a stupid thing to want to be: a yo-yo champion. That was the kind of skill, I concluded, that a guy really should keep quiet about.

Davy Crockett hats were big for a while, when Walt Disney churned out a movie about the King of the Wild Frontier. It was only posh kids who got to wear genuine Walt Disney copyrighted Davy Crockett raccoon hats, stupid round things with a tail hanging down the back. This must have been one of the first examples of movie merchandising to hit Dublin. Big excitement surrounded another movie, *The Bridge on the River Kwai*. An evening newspaper, the *Mail* or the *Press* or the *Herald*, ran a competition for children to build a model of the bridge, from ice-pop sticks. It was too difficult for someone my age, but the bridge on the Kwai, in real life the scene of terrible agony for British prisoners of war, became for us a childhood icon.

(I was too young to go to see the movie. Years later, when I worked as a projectionist at the Capitol cinema, off O'Connell Street, we showed a revival of *The Bridge on the River Kwai*. There is a scene near the end where the Japanese commander is about to discover the explosives planted to destroy the bridge. 'Kill him!', William Holden tells a subordinate. 'Kill him!', whispers Jack Hawkins. I used to stand at the back of the cinema during that scene and listen to hundreds of kids passionately screaming, 'Kill him! Kill him! Kill him!' One afternoon after the next, the scene never failed to excite the killing instinct within the children.)

A lot of things you did alone, finding out stuff. Like what it felt like if you twisted a rubber band around and around your finger until the top of your finger was turning purple and then you whipped off the rubber band and the blood flowed back down your finger. It felt cold and strange and nice. You could get a similar effect by closing your teeth on a piece of your cheek and biting hard until you couldn't stand it anymore, then you let go.

You could adopt a policy of not walking on lines in the pavement, which was an easy one to do. I came up with the far more difficult feat of not alone not stepping on lines in the pavement but always taking three steps in the space between two lines. That kind of thing can, if carried to extremes, turn you into a suitable case for therapy.

At home, there was an old sofa that was my private horse to ride, my mountain to climb, my rooftop from which to dive onto an unsuspecting German soldier, my racing car to drive and the spaceship in which I rescued Dan Dare from the clutches of the evil Mekon. There was a solid table, underneath which I piloted my submarine, crawled along iron girders on half-built sky scrapers, and hid in my private cave.

Girls' games were, of course, fit only for scorn. There was little crossover between the sexes. They played skipping, sometimes with two ropes going in opposite directions. We'd never admit it, but none of us could do anything as skilful as that. They tied ropes to lampposts and they swung wide around the lamppost, out into the street and to hell with traffic, sometimes dipping their heads, long hair skimming just inches above the pavement, twisting and rocking and somehow never slamming into the lamppost. They juggled balls, three or four flying through the air at the same time. They leaped and hopped through chalked 'beds' with absolute precision, one foot off the ground, the toe of the other nudging a shoe-polish tin packed with clay. Nah, we said, we wouldn't be interested in that nancy stuff.

Girls also made daisychains, which needed a skill we boys didn't hold in any regard. Girls would pick a buttercup and hold it under your chin, and if the yellow colour was reflected on your chin it meant you liked butter. 'You like butter', they'd conclude, as though they'd figured out some deeply hidden character trait. All we boys knew about flowers was that if you messed with dandelions you'd end up wetting yourself that night. Dandelions (it was a weed, not a flower, but we didn't know the difference) were known as piss-in-the-beds.

The official Dublin Corporation playground had a monkey puzzle to clamber up and jump off, four swings, a roundabout and a sandpit. The tarmacadam was marked out for football and tennis, and there was a handball alley and a pavilion. It's an old Dublin tradition that everything official has to have railings around it and a gate, and official opening hours. A bar of the railings around the playground was, inevitably, knocked out, to make an unofficial entrance. If the Corpo had taken down the railings and put up a few seats for older people to sit and talk in the evenings the playground might have felt more a part of the community. Instead, come official closing time everyone was shut out except the hard chaws, who climbed the railings with no bother and eventually made the pavilion the location of cider parties and the sandpit a site for bonfires.

Most days in the summer we'd kick a ball around the playground. Some of us went from time to time to see the local soccer teams, St Brendan's and Beggsboro, and in time local heroes like Jimmy Conway and Blacker Flanagan made names for themselves, but for most of us it went no further than a kickabout in the layer. The transformation of British soccer from a game into a showbiz commodity market wasn't yet under way, but there was already an amount of merchandising. I wasn't the only one in my class to send off for a signed photo of Jackie Carey. I had never seen him play, of course, and had no idea who he played for. We had as yet no access to TV coverage of soccer, and I had only the faintest of notions as to why I needed a signed photo of Jackie Carey or anyone else, but I knew that Jackie Carey was a hero, an example to us all. Kids like to belong, to sign up to a heroic idea, which makes them ideal consumers, as the Manchester United of today has twigged. Just as I hadn't a clue who Jackie Carey was (and, to be honest, I'm still not sure), so there are kids today spending a lot more money than we dreamed existed to dress themselves and their bedrooms in merchandise of football stars they idolise, while having hardly any interest in actual soccer games.

Sometimes our football became more serious than kickabout stuff, with two self-important captains taking turns picking their teams while the rest of us who wanted to play stood in a row, waiting to be called forward. I was a terrible player and was usually among the two or three shufflers that no one wanted until virtually the whole team was picked and we remnants were reluctantly taken on board. What happened in every match was that I'd run at the guy with the ball, try to take it from him, and he'd step around me and run on and I'd turn and run after him and he'd kick it to someone else and by the time that had happened fifteen times I just wanted to give up. Not that anyone would have noticed. If I tried my damnest or if I didn't bother too much the result was pretty much the same: the guy with the ball waltzing around me again.

If I happened to stumble across the ball as it ran loose you could bet money that an opponent would within seconds take it off me. I lacked whatever eye–foot coordination is necessary to control a moving ball. It's not a capital offence, but there were afternoons in the playground when it felt like one.

There was a weekend when I was assigned to defence (all the good players wanted to be up front, where the goals are scored) and I decided there was no point running after the opposition, wearing myself out. I just stood there. I didn't jig this way or that way, I didn't rush the attacker, I just stood there waiting for the guy to come to me. If he altered course I moved until I was again between him and the goal. And when he came within tackling distance I didn't try to take the ball away from him. I just lashed out at the ball and kicked it away. It didn't matter where, just away from the guy's feet.

I stood there, stunned, as our side took the ball and someone ran with it. I had stopped the attack. A few minutes later I did it again. And again. I had stumbled on a great footballing truth. You don't have to take possession of the ball, you just have to hook it away from the other guy. Where it went after that wasn't my responsibility, but the attack was stopped dead. I did it again, and again and again, six, eight, ten times. My team-mates were as bemused as the opposition. Suddenly, I was a sports hero. The other side started passing too soon, making mistakes, in efforts to overcome the problem of the guy who didn't do anything except stand there and wait for you to come and then lash the ball away from your feet. We won the match. I was told I played a blinder and I knew it was true.

A couple of days later there was a game in the Bogies and I was one of the first picked. Word had spread. *Hey-hey, Stanley Matthews!!!*

I had so impressed my peers that I was immediately told to take a forward position. I was a sporting hero now, a match-winner, a regular Roy of the Rovers, and I didn't belong at the back of the field, like some clumsy oaf being tolerated by real footballers. Truth

143

to tell, I'd impressed myself and was quite happy to take a key role in attacking the enemy. Of course, the gimmick that worked in defence was useless up front and every time I got the ball I lost it immediately. I spent the match running back down the field after those who had no trouble running rings around me as I vainly tried to take the ball back. I grew more depressed as the game went on and I watched my footballing reputation disintegrate. As the match ended I heard the phrase, from the lips of one of those who had so recently been singing my praises: Flash in the pan. It was the first time I heard the expression, but I knew immediately what it meant.

It was in or around then that I retired from football. The playground introduced succeeding generations to the game, and as television made its impact you could see the kids who scored goals turning and running back towards the centre of the tarmacadam pitch, their limbs moving in slow motion, just like in the TV action replays.

* * *

There came a time when we could stay out a little later in the evenings and we began to think of things other than cowboy games and football. Groups of boys would cluster at the edge of a green space known as the Compound, and nearby would be groups of girls. And nothing would be said, nonchalance ruled. Then a boy would stray off a couple of yards, maybe kicking a ball, doing a pratfall—and suddenly there was a rush of girls coming at him and the boys all scattered and the girls concentrated on their victim and he swerved and twisted and doubled back and they always got him and he vanished under a heap of arms and legs and hair and they held him down and no matter how frantically he shook his head from side to side a big wet, slobbering kiss was planted on his protesting lips. The phenomenon of the Kissing Girls was not limited to our generation (it happens among kids today), nor this locality (I've read an American's description of much the same thing, and over there, too, they were called the Kissing Girls). Girls develop earlier, and they were practising on us. There was an ambiguity. We were ten or eleven, being kissed by wet slobbering lips was unpleasant. But, while we ran like we meant it, it didn't stop us hanging out in the same spot the following evening, glancing down towards the Kissing Girls, wondering when they'd make their play. The hormones that would scramble our brains in the years to come had not yet kicked in, but we knew deep down there was more to this than a chasing game.

Mostly, though, our play was all cowboys and indians, soldiers, and cops and robbers. Apart from our homemade weapons we had our arsenals of toy guns. If you had to, you could make do with one of those silvery revolvers, garish things in which no gunslinger could take pride. By and by, the silver would flake off and the grey metal underneath was acceptable. At Christmas we always had rolls of caps to thread through our guns. The air was heavy with the smell of burnt caps and the sound of explosive bangs until we ran out of caps and had to make do with going 'Dar-dar!' or 'Ptchuuuu!' We could imitate to perfection the sound of a gun firing, the sound of the bullet ricochetting. We never went 'Bang-bang'.

There wasn't much about the Old West we didn't know. A Buntline Special (Wyatt Earp's weapon of choice) was a handgun with a very long barrel; its polar opposite was the Derringer, a tiny weapon you could keep up your sleeve, dropping it into your palm and blowing a hole through the louser who thought he had the drop on you. We knew the nicknames for guns: the Equaliser; the Peacemaker; and—though the casual callousness of it never occurred to us—the Widowmaker. We knew about the chaps the cowboys wore to keep their legs from being scratched as they rode through the briars and the bramble. The spurs that they used to giddyap their horses, and that made a tell-tale noise as the baddie crept up behind the Cisco Kid. The neat rows of bullets on their belts; their waistcoats and bandanas. Boot Hill was more real to us than Glasnevin cemetery. We knew how to rope and throw and brand, how to toss a lasso and build a teepee; we knew the difference between a town sheriff and a federal marshal, what to do if you got shot in the shoulder with an arrow (you don't pull it out, as the barb would take half your shoulder along with it; you break it off just where it enters your flesh, then you douse the wound with whiskey—pull the cork out of the bottle with your teeth—and that will tide you over until you can get to the drunken old doc in the nearest town, there being a drunken old doc in every town in the West).

My favourite handgun was a Christmas morning miracle, a sleek, sweptback matt black revolver, a thing of true beauty. It came without a holster, and it didn't really fit in the old holster that went with the flaked-silver handgun, but I paired them anyway, and when I rode my imaginary horse at full gallop I had to keep one hand on the black sixgun to keep it from falling out of the holster. I used a piece of string tied around my thigh to keep the holster tight against my leg, so not a split second would be lost in a quick draw. We sometimes squared up to each other, hands poised, until someone said 'Draw!' and we slapped leather, our hands mere blurs. Buck Jones was our hero. The thing about Buck: unlike nancyboy cowboys, Buck never shot the gun out of anyone's hand. You messed with Buck, he shot you dead.

There was the Durango Kid. And Lash LaRue, who used a whip to subdue the baddies. Champion the Wonder Horse, who would rear up on his hind legs and lash out with his front hooves, knocking the weapons from the baddies' hands. Rin Tin Tin, the wonder dog (and his mate from the 7th Cavalry, the boy Rusty). Bat Masterson with his derby hat and his cane. The Lone Ranger was cool, but maybe a bit posh, in his spotless outfit. You didn't need a special outfit to be Wild Bill Hickock or Buffalo Bill. No one was faster on the draw than Wyatt Earp.

Except, maybe, Shane. *Shane* was the first movie I saw more than once. Every kid I knew went back to see it again and again. Today, kids own video copies of their favourite movies and play them over and over, as though they were records, becoming familiar with every scene, reciting dialogue verbatim. Back then, a movie came

146

and it went and all you had was the memory. A movie had to be special to induce you to pay twice to see it. *Shane* was special.

Alan Ladd was Shane, a weary and reluctant hero, a quiet man running from a violent past, determinedly peaceful until the bad guys went too far. Then, he slowly strapped on his gun and they found out the hard way how fast he was on the draw. It's probably a fantasy every boy has about himself: you think I'm just an ordinary kid, but don't push me too far or you'll force me to reveal the nerves of steel and fists of iron hidden beneath my modest exterior. *Shane* is not the most highly regarded of westerns, but for us it had the depth and quality of a classic tale. Honest toil versus thievery; self-sacrifice in the name of honour. We were too young to notice Shane's reluctant and chaste love for the wife of his farmer friend, but there was that too. I can still watch it and feel a chill as young Brandon de Wilde, the farmer's son, runs across the hills calling for Shane, his hero, heading off to face down Jack Palance, the gunslinger hired to drive out the farmers. Come back, Shane, he cries, please come back, and we all sat whitefaced, sharing his fear for Shane but knowing that Shane had to do what a hero has to do, what we all would have done in the circumstances. (By the way, in the opening scene, as Shane rides towards us from the horizon, look behind him and you'll see in the distance the dust being raised by a passing car.)

John Wayne was for older people, not for boys. We much preferred Audie Murphy, who could always be relied on for a good cowboy picture. Audie was a shy Texas lad from a dirtpoor background who joined the US army to fight Hitler and received a battlefield commission as a lieutenant. He became the most decorated American soldier in the Second World War and later had a smallscale and somewhat uncomfortable Hollywood career, mostly in cheap westerns. He suffered nightmares for years after the war and died aged forty-six in a plane crash at a time when Vietnam was convulsing America and war heroes were out of fashion. A few years back, while doing tourist things in Washington DC, I went to Arlington military cemetery and visited

Audie Murphy's grave. Only JFK's grave draws more visitors. A black man about my age, visiting from out of state, came by and stood alongside me and we sheepishly nodded and said gee whizz things about poor old Audie. Neither of us was there to honour his military feats (which were truly breathtaking) but to salute a boyhood movie cowboy hero common to men of a certain age who grew up in the vicinity of a cinema screen.

And, please, no one sully the memory of those years by mentioning such cretins as Roy Rogers (the gobshite actually drove a jeep, and although he had a horse called Trigger and a dog called Bullet we all knew he preferred hanging out with Dale Evans, a cowgirl) or Gene Autry, the yodelling cowboy fool.

Mostly, handguns were our pride and joy. But much as I loved my matt black sixgun, what I really wanted was a Chuck Connors *Rifleman* rifle. *The Rifleman* series was on one of the British TV channels and I hardly ever saw it but that didn't matter. I knew what Chuck Connors looked like, and what his rifle looked like, and that the character he played was called Lucas McCain, and how he casually twirled his rifle and used the special lever to cock it and fire in one fluid motion, and no rollerblader of today wishes more fervently for a pair of Majestic Twelves with 52-inch laces than I wished for a Chuck Connors *Rifleman* rifle. Maybe in the next life.

The arrival of a slew of cheap and dubbed Italian movies featuring the likes of musclebound Steve Reeves as Hercules or Goliath (when we saw the posters for the movie we called him Golly-it) created a passing fashion for strongman games. But you could only go so far in pretending to uproot trees or toss huge boulders at your enemies, so we soon reverted to slapping leather.

When we didn't have each other to play cowboys or war games we had our lead soldiers, metal figures who waged fierce battles against each other. We had little artillery pieces that you cocked by pulling back a bolt. A piece of a matchstick inserted in the muzzle acted as a shell. You released the bolt and out shot the matchstick and if your aim was any good you hit one of your lead soldiers. You could spend most of an afternoon perfecting your artillery techniques on the stoical footsoldiers. A bit like real-life armies in real-life wars, when you think about it.

One day my Uncle Larry brought me into town, into Parnell Square, to see the soldiers go away. There were real army trucks and real soldiers with real uniforms and real guns. They were heading off to the Congo, the first Irish troops committed to a United Nations peace mission, and some of them would die terrible deaths in the jungle. Their mission marked a turning outward, an involvement with the wider world. I was fascinated by the guns, astonished at being so close to real weapons that looked just like the ones in the comics and in the movies. I had no idea of the significance of the occasion, as the country passed some kind of milestone, becoming a player of sorts in the big wide world.

*   *   *

As the smug little republic rubbed up against reality it began fraying at the edges. Within the period 1957–62 (between the year I made my First Communion and the time I had my first brush with adultery) the economic, intellectual and social misery became such that increasing numbers began to see the stagnant old policies of wallowing in frugality for what they were. Three innovations in that period would devastate the old order: the Lemass government effected a change in economic strategy, inviting in foreign capital; Irish television began broadcasting; and the Second Vatican Council began seeking ways of adapting international Catholicism to keep up with changes in the postwar world. There were other things: the paperback revolution that brought the price of books within reach of everyone; the development of a youth market and a distinct teenage culture; and the ease with which issues and causes (Vietnam, feminism, racism, civil rights) spread across borders. The Irish Catholic hierarchy assumed things would go on much as before. Archbishop John Charles McQuaid, returning from the Vatican Council, patronised

149

his flock: 'Allow me to reassure you. No change will worry the tranquillity of your Christian lives.'

Oh, yeah? Smart boy wanted.

It wasn't godless liberals who caused the Church problems over the following twenty years, it was practising Catholics quietly making choices. The economic and intellectual opening up of the country had effects. The censorship eased. Education was improved. Tens of thousands of women began taking the pill, whatever the Pope said, whatever warnings of eternal damnation the bishops gave. People were no longer taking the official line without thinking about it. There were a lot of reasons for the change in attitude, one of them being that you could press a switch and a whole other world, a wide and varied world where bishops were no big deal, came right into your living room.

* * *

More than once, I sat beside the radio and stared at it, every molecule in my body lined up and focused through my eyes onto the glass dial, a pure stream of energy willing a picture to appear there. I knew nothing of the technology, but when you're ten or eleven it makes some kind of sense to believe that if you just wish hard enough you might make something happen. Television pictures would appear on the radio dial.

There was a sense of magic in the notion of having a box in your living room on which you could watch stories being told. Going to a cinema was exciting enough, but the idea of having a kind of cinema all of your own, in your own home, promised endless riches. We couldn't afford a television, few people could, and the reception wasn't great and maybe the adults wondered was it worth it, was it not a fad that might disappear. We kids knew that television, and all it represented, was the future.

It was 1960 or so. Since 1953, when the BBC began broadcasting in Belfast and their signals could be picked up down here, TV aerials had been sprouting from rooftops, grabbing from the air the faint, snowy signals from Out There. No one on our road had a TV for a long while, but the next-door neighbours of my Uncle Larry had it and they used to ask us in. We'd gather in front of the TV set, maybe a dozen neighbourhood kids, the curtains drawn, held rapt by the miracle of the event as much as by anything on the screen. Sometimes we watched football matches, with Liverpool or Manchester United, games that must have been of some importance to the adults but which were in themselves of no significance to us. Still, we watched. We watched anything, as it sucked us out of our limited world into the vast possibilities on the other side of the screen. Sometimes there'd be something showing that held us transfixed, maybe the Lone Ranger. The guy with the neat outfit, the mask and the Indian friend, Tonto, and the horse called Silver. The Lone Ranger had silver bullets in his gun and the show was introduced with a flourish:

> A fiery horse with the speed of light
> A cloud of dust and a hearty
> Hi-ho, Silver, awaaaaaaaaaaay!

And we were straight into Rossini's 'William Tell Overture', except we didn't know it was Rossini's 'William Tell Overture', to us it was the music from the Lone Ranger show.

The belief then was that watching TV was easier on the eyes if done in a darkened room. In the daylight you covered the windows, in the evenings you switched off the roomlight. The monochrome screen created a flickering blue glow in the room, and that flicker, as seen from outside, defined the arrival of the TV age. By and by, you could walk down a street and see in one living room after another the flickering blue glow as families gathered around the electric storyteller.

A couple of times a week, my pal Frankie and I would set out on a two-mile expedition to Phibsboro, to stand outside Ren-Tel, the TV rental shop beside the State cinema. There were half a dozen TV sets visible from outside the window and Frankie and I would stand there until we got bored watching the silent flickering screens. Cartoons, usually, maybe the manic crows, Heckle and Jeckle, or Popeye the sailor man (he lives in a caravan, he'll fight to the finish 'cos he eats his spinach, he's Popeye the sailor man). Or a western, the Lone Ranger, maybe, the characters silently mouthing their lines, the Lone Ranger's gun recoiling as he fired a silent silver bullet. We'd watch the mute news if that was all that was on, or a bit of some nondescript documentary, silent images we couldn't interpret but which kept our attention. We would then cross over to Doyle's pub, at Doyle's Corner, and push open the door a few inches and peer in. This was in some ways better than standing outside Ren-Tel. The screen was farther away but we could hear the sound. However, within a minute or two a spoilsport barman would chase us away, the louser.

Then, Telefís Éireann arrived. On New Year's Eve 1961, powerful searchlights lit up the sky over O'Connell Street, where the launch was being officially celebrated. Three miles away, in Cabra West, out playing in the snow-covered Compound with my cousins, I stopped tussling and we stood there and stared up at the fingers of light probing the clouds, fingers beckoning into our lives changes we couldn't imagine.

(1961, by the way, was a special year because it was the year that was the same whether you looked at it right side up or upside down. Some of us thought that was amazing, and we worked out when was the last time the year looked the same right side up and upside down. That was 1881, we concluded. And before that 1691. And, of course, 1111. And 1001 and 906 and 888 and 818 and 808. And 609 and 111 and 101. And 88 and 69. And 11 and 8 and the year 1. Once we'd established that, there wasn't a lot to say about 1961.)

With a home station to watch, people rushed to buy or rent TV sets. Uncle Larry got one and on Saturday evenings we'd visit and watch John Payne in *The Restless Gun*, and *Jackpot*, the quiz show, and *The Twilight Zone*. A highlight of Saturday nights was *The Wonderful World of Golf*, a series featuring American professionals.

No one we knew played golf, we couldn't give a toss about the game, but we'd sit for an hour watching people named Snead and Sarazen perform for our benefit. On Sunday evenings we'd go down again to Uncle Larry's and watch *The School Around the Corner* (which had transferred from radio) and *The Flintstones*.

At home, we still had just the radio, and no matter how intently I stared at the glass dial no picture appeared. The dial had printed on it the names of exotic places: Luxembourg and Stockholm and Hilversum and Berlin and Athlone and the like. It was called the wireless, which was something I could never figure out. If you opened up the back, as I did, you found it was full of wires connecting mysterious bits and pieces. It had served us well, the wireless. *Leave it to Lynch, The Foley Family* ('Aaaaaah, Alice'), *The Kennedys of Castleross* ('Middling, only middling'), Paddy Crosbie and *The School Around the Corner*, Din Joe and his dancing programme, *Take the Floor*. We sat and listened to the sound of Irish dancers tapping and jigging and reeling away, it not seeming the least bit strange that we should be listening to people dance.

There were fifteen-minute sponsored programmes at lunchtime. A man named Harry Thullier did a show in which he interviewed people as they flew across the Atlantic to America. We heard the captain announce that the plane was about to take off. We heard the interviews as the plane travelled westwards. We heard the captain announce that the plane was about to land at New York. Ignorant of the existence of tape editing, I wondered how all this was happening in just fifteen minutes, when everyone knew it took half a day to cross the Atlantic.

On the Jacobs programme, Frankie Byrne gave droll advice to the lovelorn, in between playing her beloved Frank Sinatra records. The Waltons programme, from the Real Ireland stable, promoted homegrown music, Bridie Gallagher and John 'Count' McCormack, céilí bands, fiddles and accordions. It seemed like they played the same tunes over and over, like they had a limited supply of records. It was taken for granted that an allegiance to a stoic nationalism was our right and duty.

> 'Twas down by the glenside I met an old woman
> A cuttin' young nettles, she ne'er saw me comin'.
> I listened a while to the song she was hummin',
> Glory-o, glory-o to the bold Fenian men.

'If you feel like singing', Leo Maguire urged us at the end of each programme, 'do sing an Irish song.' And I seemed to spend half my childhood eating my dinner to the sound of 'The Whistling Gypsy' who came over the hill, down through the valley so shady. *Aw-dee-doo aw-dee-doo daw-day.*

There were some songs, presented as cute entertainment, which seemed to me even then to be quite vicious. The one about 'let Mr Maguire sit down', in which a scheming family sucks up to a man who is courting Kate, a daughter of the house.

> Don't ye know very well he owns a farm
> A wee bit out of the town.
> Get up out of that you impudent brat
> And let Mr Maguire sit down.

And as soon as he is locked into marriage to Kate the family feels free to treat him with contempt, and he is now 'oul Maguire'. This was regarded as humorous, as was 'Granny's Old Arm Chair', in which the singer is treated with derision by his brothers and sisters, who inherit all their granny's worldly goods except her old armchair.

> How they tittered, how they chaffed,
> How my brothers and my sisters laughed
> When they heard the lawyer declare,
> 'Granny has left you her old armchair.'

One day, the bottom of the chair tears open and a fortune in banknotes falls out. And the singer gloats at having bested his brothers and sisters. The traditional rural animosities born out of hunger for land and jealousy of inheritance were casually reflected in such songs. They sounded odd to our urban ears.

We didn't know what a boll-weevil was, but it seemed like there wasn't a day went by without Radio Éireann playing Burl Ives singing about one of them. That or the old woman who swallowed a fly. Or someone else singing about working for a coal mine ('ya load sixteen tons and waddya get, another day older and deeper in debt'). Or Big John, who was broad at the shoulder and narrow at the hip and everybody knew you don't give no lip. Or the plea that Katie Daly come down the mountain, with her mountain dew. And the song that urged Tom Dooley to lay down his head ('pore boy yer gonna die').

From abroad came the radio game shows, *Double Your Money* and *Take Your Pick*. Michael Miles entreated the contestants to 'Open the box or take the money!' and we joined in, calling 'Open the box, open the box!' The older people listened to the BBC radio soap *Mrs Dale's Diary* with the loyalty that is today devoted to *Coronation Street*. If you could put up with a lot of hissing and crackle you could pick up AFN, the American Forces Network, broadcasting American music and news to US troops in Europe. Radio Luxembourg 208 brought us the early efforts of the kind of music that you never heard on Din Joe's show or the Waltons programme, the first stirrings of rock and roll. A youth culture was being born, as postwar prosperity created a youth market. It used to be you were a kid, then you became an adult. The developing youth market created a distinct period, bridging childhood and adulthood: teenagehood, a distinct culture with its own music and style, its own conventions and hierarchies. Elvis Presley and the birth of rock and roll, Lonnie Donegan warning us about the dangers of leaving our chewing gum on the bedpost overnight, the movie *Rock Around the Clock* and the row it created, were on the periphery of our world. That kind of thing was frowned on by adults as 'Teddy Boy music'. A Teddy Boy was a bold boy who had grown up and got himself fancy clothes.

At 7.15 each weekday evening I could listen to Radio

Luxembourg's serial, *Dan Dare, Spaceman of the Future* (and follow Dan's adventures in the *Eagle* comic which my Aunt Kathleen sent from London every week). When Sputnik, the Russian satellite, was launched in 1957 I couldn't understand the fuss over a glorified basketball with a few aerials sticking out of it. When Gagarin and Shepherd and Glenn and the rest of them were sent up on tentative flights and the space age began I was puzzled. Surely Dan Dare had been up there for years, fighting against the Mekon for intergalactic freedom? I had my own Dan Dare ray gun and my Dan Dare radio (a piece of plastic that you spoke into), Santa had brought me a Dan Dare annual just a year or two back. The truth dawned slowly, and sadly, that there was no Dan, that there were no battles in space, that we had just about figured out how to blast an astronaut a few miles into the air, where he would hang momentarily before falling back to earth.

The homegrown station was, like everything else, well impregnated with the Catholic ethos. In 1950, on the suggestion of John Charles McQuaid, Archbishop of Dublin, Radio Éireann set up an elaborate arrangement to broadcast the ringing of the Angelus bell at 6 p.m. (it's still being broadcast at 6 p.m., of course, and for a long time now at noon as well). It wasn't enough that any old bell be gonged in the Radio Éireann studio, to call on the faithful to say the Angelus; it had to be the bell of the Dublin Pro-Cathedral in Marlborough Street. A Post Office engineer designed a special microphone and amplifier in a weatherproof box on the roof of the Pro-Cathedral, close to the bell. A master clock in the GPO received a signal from Dunsink observatory, indicating it was exactly 6 p.m. The master clock activated a machine which sent a signal along an underground line to the Pro-Cathedral, starting the bell ringing the Angelus. The sound was picked up by the microphone in the weatherproof box on the roof and sent back down another underground line to the Radio Éireann studio in the GPO, which broadcast the ringing of the Angelus bell to the nation. The complex device first went into action on 15 August 1950, the Feast of the Assumption.

Radio became strictly a daytime thing once we finally got a TV set. The TV had a portable aerial on top of the set, rabbit's ears. The technology was fairly basic and it sometimes seemed that all it needed was for someone to cough too loudly and the picture would slip or twist and you had to jump up and poke around the back of the set to adjust the 'vertical hold' or the 'horizontal hold'. You also had to experiment by moving the rabbit's ears to different positions in attempts to improve the always-dodgy reception. When you switched the set off the picture collapsed into a dot at the centre of the screen that lingered for ages before fading. The set was rented from the Ren-Tel shop in Phibsboro to which Frankie and I used mount expeditions. A set cost something like £70 to buy, and it would have taken my mother a month or two to earn that.

From the glowing screen poured a succession of images which might today be considered primitive and quaint but which for us signified a new world. Short-lived and long-discarded US series became for us the cutting edge of television: *Our Miss Brooks*; *The Aquanauts*; *Ripcord*; *The Rough Riders*; *Yes, Yes Nanette*. We followed the Wild West adventures of Kit Carson, the Cisco Kid and his mate Pancho, and the swordplay of Zorro (who carved his identifying initial, Z, with three quick flicks of his rapier). Each Sunday afternoon we were transported to one or other aspect of the *World of Walt Disney* ('When you wish upon a star, makes no difference who you are . . .'). Sometimes animation, sometimes film of animals, impeccably edited into a drama. Sergeant Joe Friday cleaned up the underworld every week in *Dragnet* (if we said or did something cool, we immediately did the 'Denn . . . de-den den' music from *Dragnet*). *Mr District Attorney* prosecuted the villains. Lloyd Bridges fought the bad guys underwater in *Sea Hunt* and, out in the Florida Everglades, Lincoln Vail was keeping law and order, zooming around on his air boat. We got the best of American comedy in the likes of *The Jack Benny Show* and *The Honey-mooners*. And the worst of it, in the simpering shape of the inexplicably popular Bob Cummings, in *Love That Bob*. And each was swallowed just as eagerly, and if *Car 54, Where Are You?* wasn't classic comedy you could have fooled us. There were the adverts. Bing Crosby singing about how he wanted to keep going well on Shell, Shell, Shell. There was a beer advert in which some prat would call out 'Mabel! Black Label!' and a barmaid would smilingly pour him a glass. The Esso Blue song. I can sing it today, or the song from the Rael-Brook shirt advert ('Rael-Brook poplin, the shirt you don't iron'). I can even do the song for Constellation bedsheets:

> Lovely lasting sheets for you
> Smooth crisp pillow cases, too
> Beautiful for five whole years
> Constellation promise you.

They take you back, those TV adverts.

Have Gun—Will Travel left us wide-eyed and slapping leather. The great Richard Boone, as Paladin, a gunslinger for hire, wandering the Old West, dressed in black, his deadly skills inevitably put at the disposal of the underdog. We didn't know then, or need to know, the legendary associations of the name Paladin, harking back to Charlemagne. Later, *The Virginian*, making heroes for us of small-beer Hollywood actors such as James Drury and Doug McClure (good old headstrong Trampas), would hold us rapt as its ensemble cast dealt with the never-ending problems of nineteenth-century ranching. The cowboy drama was a weekly morality play, designed for the lowest common denominator, which is what we were. And from it and its like, in perpetually recycled plots, there trickled down to us a diluted sense of all the great tales and themes of both popular and classical literature.

Beyond the reach of our rabbit's ears aerial there were such wonders as *Rawhide*, *Bonanza*, and *Wagon Train*, glimpsed occasionally in the houses of friends with rooftop aerials that could pick up crosschannel stations. And, of course, the adventures of Lucas McCain in *The Rifleman*. (And the likes of the BBC's *Blue Peter*. I sat mesmerised in front of the screen one afternoon in someone else's house as a presenter showed us how to make things. Give me a length of wool, a piece of cardboard, some thread and a scissors and to this day I could make you a bobble for your woolly hat.)

The British channels were foggy even if you had an aerial attached to your chimney. Telefís Éireann ('bealach a seacht') was clearer and it had people who looked and sounded like us. *Broadsheet*, with John O'Donoghue, and John Molloy with a scarf around his neck, doing a Dublin taxi driver commenting on the issues of the day. It was magic to have someone like John Molloy doing a turn right in your own living room. Cookery, with Monica Sheridan licking her fingers, challenging our culinary ignorance by demonstrating how to make such exotic meals as hamburgers or how to do saucy things with crabs; *Just for You*, a musical programme; *Kino* reviewed the movies, and the presenter told us that the programme's name was the Greek word for 'movement'; you couldn't help but learn things, watching TV. *Silents Please* revived the silent movie antics of Charlie Chaplin and Buster Keaton and the Keystone Kops. *The World of Tim Fraser*, a British crime serial, kept us hanging on for weeks as the mystery unfolded. For kids, there was *Bláithín*, teaching us how to draw. Charles Mitchel, an actor of no great note, found the precise role to fit his voice and face, falling into what became in a real sense the role of a lifetime, reading the TV news with authority, reliability, *gravitas*.

There was *Dáithí Lacha*. Now that was a crazy mixed-up duck, a casualty of the Gaelicisation strategy. Dáithí Lacha was a cartoon, very minimalist stuff. No animation, just a bare drawing of a duck, and if he was supposed to be running the camera panned across his still figure. Someone had spent some time thinking up a name for the duck. Fred Duck? Joe Duck? Mary Duck? Peter Duck? Dickie Duck? Better, but not quite right. David Duck? That's more like it. David Duck. The alliteration worked for Donald Duck, for Mickey Mouse. So, David Duck it would be. Then, the imperative being to take every opportunity to promote the Irish language, particularly among children, the name was translated into Irish, becoming

Dáithi Lacha, and it doesn't appear to have dawned on them that they were losing the alliteration they had so carefully chosen and no one had the wit to rename the thing Lorcan Lacha.

You could immediately identify a home-produced programme. The titles were pale, almost transparent, white overlaying the picture, like something produced by an amateur film club. Programmes from America and Britain had solid, professional-looking titles.

There was a weekly series about Paris, *Mademoiselle de Paris* it was called, with accordions playing and people strolling along the Seine and I wanted so much to go there and twenty years later the accordions were playing in my head when I strolled through the Tuileries. And a series of tennis games, which is how I came to win a small fortune on the 1963 Grand National. The tennis programme was on every week and I, who have to this day never waved a tennis racquet, came to know the regular players as though they were the cast of a soap opera. One of them was called Louis Ayala, a favourite of mine who battled and won and lost over the weeks. I've never heard of him since, but when it came to my attention that there was a horse called Ayala running in the 1963 Aintree Grand National I gave my Uncle Larry a shilling and he put it on for me and Ayala came in first at a ridiculously massive price, 50–1 or something like that. Television was not alone a source of knowledge but of riches.

The random information pouring out of the screen had its effects. We saw New York, London, Paris, we saw mountains and jungles and deserts and seas. Walter Cronkite, the legendary American broadcaster, presented a weekly docu-drama called *You Are There*, which reconstructed historical events and showed you the very dust stirred up by the gunfight at the OK Corral and the very pavement on which John Dillinger was gunned down. In such epics of domesticity as *Father Knows Best*, *My Three Sons*, *The Donna Reed Show*, *Bachelor Father* and *Leave it to Beaver*, we saw the television version of white American middle-class family life, where the daddy said things like, 'Would you like to pass the milk?'

160

(how incredibly gentle, that 'Would you like to') and the son said, 'Yes, sir.'

It was mostly America we learned about. A bright, shining country where everyone was mannerly and cheerful, except the bad guys, who were readily identifiable because they scowled and were badly shaven. They were always arrested before the end credits. A country where you just climbed out of your car and closed the door behind you, never locking it. A country where Sergeant Joe Friday wanted just the facts, ma'am. And the announcer told us in stern tones that *Mr District Attorney*, played by David Brian, fought to defend Americans' constitutional entitlement to 'life, liberty and the pursuit of happiness'.

What a nice thing to put into your constitution: the right not only to life and to liberty but also to the pursuit of happiness. Now, that's something de Valera never would have considered sticking into his 1937 constitution. And one can be damned sure that had he thought of it the bishops wouldn't have been too impressed. Very unCatholic, the pursuit of happiness.

Other things came through, names of distant places. Laos, Vietnam, troubled people doing desperate things. Names, the significance of which we could only guess: Pathet Lao; Profumo. Scandalous snippets from the adult world: a drunken Brendan Behan being arrested; the Shanahan stamp fraud; Marilyn Monroe found dead (we had a rhyme about her: 'Marilyn Monroe, if you're able/Please take your leg off the table;/The table's for food and you're in the nude/So, Marilyn Monroe, if you're able').

The focus of attention in the living room changed. The chairs which used to face the fireplace now faced the television. We were learning more, seeing more, than people at any other time in history. We, who had never set foot outside Ireland, could experience close up the look, the sound, the atmosphere of more foreign lands than the greatest travellers of the previous centuries. The daily hurly-burly of a wide world was funnelled into our homes, a wide world going about the business of life. We were not passive watchers, we talked about what we saw and heard. Among the homemade programmes a stopgap effort (a filler until something better came along) called the *Late Late Show* was created in 1962 and every Saturday night we were seeing people chatter and joke and sing and argue and get angry and over the next few days, at school and in work, people would talk about what had gone on. Later, the arrival of cable and the proliferation of channels would fragment the audience. But for a few crucial years Telefís Éireann was the channel everyone watched, and if there was a row on the *Late Late Show* it was one into which the rest of us were drawn.

By 1967, three-quarters of Dublin homes had TV sets.

The television service was as locked into the Catholic ethos as was the radio station. On the evening in June 1963 that Pope John XXIII died the television news told us at 9 o'clock that our pontiff was dead. And then, as a mark of respect, the television service closed down for the rest of the evening. A few days later, on the day of the Pope's funeral, Telefís Éireann came on at teatime to cover the funeral and having shown us the ceremony immediately switched off for the rest of the evening. On Good Fridays the ordinary radio schedule was dumped and the station played solemn classical music all day.

But the ethos now had to compete within a bigger world. Television was pouring forth with prolific recklessness a wild flow of images both profound and shallow. Po-faced American actors fighting crime, tennis, golf, football, cities and villages, Asia and Europe and West Cork, music and sport, news and chat, celebration and protest. Its very existence, its variety, the various worlds that it showed us were out there—not fantasies like in the cinema, but the exotic mixed with the humdrum, the exciting and the mundane—undermined the walls built up around us over the decades. The cinema showed a world populated by movie stars. Television showed a world to which we could aspire. As we had suspected, the world was bigger than the grownups had let on (bigger than most of them knew), more varied. And in that bigger world the priest and the bishop and the GAA man and the schoolmaster and the Gaeilgeoir and the TD did not loom as large as once they had. No more could one point of view be handed down as the entire truth. Our smug little republic was being put in perspective.

Eight

I didn't know about the Civil War until I was nineteen. I found out about it watching the *Late Late Show*. I've looked it up since and the date was 16 November 1968; the *Late Late Show* was by then a settled programme, a centrepiece of RTÉ's schedule, mixing entertainment and serious discussion. Actress Susan Hampshire was the best-known guest and someone did something from *Finian's Rainbow*. One of the guests that evening was an Australian writer named Calton Younger. He was there to discuss his book, titled *The Irish Civil War*. I watched, slightly puzzled at first, then more than a little agitated.

What civil war?

I had lately turned nineteen, five years out of school, making my way in the world, and I'd just discovered that there had been a civil war in my country only twenty-six years before I was born.

What's more, the people on the TV seemed to be discussing the Irish Civil War as though it was a matter of common knowledge, like 1916 or the War of Independence. How could it have escaped my attention? Mr McAuliffe was hard pressed, it is true, to teach us some history and geography on top of teaching us English and Irish and arithmetic and making time for our religious instruction. But we had definitely done some history, and he could hardly have just plain forgotten to mention the Irish Civil War. Perhaps I had been out sick on the day he mentioned it.

The day after that *Late Late Show*, I went digging down into a big old suitcase and pulled out my primary school history book. *A Junior History of Ireland*, by James Carty, published in 1959. It was from Mr Carty's history book that I learned all about 1916 and the leaders of the Rising: 'The greatest of these leaders and one of the noblest characters in Irish history was Patrick H. Pearse', he wrote. I had learned that 'the Volunteers fought with the utmost bravery', and how 'more than one position only fell when the last man defending it had been slain'. History, I concluded, was a series of ripping yarns, heroes, villains, insurrections, fights, flights and betrayals. I drew a Hitler moustache on the picture of Cromwell on page 21 of Mr Carty's book.

Wolfe Tone and Daniel O'Connell were in the book, and on page 84 I added a hat, cigar and bootlace necktie to a guy in a picture, scribbled over the identifying caption (Michael Davitt) and rechristened him Doc Holliday, one of my western gunman heroes. The Land War was there, and the Famine, the Treaty of Limerick, Parnell and Home Rule. Chapter 18 told us about Easter Week. Chapter 19 was titled 'From Easter Week to the Treaty'. And there endeth the lesson.

There followed four general chapters about Irish customs, trade, agriculture and such important matters as the Eucharistic Congress of 1932. But, although we were told that the Treaty ended the War of Independence there wasn't a single word in the book or in my schooling about the bloodshed that led from the Treaty and the split which created the dominant political culture of the decades that followed.

The final page of the *Junior History* had a chronology, 'A Review of Great Events in Our History', beginning with the Flight of the Earls. It went on through the centuries until it came to:

1891	Death of Parnell
1916	The Easter Week Rising
1914–18	The First World War
1921	Anglo-Irish Treaty
1937	New Constitution of Éire

Somewhere in that chasm between 1921 and 1937 my innocence, along with the Irish Civil War, went missing.

Why was the Civil War left out of our history book? Could it be that when Mr Carty went to school his own schoolbook skipped over it and he just didn't know about the Civil War? Maybe he'd forgotten to mention it, it slipped his mind or he mislaid his notes. Perhaps there wasn't space.

Years later, by chance, I came across some schoolbooks in a secondhand bookshop and I realised that my *Junior History* was an abbreviated version of Mr Carty's four-volume *Class-book of Irish History*. And where our *Junior History* ended with the Treaty the senior book added a single paragraph in which Mr Carty wrote that 'civil war broke out'. No background, no explanation, just one sentence: 'The Republican minority still continued to oppose the Treaty', and 'civil war broke out'. No cause, no one made decisions, it just kind of happened. It just 'broke out'. Like it was a case of measles.

The list of Important Dates at the end of the senior book had the same gap where the Civil War should have been.

So, Mr Carty knew about the Civil War, but he was a bit shy about mentioning it. Forty years after the event, the Civil War was still a sore wound. It wasn't talked about. Even in a four-volume textbook it would merit but a single paragraph. For the smaller volume, used in national schools, the state's educational authorities quietly decided it would simply be better for us not to know about the Civil War. It might confuse us, it might take a bit of the shine off the picture painted for us of a happy, holy Ireland, the family of the Gael broken free from the yoke of the Brit. Better to edit the little family squabble out of existence. Like sex, the Civil War was a yucky subject which could not be raised without embarrassment, so it was best not mentioned at all. And, like sex, the Civil War was left as something we would find out about ourselves, in God's good time.

They showed us what they wanted us to see of the world, and they kept the unfortunate bits under wraps. The politicians and the priests and the Irish language people, the grey men who ran the country, gave us a version of the world they wanted us to see, the Real Ireland, a sealed, frugal, self-sufficient nation with a glorious past, a self-satisfied present and more of the same for the future. Perhaps it was the world as they had come to see it, perhaps they believed that the vision they were passing on was the way things were or the way they should be.

Mr Carty's book belatedly and unwittingly taught me a lesson in a subject that wasn't on the curriculum: scepticism. Since discovering the missing Civil War I have never totally believed the official version of anything.

* * *

If we missed out on the stories of Civil War derring-do we weren't short of violent national legends to re-enact, from Cúchullain to Pearse. I was too old for such playacting when, in 1966, the state celebrations of the anniversary of 1916 helped turn the rebels into action figures worthy of emulation. Younger kids re-fought on the streets the battle of Mount Street Bridge and the Alamo-like stand at the GPO. Mythic figures were now made more real by the power of television. RTÉ's drama series reconstructing the Rising, *Insurrection*, turned historical characters into gunplay heroes more plausible than John Wayne and more immediate than Audie Murphy. The re-eruption of the Northern conflict was a bare two years away.

The connection between boys and toy guns is so deeply woven into our culture that parents seeking to steer kids away from such activities have little chance of success. To be a gunslinger of the Old West, or an American GI sneaking up on a German patrol, a stealthy Indian with a wooden knife between your teeth, or a 1916 hero proudly holding aloft your gun as you waited for inevitable failure or death, was to rise above the smalltime world in which you were a figure of little consequence.

The only occasions on which we came close to anything like a real gun was fondling someone's big brother's pellet gun, or firing a pellet rifle at a fairground. The last time I fired a pellet rifle at a fairground I was maybe twelve. I broke the rifle open, put in the tiny lead slug, closed the rifle, took careful aim at the target and fired. The tiny piece of lead went through the paper target, disintegrated as it hit the metal backdrop and flew all over the place. Immediately after squeezing the trigger I felt the sting of a fragment of lead hitting me right between the eyes. The lead lodged under the skin, painful to touch, and it was weeks before I was able to ease it out with a fingernail.

Years later, when I was grown up, the playground where we fought our football battles was the scene for a row between some young men. A row over a bike, I think. It happened in the small hours of the morning. One guy went off and got his brother's shotgun. Lord knows what combination of images of himself were shaped inside his angry head by the casual accumulation of legends of gunplay, the strain of the argument and the availability of a weapon. He came back to the playground and poked the gun through the railings, took aim and shot a young man dead. I heard the bang and the screams, rang for the police and an ambulance and ran over to the playground, where the young victim's friends were standing in shock. The body was sprawled on the tarmacadam, yards from where we had played football. Next day, the cops examined the scene carefully, under a fading graffiti slogan carefully painted in huge letters along the top of the handball alley: ALL COPPERS ARE BASTARDS. They, of course, nailed the guy who used the shotgun. He got three years in prison. At the funeral of the young man who died, the hearse slowly drove out of the grounds of the Church of the Most Precious Blood and then the cars carrying the lad's family. At the top of Inver Road a half-dozen of his mates lined up on their horses, pet horses having by then become a pastime of working-class teenagers. Their leader gave a wave that John Wayne would have been proud of, and the horsemen wheeled in behind the family cars and trotted after the hearse as their friend was taken on his final journey through the neighbourhood. Shoppers stopped and stared, lamenting the death of a neighbour's child and at the same time struck by the dignity of the kids on horseback as they made live on our streets an image born in Hollywood.

* * *

As I write, it's two days before Christmas, Monday 23 December, and the Big Push is at full throttle. There is anticipation, celebration and fear. A fear of forgetting something. A fear of forgetting to buy a present for a cousin or a nephew or a niece or a friend; a fear you haven't got in enough drink; or mince pies; Santa is bringing too little, or too much; will I forget thyme or parsley or something else essential for the Christmas dinner and The Day arrives and it's too late.

The Christmas tree, a splendid non-shedding variety purchased for £25 and put up two weeks ago, is not alone shedding its needles all around the base, but its branches are drooping, brittle; it has for the past few days been in the process of shuffling off this mortal coil. If this tree were a human it would be in intensive care with the consultant taking its family aside and shaking his head the way they learn in doctor school.

A Christmas tree is an essential ingredient of the season. There are few sights which as easily press the nostalgia button as a well-lit Christmas tree seen through a window from the street. What to do? Scrap the tree at this late stage and get a new one? Or pretend we don't notice it has popped its clogs?

Already, there is angst in countless households, a certain knowledge that there will be disappointment on Christmas morning. This year's must-have toy is Buzz Lightyear, the space ranger from the movie *Toy Story*. A few months ago Buzz was a slow mover. Then the word went through the secret communication channels which seem to run through kiddie circles from Bangkok to Ballinspittle, from Indonesia to Idaho, and suddenly Buzz the action figure became the thing to have. By the time most parents realised that their darlings would be heartbroken if left Buzzless on Christmas morning, the toy had long vanished from the shops. The action figure Buzz flew off the shelves immediately, and a couple of weeks ago even the teenchy little Buzz that doesn't talk could not be found. Buzz's rival and friend, Woody, disappeared with the same

169

swiftness, a consolation prize for the kids who failed to get their Buzz. The manufacturers, having underestimated demand, are mourning the millions of dollars in potential sales now lost. They will saturate the market next year and the things will grow dusty on the shelves, having missed the tide in the affairs of toys which must be taken at the flood.

When, through whatever combination of marketing, schoolyard gossip and kiddie fantasy, word spreads across the world that this or that toy is this Christmas's must-have it vanishes before word gets to the grownups. We search for substitutes, but they won't do. You can get pencil cases and colouring books and games and selection boxes with pictures of Buzz Lightyear on them, you can get toy versions of *Toy Story*'s Hamm the pig or Rex the nervous dinosaur, but such substitutes, such lesser Buzzes, would be an insult to a child who has asked Santa for a Buzz Lightyear action figure.

Christmas morning, the kid will be joyful over what he gets, and there'll be some explanation ('maybe Santa's sleigh was too full . . . or maybe he made a mistake with the number of Buzz Lightyears he ordered from the elves'), but it won't work. Behind the joy, maybe later that evening, maybe next day or next week, when he has time to think, the kid will puzzle it out. Santa is magic, Santa could magic up as many Buzz Lightyears as he wants. There must be a reason why Santa decided not to bring me one.

Two or three years ago it was Mr Frosty, the ice-making machine (why the hell would kids want an ice-making machine?) and then it was Power Rangers, action figures based on the kids' TV show. They too disappeared with the speed of a brown envelope vanishing into a TD's pocket. The stores filled up with rip-offs, Cosmic Rangers and Power Fighters, but you couldn't fool the kids. They wanted the real thing, and they knew the name of every Ranger and the type of fantastical mechanical monster he or she magically turned into when the magic phrase was shouted: 'It's morphing time!' The kids knew the Powerzords and the Megazords and how they fit together and what they chanted when they were morphing ('Go-go Power Rangers, Mighty Morphing Power Rangers!')

Just before that Christmas, in a toy store, I stumbled upon a box containing the unobtainable Megazord, which a nephew was confidently expecting from Santa (far more confidently than his parents). Simultaneously, a six-year-old appeared from nowhere, his eyes lighting up as he saw the box. We were each maybe four or five feet away from the box. I looked from the kid to the box and back again, computing the speed with which I would have to move in order to whip the thing from under his chocolate-stained chin. He moved forward, so did I, he reached for the box, I got there first. My adrenaline rush spluttered and died as I noticed a handwritten note on the side of the box, explaining that there were some pieces missing. I relaxed, let go, and the little kid grabbed the box, chanting 'Megazord! Megazord! Megazord!' I wondered what I would have done had the thing not been faulty, would I have wrestled the six-year-old for it?

In the toy department in the new Debenham's store in the Jervis Street Centre this morning ('off we go with a hop, hop, hop'), I was looking for a soft toy, unable to make up my mind between a tiger and a monkey. Like an ancient knight stepping out of the woods and suddenly finding the sword Excalibur sticking up out of a lake, I turned and found that I was standing in front of a Buzz Lightyear toy. A single box, standing alone on a shelf, obviously the last one, the one and only Buzz for sale in the whole and entire toy world. The big one, not the teenchy little thing that doesn't talk. Before I could think, my hands had dropped the bags I was carrying and shot forward and grabbed Buzz. I stood there, looking this way and that, fearful that someone might come and challenge me for the prize. That I should, in the midst of a notorious Buzz shortage, stumble across him the day before Christmas Eve seemed unbelievable. I stood there, the undeniable fact now dawning on me that I hadn't been looking for a Buzz Lightyear. I didn't need a Buzz Lightyear. No one I knew needed a Buzz Lightyear. The one nephew who had asked Santa for a Buzz was seen to, his parents had some weeks ago managed to get their hands on one. Yet, here I was clutching the prize for which adults in this country and in countries across the world, frantic to defend their children's belief in the magic of Santa, would kill. To simply put it back on the shelf would surely be an act of unthinkable contempt for the importance of Buzz, the urgency of childhood fantasy, the magic of Christmas itself. I mentally shuffled through the names of the children of relatives or friends, acquaintances, trying to identify someone in need of a Buzz. Maybe I should buy the thing anyway, in case I hear tomorrow of someone going frantic. Of course I had to buy it, I'll give it to someone, anyone, there isn't a kid alive who wouldn't be delighted to wake up on Christmas morning to find Buzz at the bottom of the bed.

While all this was zapping through one part of my brain, other cerebral synapses were trying to process the information that while the Buzz I was clutching might be the same size and shape as the elusive Buzz being searched for on five continents, it wasn't the Buzz I had thought it was, it wasn't the action figure. As the message got through, my shoulders slumped, I shrunk two full inches. This was a Savings Bank Buzz, same size and general shape as the action figure, with a slot in Buzz's back into which kiddies were supposed to put their spare cash. This Buzz didn't talk, nor did his wings spring into place with a satisfying click, nor did his arm perform a karate chop when you pushed a lever on his back. This was a lesser Buzz. Only seconds had passed since I came across this thing, and only those seconds ago I had not needed or hoped or wished to find a Buzz Lightyear action figure, yet now I felt real disappointment. And I felt a bit foolish. Imagine being so gullible as to think you might find a Buzz Lightyear action figure on a shelf two days before Christmas. I put the box back on the shelf, picked up my bags, and turned back to the soft toy section, hoping no one had noticed my moments of extreme emotion.

* * *

Postscript on Power Rangers. The mighty Rangers, marketed via a cheapo-cheapo TV series aimed at kids, earned billions for their creators. You could watch the TV show, buy the action figures, buy their images on lunchboxes and pencil cases, buy a Power Ranger flashlamp, Power Ranger comics and outfits and swords and helmets, and by and by a stage show featuring the Power Rangers came to Dublin and the kiddies flocked to it. On TV the Power Rangers dealt out punches and kicks in the name of Truth and Justice, defeating a shower of nasties, one of whom had a television screen in his belly and all of whom were disgusting to look at. On TV the punches and kicks were delivered in synch with the satisfying crack of flesh hitting flesh.

In the stage show, the fights were daintily choreographed conflicts, energetic dances, the kicks and punches clearly not connecting, to the great disappointment of many youngsters. The Power Rangers were revealed to be a bunch of softies. Henceforth, in certain kiddie circles, the saviours of the universe became known as the Flower Arrangers. The following Christmas, in Dublin at least, no one was in danger of having to wrestle anyone over the last Megazord. You couldn't give them away.

*　*　*

The rattle of the puddings. That rattle was the soundtrack to the preparations for my childhood Christmases. Weeks before Christmas my mother put together enough ingredients to make half a dozen Christmas puddings, so there'd be sufficient to give to relations or others who hadn't the pudding knack. 'You'd never know who'd be stuck.' Each had to be made in a pudding bowl, the top covered with a double layer of greaseproof paper that was held firmly in place by a tightly wrapped circle of string. The bowl was put into a big saucepan of water, with an upturned saucer acting as a trivet, and the water was boiled. The puddings had to be boiled endlessly, the bowls rattling away inside the saucepans for hour after hour, the sound a constant pre-Christmas background noise. Once the puddings were made the baking of the Christmas cakes got under way (cakes plural: 'You'd never know who'd be stuck').

None of your sponge cake with a thin layer of soggy icing. That generation made real cakes, with rich fruit, almond and proper royal icing and a little Santa on top. It was a moment of tension when the oven door was opened: the cake might have collapsed (turn it over and use the flat bottom as the base for the almond and icing), it might be slightly burnt (scrape off the burnt edges), but almost always it came out right.

The paper chains were unfolded from the storage boxes. The glass balls for the Christmas tree were fragile things. If dropped they smashed into a million tiny dangerous fragments. Today the shining balls look the same, but you can bounce them on the floor and they won't break. We had a little frosted glass angel, carefully unwrapped every December and hung from the tree. It vanished sometime during the years when I wasn't paying much attention to such things. Today, around Christmas time, I see glass angels for sale and sometimes they're pretty similar, but not really.

Things which to adults are transient and temporary, decorations and ways of doing things, become for kids fixed elements of Christmas. Over the past few years many people have been putting in their front windows a decoration in the shape of an upside down V, lined with electric candles, a candle bridge. This decoration was dreamed up by someone looking for a quick buck, made in sweatshop factories in the Far East and imported by someone chancing his arm. Forty years from now today's kids will fondly remember such things as fixed, permanent elements of their childhood Christmas, imbued with the gravity of tradition.

When we were kids it was a big deal to visit town and marvel at the lights in Henry Street and the crowds and the carol singers. On the facade of McBirney's department store, now the Virgin Megastore, a huge lighting display went up each year, depicting Santa and his sleigh. In the Church of the Most Precious Blood the crib was installed early in December, but the manger was empty. Baby Jesus wouldn't be placed there until Christmas morning. We visited the crib to look at Mary and Joseph and the kings and the shepherds and the cow and the sheep gazing in awe at an empty space.

Each Christmas the Blessed Martin people would set up their Moving Crib in the basement of a building in Parnell Square and we'd go visit. It was even better than the moving figures you saw when you went to see Santa at Clerys, except when you reached the top of the queue at Clerys Santa gave you a parcel. Being personally handed a present from Santa was one of the centrepieces of the season, and the fact that it was a cheap toy that might break before you got it home never lessened the magic.

There was one Christmas, I was twelve or thereabouts, I had saved fourteen shillings and sixpence and I carried it in my pocket, riches of the kind previously seen only at First Holy Communion time. Christmas Eve, having gone for the messages, hauled home huge amounts of Taylor-Keith's orange and lemonade (and lesser quantities of Mi-Wadi, the orange drink you had to 'dilute to taste'), I got together with my cousin Tommy and we decided to go into town. It was a casual, unplanned thing, and we talked about it for months afterwards. Woolworths in Henry Street was so packed it felt like maybe you could lift your feet off the ground and the crush of the crowd would hold you up. I tried it and it worked. For a few moments I floated, held aloft by the pressure of arms and sides and elbows.

We ate in Woolworths' café, over the Henry Street store, we bought whatever we wanted (Tommy, nearly two years older, bought a cigar) and we went to a movie in the Regal cinema and we walked home and I'd spent every penny of my fourteen shillings and sixpence. There was so much magic in the day that we resolved to make the following Christmas Eve even better, and saved for months so each of us had a lot more than the likes of fourteen shillings and sixpence. And we went into town the following Christmas Eve and it was no big deal. The spontaneity of the previous year was missing, and the sense of discovery. The conscious need to enjoy ourselves, to match the happiness of the previous year, let us down. Lesson: you can't plan that kind of magic, not for yourself.

The commercial heart of our Christmas was Henry Street, the

dealers with their stalls, cheap decorations and cheap toys. We were urged to 'Get the last of the Cheeky Charlies', some kind of monkey on a stick or a string. Around the corner, in Liffey Street, Hector Grey had for years been bringing in supplies of cheap toys from the Far East. Apart from his shop, he did a street selling gig each Sunday morning. He didn't need the money, but he obviously loved the ritual. Some Sunday mornings my Uncle Larry brought me down to the pitch beside the Ha'penny Bridge, where Hector set up for business. He stood on a box, head and shoulders above the bedazzled crowd, offering flashlamps and garden shears, collapsable tables, hammers, gadgets for sweeping crumbs off the tablecloth, sets of screwdrivers, fancy mirrors, tiny folding scissors, hairbrushes, footpumps, jewellery boxes, whatever he thought he could sell. And Hector thought, quite rightly, that he could sell just about anything. He loved selling alarm clocks, demonstrating that these were not your cheap and nasty efforts that couldn't wake a hungover mouse. He would set the alarm off and hold the clock up as it shrilled away: 'If that doesn't wake you you're not asleep, you're fucking dead!'

'I'm not asking for five pounds!', he'd howl, holding up something that everyone knew was worth, oh, maybe ten shillings.

Hector Grey was a trade name but he answered to it. Alexander something or other was his real name, I think. He was a big, heavy man, balding, glasses, a strong Scots accent after decades in Ireland, a distinct voice honed on years of street selling.

'I'm not asking for three pounds or two pounds! I'm not even asking for a pound!' And we knew he was going to bring the asking price down to ten shillings and the adults considered the wisdom of making a purchase. Yes, it was reasonable value at ten shillings, but did they really need it?

'I'm not asking for eighteen shillings or fifteen shillings! Twelve shillings, no, I'm not asking for twelve shillings either!' And he let the shiny naked hook of a bargain dangle over the crowd, glistening. Maybe he'd bring it down beyond ten shillings, maybe to nine, and that would be tempting. The crowd were mostly men, it being Sunday morning. The women were at home, cooking the dinner.

'Ten shillings!'

And one or two people would tentatively raise a hand.

'No! I'm not asking for ten shillings! Nor eight shillings, and I'm not looking for seven and sixpence, nor am I asking for six shillings, either!' Pause to let the hook glisten one more time. 'I'm offering two of them for five shillings!'

And the crowd, the hook well and truly swallowed, all hesitation gone, waved their money in the air and besieged Hector, thrusting their cash forward, over the heads of those in front, fearful that Hector would sell out before they got their bargain. Hector would never sell out, he had countless boxes of the things, whatever they were, in his van, more in his stores. And he probably got them for eight shillings a gross.

At Christmas he would confine the sales to toys and decorations, and many homes would have been Santa-less without the cheap guns and cowboy suits, the tin trucks and the bright rag dolls, the teasets and the Christmas stockings, brought from far-off sweatshops.

(There were others who sold stuff close to Hector's pitch, making a living from his overflow. From one of those guys, at the age of fourteen, for five shillings, I bought a comb and blade gadget, designed for DIY haircuts. He had a gap-toothed assistant whose job it was to help demonstrate the efficacy of the gadget. The assistant's role was to stand there each Sunday morning, grinning happily while the street seller trimmed more and more from his vanishing hair. After years of having my head mauled by Ernie and Joe, at the local barbershop, I hated getting my hair cut. For the next twenty-five years I used the gadget to cut my own hair. By the time I finally went to have my permanently-chopped-up-looking hair properly cut, barber shops were no more, and there were twenty-year-old women to massage your skull, style your hair and ask you where you're going on your holidays.)

We called him Santa and Santy, we never called him Father Christmas.

'What're you asking Santa for?'

'A doll, a drum, a kick in the bum, and a chase around the table.'

Back then, Christmas expectations were low by today's standards, but sufficient unto the day. A gun, maybe, an aeroplane, a truck, a board game. I always wanted an annual and a flashlamp and I usually got them. An annual, the hardback once-a-year version of a favourite comic, or a whole thick annual devoted to a single hero. I got a last-minute yen for a Buffalo Bill annual one year, a need as great as any kid this Christmas feels for a Buzz Lightyear action figure, and on Christmas Eve my aunt Eileen walked the streets, trying every little huckster shop and newsagent in the three miles between Cabra West and town before she found it in a branch of Banba Books.

Christmas Eve, the turkey stuffing was made and the trifle, and I got to take a spoon to the leftover custard in the saucepan. My mother had her annual bottle of Guinness. I hung a token sock from the mantlepiece, into which some nicknack would find its way by morning. In later years we might go to Midnight Mass, and there was something majestic about the hymns and carols filling the air above our heads as the Blind Man, Mr McElroy, accompanied us in our Classic Religious Anthems.

Out in the church porch there was a smell of drink, the hard chaws having fallen out of the pubs and up the steps to the Church of the Most Precious Blood to get Midnight Mass so they could have a lie-in next day.

On Christmas morning, maybe 5 a.m., 6 a.m., you woke, realised what day it was, your feet probed for the weight of the presents at the end of the bed, you rolled out onto the floor, diving for Santa's goodies. The gun, the annual, the Christmas stocking from Hector Grey, bulging with nicknacks made of card, paper and plastic. And, when you were really lucky, a flashlamp. Best of all, the flashlamp with the curved plastic shades, green and red, that swung in front of the bulb, so you could have an ordinary light, a red light or a green light. Why you would want a red or green light was not a question that crossed your mind. You never knew when you might need to flash a red light at a train full of orphans that was chugging towards a bridge washed away in a storm.

Back into bed, under the covers with the annual and the flashlamp, reading in the cosiest cave on the earth. Pure, unalloyed happiness.

Out of the bed again, check, just in case there was something you'd missed. A Chuck Connors *Rifleman* rifle, maybe? No. What matter. A flashlamp, an annual, and the whole day ahead; out on the street, first thing, to check out what Frankie and Jimmy and Charlie and Willie and Gus and Blackie got from Santy; then the fried breakfast, the only day of the year we bothered; the smell of the turkey cooking, gradually permeating the house; the carefully laid table for the turkey and the stuffing and the sprouts and the roast potatoes and the trifle; my mother's annual glass of Sandeman sherry; the evening with Uncle Larry and Auntie Mary and the adults getting the deck of cards out to play Sevens and the kids, allowed to stay up until all hours, filling the air with the smell of exploding caps and the sound of makebelieve gunfights; the noise and the smiles and the hugs and the taste and the smell and the sheer joy of it all.

Nine

We are now in the winding down period, the sated days between Christmas and New Year, the calm after the storm. There are the usual mutterings about how we make too much of the break, about how it goes on and on, but the climax of The Day Itself needs an afterglow, a few days in which friends visit, we kick back and let the dust settle.

Early on Christmas Eve morning, on the radio, John Creedon read out a list of things that most commonly cause the domestic fires that happen around this time of year. Faulty lights, cigarette ends after parties. And Christmas trees that have died, grown brittle and dry, vulnerable to any spark. Each Christmas there's usually a tragedy or two. Every year we wince as the RTÉ television news shows us blackened walls, smashed windows, neighbours saying they were a lovely family. We went out that morning and bought a new tree, stripped the dead old one of decorations and dumped it out the back.

Christmas Eve was spent cursing the Early Learning Centre. Santa was bringing my daughter a kitchen centre. It looked great on the box. I opened it and found not a kitchen centre but a kit for a kitchen centre. These days, manufacturers like to reduce costs by closing down the section of the factory that puts things together. And by simply cramming the unassembled components into a box they can squeeze more units into the containers which carry them to the shops, thereby cutting transport costs. It's left to the purchaser to assemble the product. There was, of course, nothing on the box to indicate that Santa needed a degree in engineering in order to finish off the manufacturers' job for them.

The toy kitchen was in no less than thirty separate pieces, not counting the screws and bolts, with another dozen or more decorative stickers to be tediously put in place. It took almost three hours to put the damn thing together. Anyone leaving it until late on Christmas Eve to open the box would have been up halfway to breakfast doing the manufacturers' work. Maybe this is someone's idea of helping us bring the personal touch back into Christmas. You get to make the thing yourself, like a 1920s father knocking together a doll's house or a rocking horse. And you get to pay 1990s prices for the privilege.

The tree didn't go on fire; I didn't forget the parsley or thyme; we didn't run out of mixers; the turkey came out okay; Santa's toy kitchen was assembled on Christmas Eve with time enough left over to open a couple of bottles of Sam Adams; the ladder gave way when I was coming down from the attic with the crackers, but I hung on, no bones broken.

The big day came and it went, the magic worked again.

* * *

THE TWELVE CLICHÉS OF CHRISTMAS

1. What is the traditional post-Christmas query, in which the Yuletide festivities are likened to a farmyard gate or a bad dose of the flu?

   How did you get over The Christmas?

2. Using the traditional response, what was the decibel level of The Christmas?

   It was quiet.

3. What is it said that, when you think about it, it is ridiculous to have so much fuss over?

   Wan day.

4. What elderly feathered thing is it, when all is said and done, that there's nothing like a bit of?

   The oul turkey.

181

5. By 26 December, at the latest, in what words should one describe the fowl illness with which one is visually afflicted?

I'm sick of the sight of turkey.

6. Consequently, what taxidermal behaviour does one now regret?

Stuffing meself.

7. On what enclosed and benighted rectangle was there nothing worth a tinker's damn over The Christmas?

The box.

8. What species of gory foolhardiness describes those who spend Christmas Day queuing outside Clerys and Arnotts to be first in line for the post-Christmas sales?

Bloody eejits.

9. In whose 24-hour period were we satisfied if on Christmas morning Santy had left an electric flashlamp and a plastic cap-gun?

My day.

10. What expensive gadgets was it far from which we were reared?

Compewters.

11. Ah, but sure, what sub-species is the whole thing really only for?

Ah, but sure, it's really only for the kids, God bless them.

12. What won't we feel it now until?

Next Christmas.

* * *

Tomorrow is New Year's Eve, and what matter if we have forsaken the debaucheries once associated with that night, the quiet evening by the fire is more than enough compensation. We'll crack open a bottle of something nice, and fling wide the door at midnight to welcome in the New Year. And as the midnight hour approaches I won't hardly be scared at all.

*   *   *

It was 1960, unless it was 1959, sometime in around there, that Jimmy Doyle's big sister told me that the world was going to end at midnight on New Year's Eve. She said it casually, like it was something everyone knew. No big deal. Then she went off about her business. It was something she heard from someone and she more than likely passed it on just as something to say.

I was stunned. Talking about it, asking about it among my peers, would make me look a fool, believing that kind of thing from a girl. It couldn't be true. If it was true everyone would be talking about it. Yet, I half believed it. Jimmy Doyle's big sister was a few years older than me and this was the kind of thing that an older kid might know, something that would be kept from the younger kids (like the truth about Santa Claus). I thought of who I might talk to about this. Kids wouldn't know; grownups would deny it. Even worse, they might casually confirm it. 'Oh, yes, we were meaning to tell you. The world ends at midnight on New Year's Eve. Big bang, off we go, not to worry, offer it up for the souls in Purgatory.'

I kept my mouth shut. As New Year's Eve approached I lived in hope and dread, keeping an ear open for a word that might betray the secret that the grownups might be keeping.

New Year's Eve was always a low-key event. Crowds gathered at Christ Church, drunk and singing and swearing and occasionally fighting, but that wasn't for us. The church bells rang out across the city; from the docks, the sirens of the boats could be heard. Some families, including mine, had the tradition of opening the front door at the stroke of midnight. You opened the door and let the

Old Year out and the New Year in. You waved to neighbours who stood at their doors doing the same thing. You hoisted a drink (lemonade in our house) and clicked glasses with the rest of the family and said, 'Happy New Year', and that was about as exciting as it got.

I trembled that night. The door open, the bells ringing. I said, *Okay, right, that's it, let's go in.* And my aunt and my mother stood and waved across at the O'Neills and the Kavanaghs, the McKeons, craned around to look down and see if the Hogans were out, Mrs Doyle and the Whites. And someone had left a cylinder, some kind of gas cylinder of the type that are used in the cellars of pubs, in the O'Briens' front garden. And as the families waved and the bells rang and the sirens moaned, the cylinder erupted and some kind of gas or steam spurted from it.

I ran back into the house, threw myself face down on the sofa and waited to die. I turned and called back out into the hall. *Come in, come in,* and eventually they did, the New Year tradition fulfilled, and they closed the front door and they asked was I alright. *It's very cold,* I said, *we were out there too long, the house is freezing now.* My mother poked the fire and shovelled on some fresh coal.

I hid my trembling. And the minutes went by and the world didn't end. I went up to the landing window, where the luminous plastic statue of the Blessed Virgin stood on the windowsill, and I looked across at the cylinder in O'Briens' garden, still hissing. Now that my panic had eased, the cylinder seemed a feeble mechanism for the purpose of bringing an end to the world. I went downstairs and as the minutes passed and no angels lit up the night skies, their trumpets blaring an end to humanity, I slowly calmed down.

The incident left its marks. On every New Year's Eve after that I felt a cold pool of dread welling up about two inches above the back of my shirt collar. At least a decade would go by, each New Year's Eve ending not with a bang but with a whoopie, before that pool of dread would drain. Even then, the sense of unease never fully went away.

The panic might seem out of proportion but it wasn't. I was about ten, still a believer in magic, still just about hanging onto the Santa Claus legend. The notion of the world coming to an end, the magic involved in an apocalyptic event at the last second of the last minute of the last day of the old year, seemed entirely within the possibilities of life as I knew it.

We had at that time, for other reasons, become accustomed to the idea that there might be a sudden violent end to the world. The Cold War was real, even we ten-year-olds knew about it, and we knew about the atom bomb. We knew about Russia and America pointing weapons at one another. Madmen waving guns in a room full of dynamite. We knew about missiles and mass destruction, and how the next war would be the last one, and if we hadn't yet come across the phrase about how the survivors would envy the dead, we understood the sentiment.

We knew about the Four Minute Warning. The technology existed to detect hostile missiles approaching from the Communist East and the Americans had developed a system whereby there would be four minutes between their radar detecting the Russian missiles and the missiles hitting their targets. It all seemed very real, immediate. At any minute of day or night there might be an announcement that the White House had just heard that the Russian missiles were on the way and we had four minutes before our world ended.

It didn't occur to us that informing the Irish government of the launch of Russian missiles mightn't be high on the Americans' list of Things To Do When The War Starts. And, even if they wanted to pass on the warning, by the time word of the impending missile strike got to the Irish government, and word was passed back through the secretary to the cabinet, the under-secretary for emergencies and the deputy assistant secretary in charge of Four Minute Warnings, the Minister for Defence, the Minister for Justice, the Tánaiste and everyone else who would get upset if their place in the pecking order was not respected, we would all be history.

We just assumed that we would get the Four Minute Warning

along with the citizens of Ohio and New York and Illinois. And four minutes later our world would end.

Around the end of 1960 Aer Lingus got its first jet planes, and even we who lived miles from Dublin airport could hear the sudden loud roar of the engines throttling up. It might, for all we knew, have been the sound of an atom bomb blowing Navan back to the stone age. Until we got used to it, it was a frightening sound for those of us with part of our minds half expecting Armageddon. The whole feel of those years was edgy, a normality based on shaky foundations. And we felt it, it frightened us.

Towards the end of 1962, October, we by all accounts came close to finding out what the Four Minute Warning sounded like. The Americans discovered that the Russians had positioned missiles on Cuba, pointing at the Yanks. President Kennedy ordered a blockade of the island. The fact that the Americans had missiles positioned in Turkey, targeting the Russians, was something no one liked to mention. Logic didn't matter, what mattered was that Kennedy not appear weak. Russian ships were steaming towards Cuba. The clock was ticking, the madmen were cocking their guns, apparently unconcerned that the first shot would set off a chain reaction that would wipe us all out.

We talked about it in the grounds of St Finbar's. Kevin Grogan, Brendan Brady and me. I said that when the war started we could look up and see the missiles passing over us. The American ones would come from the Broombridge Road direction, on their way to Russia; the Russian ones would come from the direction of Phibsboro, on their way to the USA. We'd just have to look up— I looked up—and we'd see them passing, right up there.

I found myself looking at the metal sign high up on the side wall of St Finbar's: Trespassers Will Be Prosecuted. I cannot, to this day, thirty-five years later, see such a sign without thinking of nuclear destruction.

Brendan Brady said I was wrong. The missiles wouldn't come over our heads at all. They wouldn't even pass through this part of the world, across Europe and the Atlantic; they'd go the other way, westwards from America, across Alaska to Russia. I said no, we'd see the missiles. Kevin Grogan sided with Brendan, I shook my head at their ignorance. Geography was never my strong point.

The Russians blinked, and Kennedy didn't have to prove his manhood by sinking the ships and starting a worldwide conflagration – for which we were somewhat grateful. When Kennedy visited Ireland eight months later half the country turned out to wave at the local boy made good. I sulked and refused to join the cacophony of welcome. Back in 1960, when John Kennedy won the presidency by a handful of votes from Richard Nixon, Irish sentiment had, of course, been heavily weighted towards the Irish Catholic. I wasn't a Kennedy fan. It would be nice to claim that even then I was suspicious of how JFK's old man's money bought Mayor Richard Daly and the Chicago vote and stole the election. But I was against Kennedy because one of my schoolmates, a member of our gang, was Noel Dixon. Dixon, Nixon, it was close enough. It was like when I put a bet on Ayala in the Grand National, because the name meant something to me. So, I was in my innocence an early supporter of Richard Milhaus Nixon, commie-baiter, crook, mass bomber, liar and all-round bad taste champion. I remember listening to the election results on the radio, sitting watching the rain dribbling down the back window, and feeling sorry for poor Dick Nixon.

There was another reason for not being overfond of Kennedy. His arrival in Ireland meant that the Telefís Éireann schedules were torn apart to accommodate live coverage of the visit. Telefís Éireann was proud of its achievement in mounting such a huge outside broadcast operation within eighteen months of coming into existence and cheerfully swept aside its regular programmes. I was outraged. Okay, so they had to show this Kennedy guy shaking hands and making speeches, but did they really have to cancel *Bat Masterson*? They dumped it, along with grouchy Broderick Crawford tracking down jewel thieves in *King of Diamonds*. *The Wide Country* got the knock, and *Mr District Attorney*, *Dragnet* and *Sergeant Bilko*. To a thirteen-year-old, the fact that they would

187

deprive us of such treasures in order to accommodate those who wished to gawk at a visiting politician seemed nothing less than cultural vandalism. (Come to think of it, I feel pretty much the same today.)

As the TV commentator announced that the presidential plane was about to land at Dublin airport my mother and aunt went out to the front door to see if they could see the plane approach the airport in the distance. They saw a plane, which may or may not have been Kennedy's, heading in towards the airport. I stayed inside, partly out of annoyance that this Kennedy prat was responsible for me missing some of my favourite TV shows; partly because I was reluctantly fascinated by the novelty of being able to watch the event on live television.

In truth, the British empire had given way to the American one and the young master was on a tour of his new estates. Ireland's previous independent line in foreign affairs had been abandoned, under US economic pressure, and we had come on board as a client of the strongest player in the new world order. But we knew little of that back then and he won us all over, with his helicopters and his limos and his cool sidekicks in their crew cuts and dark glasses. He was young and smiling, he cracked jokes and wore his responsibilities lightly. We were discovering that politicians didn't all have to be old men scowling.

Five months after Kennedy visited Ireland I was lying on the floor in front of the TV, watching *The Thin Man*, a half-hour humorous detective show, when newsreader Charles Mitchel cut in and told us that President Kennedy had been shot in Dallas and was seriously wounded. I was shaken by the news but also fascinated by the coincidence that it should interrupt *The Thin Man*, which starred Kennedy's brother-in-law, Peter Lawford. Fifteen minutes later, when *The Thin Man* ended, Charles Mitchel came back and told us Kennedy was dead. In the days that followed we watched the mourning, the widow and the children; Jack Ruby killing Lee Oswald; the funeral, the horse with the empty saddle, the boots reversed; the coffin resting on a catafalque. It's odd, the

188

things that stick in the mind. I will always know, because my childish mind was paying attention to such details in those strange, impressive days, that a catafalque is what the coffin of a distinguished person rests on during a funeral service.

It was the first news event that linked so many millions of people, hearing about it simultaneously around the world, and watching it on television, the sense of shared shock multiplying the impact. Mingled with the shock I felt more than a little guilt, that I had been so annoyed at Kennedy for screwing up the TV schedules just five months earlier. A year or so after that, when an official JFK memorial exhibition came to town, I queued with thousands of others at Parnell Square and stared respectfully at the props of the presidency. You could see the very notepads (they were large yellow legal pads) on which JFK scribbled his thoughts. I was hugely impressed, my feelings of guilt compounded.

The impact of the Kennedy visit, and his dramatic death so shortly afterwards, had something to do with us realising how big the world was and, yet, how things were connected and how we all, even in little Ireland, were wired into something bigger. The parochialism of just a few years earlier was peeling away.

Of course, becoming part of the excitement and variety of something bigger meant that its problems became ours, and one of those remained the possibility that at any moment we might be given that Four Minute Warning.

* * *

The fear of nuclear war was so real, so much a matter of fact, that sometime in or around then the government decided they should prepare us for the eventuality of the Cold War suddenly hotting up. They must teach us what to do when the earth shook under us. They issued a booklet. It was called *Bás Beatha* and it was distributed to every home in the country. It was a little 64-page thing, with red and green coloured illustrations drawn by David L. Murphy, Dip. A.I.C., A.N.C.A. (Design). Red

189

dots, masses of them, were used to signify the radioactive fallout of which we must beware. 'It can come to us on the wind from other countries. It cannot be seen or felt.' There was an Introduction by Gearóid Mac Phartaláin, who in real life was Gerry Bartley, the Fianna Fáil Minister for Defence. 'The risk of war', wrote Gerry, 'which has caused the Government to issue this booklet specially for householders, may remain for many years. So keep the booklet carefully. Hang it, or place it, where you can easily find it in an emergency—it could mean the difference between life and death for you and your family.'

To facilitate us in hanging the booklet where we could easily find it in an emergency, the government punched a hole in the top left corner, ideal for hanging the booklet from a nail. Presumably the idea was that when the Four Minute Warning was sounded we would rush to our booklet and flick through it to refresh our minds with tips on surviving a nuclear holocaust.

And when we tore open the booklet what would we find? Let us turn to page 42, where the government shared its research on what to do at the moment of explosion. That's the subheading of the section: What to Do at the Moment of Explosion. And here the booklet, in order to stress the importance of the advice it was about to give, went into capital letters:

TURN YOUR BACK TO THE FLASH.

No kidding. Turn your back to the flash. This advice on how to survive a nuclear explosion was in all seriousness written down by the Fianna Fáil government and sent to every home in the country. Turn your back to the flash.

'Bombs away, skipper!'

'Too late, damn it, the wily buggers have turned their backs!'

Page 43 has further insights into how the fast-thinking citizen might survive a nuclear holocaust: THROW YOURSELF FLAT ON THE GROUND, it says.

PROTECT YOUR HEAD AND THE BACK OF YOUR
NECK WITH ANYTHING YOU MAY BE CARRYING (an
overcoat for example), OR WITH YOUR COAT COLLAR,
ETC.

Turn up your coat collar to protect the back of your neck from the
blast of a nuclear explosion. I'm not making this up.

Radioactive fallout would be a major problem, and the booklet
went into great detail on this. 'Get rid of the dust from your
surroundings. Your vacuum cleaner could be very useful for this
purpose.'

Leaving aside the fact that, whatever about Gerry Bartley's
domestic circumstances, vacuum cleaners were not common in
Irish households of the early 1960s, the enlistment of household
appliances in the fight against nuclear fallout had at least the
benefit of novelty. It is a wonder that vacuum cleaner manufacturers didn't, in their advertising, exploit this additional use for
the product.

We were warned that we should create a 'refuge room' in which
we must gather our family, stock our food and water, and have a
radio constantly tuned to Radio Éireann. There was an illustration
of a man sitting on a chair, under a table. The table had been
raised, with books or bricks under each leg, to give the man room
to bring his chair in underneath. The man just sat there under the
table, waiting for the fallout to go away.

There were illustrations showing us how to fill boxes and
suitcases and crates with clay dug up from the garden. These were
to be stacked in front of the windows, in order to place a solid
barrier between us and the deadly rays emanating from the
radioactive fallout. One illustration showed a wardrobe being filled
to the top with clay. The wardrobe would then be stood in front of
the window. I spent ages staring at that illustration, wondering how
long it would take me to fill the wardrobe with clay and then
manoeuvre it in front of a window. How I'd shift a heavy wardrobe
stuffed with clay was something to which I gave much thought and

which caused me some worry. Maybe I should first put the empty wardrobe in front of the window and then fill it full of clay, carrying the clay inside by the bucketful. I never resolved this dilemma, knowing in my heart that whichever approach I took would require a lot longer than four minutes.

We read dozens of pages of detailed, if sometimes absurd, instructions on protecting ourselves from flying glass and fallout; we read about the weeks we might have to spend sitting in a shielded corner of the refuge room, drinking water from stocks kept in the bath, shitting in a bucket and trying to avoid breathing in radioactive dust; and it all confirmed our fears that we might at any moment be plunged into a living hell. The booklet was never recalled, the warnings were never qualified. As far as the state is concerned *Bás Beatha* still hangs from a nail by the door in countless homes, as it may well do, awaiting the announcement that mass destruction is but four minutes away, giving us just enough time to find page 43 and turn up our jacket collars in order to ward off the heat from any thermonuclear device which might detonate in our vicinity.

To come to the age of reason in that atmosphere was to believe that the horrors of nuclear blasts, radiation death and the destruction of everything stable, ordered and civilised might well occur with a warning of only minutes. It was a disconcerting knowledge, if you were of a mind to pay attention to such matters (and many were not). It was an acid that quietly ate away at our sense of security.

The younger kids knew little of this. The grownups came to terms in their own ways with the possibility of mass annihilation. For those of us who were ten or twelve or fifteen, just beginning to understand how little we understood of the world in which we would have to make our way, the revelation that at any moment we might all be vaporised was, to say the least, unsettling. With some of us it left a residual uneasiness.

Only as the years passed and international relations changed and *Bás Beatha* became something to be looked at as a joke from a strange time did the fear that soaked into our fibre slowly evaporate.

I still have *Bás Beatha*. Just in case.

* * *

It's nighttime, you are not quite asleep but tiredness has dimmed your mind. The light from the landing softens the darkness of your bedroom, creating familiar, comforting shapes and shadows. Your eyes close, open again for a moment, as though you're checking that the room is still there, and then they slowly close again. Wisps of your world drift into and out of your consciousness. Tastes, shapes, feelings, the flotsam of the day. Way off in the distance you hear the long, whining, creaking noise from the hinge on the living room door. The noise that means that the door is opening. Noises that mean someone is in the parlour, the whine of the hinge again, the sound of the door closing. Voices. A tap running. A bump, a noise you can't identify. Laughter. The murmur of conversation that fades as your mind sinks below the threshold of sleep.

Subconsciously, you have learned one of the basic facts of life. There are other people in the world, people who have lives separate from yours, lives that are not always concerned with you. Your parents, the people closest to you, have aspects to their lives which have nothing to do with you. Their lives go on while you sleep.

You have started to learn that you are not the centre of the world, that you are part of something.

Without knowing it, you start to learn something else. That the world goes on without you. And this knowledge deep inside, that you hardly know you possess, will help you to understand later on—much later on—about mortality, about how the world will go on without you when you die.

* * *

I can think for a moment and summon up Dáithí's face, dead the best part of forty years. And Jimmy and Joseph. Three kids I played with who died before we got out of childhood. It seems a lot now, and maybe there was a higher death rate for kids back then, in the alleged rare oul times, maybe not.

'Yes, she had seven, five of them lived.' It was the kind of remark you heard often back then. Polio and diphtheria and TB and other things we didn't know the name of took people away.

There were things you don't see so much today. Maybe it was diet, maybe it was a condition left untreated then and treated as a matter of course today, but there seemed in that time to be far more kids with misshapen legs. The word was bandy. *Hey, bandylegs*, we smirked with casual cruelty. (It has just occurred to me that maybe we saw so many bandy legs simply because we all wore short trousers.)

'You'll catch your death of cold', was the improbable warning as we were told yet again on winter days to button our overcoats, and here's your scarf, the damn thing tucked in all around your collar as though you were off to conquer the Antarctic instead of going down to the shops for a quarter stone of potatoes, three-quarters of a pound of round steak minced and a vienna roll. Capped, scarfed, gloved, pullovered, jacketed, overcoated, with socks pulled up our shins to our knees: but still wearing short trousers. Go figure.

Keep your overcoat buttoned. You were warned that the least you could expect was chilblains. And if you were careless you might be snatched away by something called pleurisy.

Mostly, we didn't die. Mostly what happened was that we got our tonsils yanked out. These two pieces of tissue at the root of the tongue in some kids get so inflamed that they have to be surgically removed. Today, tonsils are removed if there is a medical reason, otherwise they remain where they are, doing no harm to anyone. Back then, whipping out a kid's tonsils was almost a rite of passage. Give a doctor the slightest excuse, or none at all, and the tonsils would be given a death sentence. There didn't have to be anything wrong with your tonsils. If your brother was having his tonsils out

194

the doctor could decide that you too might as well have the operation done, get it over with.

I can't remember which hospital took mine out but I remember the dirty trick the nun played on me. I clung to my mother and my aunt Eileen, refusing to let them leave. 'Would you like to see the fishes?', asked the smiling nun. The fishes? 'Here they are, over here', and she led me to a fishtank, wherein moped a handful of miserable goldfish or pinkeens. I looked for a moment at this tawdry entertainment and turned back and my folks had gone. 'Right, now', said the nun, and as I screamed she took me in a grip that Lugs Brannigan might have envied and hauled me off to a ward. My mother and Eileen stood out in the corridor, listening to my screams, both of them teary-eyed. Few of us got chilblains or died from pleurisy, but most of us went through the trauma of tonsillectomy.

When someone in the neighbourhood died there were customs and rituals. The woman who specialised in laying out the bodies of those who died at home (did she really put pennies on a dead person's eyes, to keep them from opening?). The black cloth diamond that a man wore, sewn to the sleeve of his jacket. The women dressed all in black—scarf, stockings, blouse, skirt and coat—in mourning clothes for months if the deceased was a close relative. Usually, the woman's best overcoat was dyed black. The memorial card, with its little photo of the deceased and the prayers for a happy death and a speedy entry to Heaven and the injunction from Saint Ambrose: 'We have loved her in life, let us not forget her in death.' A black-rimmed card pinned to the front door, announcing the death of one who lived there. The curtains drawn or the blinds pulled down and the house in darkness until after the funeral.

Macker, the neighbourhood predator, coming in the window, doing several houses in a row, on the day of a funeral, knowing that the neighbours would be at church, paying their respects, and most of the houses on the street would be empty and ripe for breaking and entering.

I was in my cousin Liam's house, over in Kevin Street flats, when the news came on the radio and the newsreader said a young boy from Cabra West had died when he fell from a cliff. Falling off a cliff was the kind of thing that was so exotic that it didn't belong in our lives and when I found out next day that it was Joseph who had died, the Joseph I'd chased and been chased by, shot and been shot by, Joseph who had run so fast from the Kissing Girls, my mouth hung open. I can't remember being horrified. I can't remember imagining what it must have been like to die that way, what a child would think in those seconds, or if he had time to think. Today, when I think of Joseph I think of the wave of horror that must have washed through the lives of his parents, his family, the young and the old. I imagine the slipping, the letting go, the tumble, the smack, the life being snuffed out of a child, the panic and horror of those around as they realised a line had been crossed and there was no returning.

Back then, I didn't have the imagination for that, I didn't have the sense of personal vulnerability and fear that such thoughts need. All I can remember is the sense of amazement that such an exotic—hell, such an exciting—thing could have happened to one of us. There were no intimations of mortality. We continued to jump off walls that were too high for jumping off, we continued to dart in and out of traffic. Without a care in the world we casually did things which shred the nerves just thinking of them today.

Then there was Jimmy, who had been touched by polio, something a lot of kids had back then. He had callipers on his legs. In those days, I think, a lot of kids had callipers. I can see him now, hopping along after us, as we chased or played football, smiling his smile and one day he just wasn't there any more.

*　　*　　*

Children believe themselves immortal. The concept of a life ending, the person being no more, if that person is oneself, is impossible for us to grasp at that age. The notion of Heaven and

196

Hell helps us accept some sort of transformation in which the person becomes some ethereal thing, borne aloft to a wistful eternity or cast down to eternal pain. The provision of this alternative to oblivion eases our fears. It also allows the provider of the alternative, the religious organisation, an influence in our lives.

The Heaven they promised wasn't the Heaven we wanted. Heaven was having chips when and as often as you wanted them. Ditto for ice cream. Heaven was having an annual to read any time of the year, not just at Christmas. Heaven was a Chuck Connors *Rifleman* rifle.

As given to us, Heaven was a bit on the Hollywood side, with angels sitting on clouds, perfection all around, all of every day spent adoring God. I didn't want to go to Heaven. It seemed such a boring place. Who wants to spend eternity adoring someone? I felt no closeness to the god I had been born to worship. I feared him. His threat of eternal damnation for relatively trivial offences seemed the act of a self-regarding despot. The choice between boring Heaven and painful Hell was a limited one. If I had to go to Heaven it would be reluctantly, out of fear of the alternative.

I seldom thought of such things. The hour of my death seemed eternities away. And I didn't like to think of the state of my soul, blackened by years of inventing sins in Confession. Like most Catholics, I put my trust in the rule of the Last Minute Reprieve. This says that you can do pretty much what you like as long as you make a full and honest Confession, thereby wiping your soul clean, just before you fall off your perch.

In my head I knew about mortality; but in my bones I knew I would, must, live forever. So difficult did I find it to grasp the idea of my ceasing to exist that gradually, tentatively, I concluded that there truly was a chance that the person had been born who would cheat the gods, who would be an exception to the rule of mortality. I would live forever, or at least a couple of hundred years, which was much the same thing.

It is hard for the young mind to grasp the fragility of life. A thoughtless moment, a slip, and the magic is gone. The remains—

a bleak and dreadfully accurate word—lie waiting to be taken up and carted away. What was full of movement and joy and fear and hope and frustration breaks instantly and becomes something still and cold and unknowing. On a cliffside, a foot this way or that way, a firmer grip, and a boy's life wouldn't stop right there, sealed and over, a memory for the rest of us who lived on through the decades.

Climbing up onto the bridge over the disused railway line at Connaught Street, on the way back from an expedition to foreign Phibsboro with Frankie. We used to sit and inch our way along the parapet. Sometimes we would stand and walk confidently along the parapet like it was a foot off the ground. That day, for some reason, I turned at the last minute so I was facing out towards the pavement. When I slipped I fell out onto the pavement, not the thirty feet onto the railway line. I stood there for a moment, then I turned and ran after Frankie. We laughed and chased and talked our way home, as usual.

It was no big deal, a nothing event. But in the seconds I stood on the bridge, having landed on the pavement, I knew that had I not swung around to face away from the railway line I would by then have been lying dead on the tracks. There was no rush of shock or feeling of escape. Just a sudden, deeply felt knowledge, which I could not then or for years after attempt to articulate, of the fragility of life, the ease with which we can crumple into not-being. I still took absurd chances, with traffic and with jumping off things, but the half-belief that the person had been born who would beat the mortality rap vanished on the bridge that afternoon.

One of the shocking things about death is that it is so mundane, nothing at all like what happens in the movies or on television, nothing like the dramatic deaths we played out in the Bogies. Death is about little things, tiny actions with enormous consequences, slips and falls and moments of distraction, people who go away one day, same as usual, and it never occurs to you that they're not coming back.

* * *

Dáithi was dying when we met him, though we didn't know that. One year—perhaps 1959, 1960, somewhere along in there—we came back from holidays and Mr McAuliffe said he wanted to introduce a new boy. His name was Dáithi, and here he was.

This was in itself unusual. When a new kid started in class he just turned up and joined in and before too long he wasn't a new kid any more. Dáithi was different. He was smaller than us. Mr McAuliffe told us that Dáithi had been ill, that he was still delicate. I believe it was the first time I heard the word delicate, and it was exactly the right word for Dáithi. Little guy, thin, little shy smile. Looking back, I know that Dáithi's parents must have known he was dying, must have wanted him to have what he could of a normal childhood, must have told the school, must have got advice.

'I want you to look after Dáithi', Mr McAuliffe said to the class of Room 4.

And we did, every single one of us. Even the hard nuts, the borderline psychopaths, the ones who in other circumstances might have seen Dáithi as easy meat. There was something about how we had been given responsibility, probably for the first time, and it brought out the best in us. It had to do with the fact that he was smaller and weaker, that he had been ill, that he needed our support. But mostly it had to do with the fact that to some extent he had been put in our trust and we were on our honour to live up to that trust.

Dáithi had a best friend, Martin, a red-haired bodyguard who seldom left Dáithi's side. Thinking back now, maybe Martin knew something we didn't know. Martin was his best pal, but Dáithi belonged to all of us. We included him in our games, we made him part of our gangs. Maybe we patronised him, but I don't think so. He had a personality of his own and he would have fitted in anyway. He was nice to be with, he joined in. But above all he was our Dáithi, our trust, and each and every one of us felt a responsibility for his well-being.

On one occasion during a schoolyard break Dáithi fell foul of someone from another class, another gang. Nothing big, just a push or a snarl or a threat. And word swept through the schoolyard and every soldier from Room 4 who heard it dropped what he was doing, locked and loaded and turned and ran towards the danger. This was unique. If I was getting grief from some gobshite from another class I knew that if word got to Kevin or Brendan or Vincent, to John, Paudy or Joe, I would get help. I knew there were others, Johnny or Riggs or Geoghegan or Kavanagh, for instance, who would shrug. They owed me nothing, the hell with me. But for Dáithi there were no barriers, there was no gang or group or individual headbanger from Room 4 who didn't hear the call.

As a result, some poor eejit from another class who didn't know that Dáithi was a special person, a protected one, who saw the little guy as a pushover, was covered in furious avengers from Room 4 and got the crap kicked out of him and probably to this day can't figure it. Word spread. Leave the little kid alone. He's connected.

Dáithi added something special to our lives. We protected him, joked and laughed and ran and tumbled (but gently) with him, and in a very real way we loved him, and in return he gave us our first real reason for feeling good about ourselves in a little bit of a grownup way.

And then one time we came back from holidays and Dáithi wasn't there. No one told us why. After a while we asked and we were told that Dáithi had died. And we realised just what Mr McAuliffe had been saying when he told us that Dáithi was delicate. I think I knew then what I know now, that that year or so was a special time, a good thing to be part of. We had been invited to share Dáithi's final days, the very important days for Dáithi and dreadfully and terribly important for his family, and we had instinctively responded properly and we behaved decently and we helped make the best of a painful time for them, and probably Dáithi didn't know what was coming and we were a part of making his short life happier, close to normal. And in return he gave us a little sense of responsibility and unknowingly brought us a little further along the road to an adulthood that he would never reach.

Ten

One of the enjoyable things about starting a new year is the opening of a fresh haul from the state archives. It's a week into January and the musty files from 1966 have been opened.

Under the Thirty Year Rule, state documents of thirty years ago are released by the National Archives into the public domain, the unveiling taking place at the beginning of each year. The documentation is limited, and no archive can preserve the nods and winks, the deals done in holes and corners, the alliances cemented at country funerals and southside dinner parties. There will be no smoking guns. No memos agreeing to do this in return for that. But there is enough to give us some flashes of insight into how things work.

It's important for historians, but for the rest of us it's great fun. It's like we get to peek behind a curtain, to see not the image of Ireland they were creating for us back then—the people who could edit out of existence a whole civil war—but a bit of the machinery behind the image.

You never know what's going to pop out. Here's a letter from March 1966, to Taoiseach Seán Lemass, from a woman who is proud of her station in life. She's major league pissed off about the *Late Late Show* and she wants something done about it. The self-assurance of the Catholic middle classes, their belief that it was their country and it should be run according to their ethos, seeps out of every line. The letter is from a chemist shop in a rural town (no names, no pack drill, let's spare the family's blushes). It's written on headed notepaper which assures the reader that the chemist is the 'appointed agent' for, among other things, 'Old

Spice for Men' and Tabac aftershave ('All Leading French Perfumes Stocked').

'We are a Catholic nation', she writes, and *Late Late Show* 'panel members' on 'our station' have in recent weeks 'left much to be desired', and one of them had indulged in 'a great discourtesy to our Bishops', so it is 'time that higher authority intervened'. So self-assured were these people that they assumed that if they came across someone saying something they disagreed with they merely had to send a letter to the Taoiseach and he, once he realised he was dealing with solid people (appointed agents for Old Spice, for instance), would arrange things as they ought to be.

Another letter in the archives was from a similar worthy who wrote not to the Taoiseach but to the great de Valera himself, demanding a curb on the impertinence of the *Late Late Show*, which was 'being used to ridicule our beloved Hierarchy and Priests'. He concluded: 'If this is what you, the President, and your colleagues fought and died for it was in vain.'

A rural parish priest wrote to Lemass, demanding action. A Galway doctor sent a long telegram to the Taoiseach demanding an immediate announcement by the Government Information Bureau that the *Late Late Show* was being 'put off the air for one month. Gay Byrne must go. I find him utterly out of sympathy with the great majority of my own people . . . dastardly outrage of my ruling people . . . He must be suspended for one month and then we will give him another job where he will learn to align himself with the thoughts and feelings and with the majority belief of my own dear country North and South.'

Note the 'we' who will 'give him another job', the assumption that the world is made up of those who matter, and who therefore run things, and the lowlifes such as Gay Byrne and his TV people and panel members who can be put in their place if they get too uppity.

The anger had been stirred up by the appearance on the *Late Late Show* of Brian Trevaskis, a young man who played a pivotal role in pushing back the boundaries of acceptable criticism of public figures. He earned a significant place in the memories of those of us who emerged from childhood in the 1960s. Trevaskis said it was disgraceful that John McGahern should lose his teaching job for writing a novel of which the bishops disapproved. This kind of thing was okay coming from literary types writing letters to *The Irish Times*, a Protestant enclave from which one could expect no better. But for it to be articulated on what had become a national forum, the *Late Late Show*, where all sorts of innocents might get the wrong idea, churned the blood of the faithful. Trevaskis slagged off the Christian Brothers and their fondness for hitting kids; he questioned the value of trying to revive the Irish language; he noted that university education was the preserve of the middle classes; he came out for Noël Browne, defeated architect of the Mother and Child scheme, and against Archbishop McQuaid. For some of us, Trevaskis was hitting targets long overdue a pasting. On issue after issue, exhilaratingly, he was saying just what we felt.

Trevaskis denounced the architecture and cost of the new Catholic cathedral in Galway and called Bishop Michael Browne of Galway a moron. Trevaskis was wrong. Bishop Browne was not a moron, he was a moderately intelligent man with a limited view of the world and an undeserved belief in his own capacity to judge what was best for others.

A member of the studio audience reprimanded Gay Byrne for allowing Trevaskis to have his say, and Byrne retorted that there was free speech on the show, and anyone was free to express disagreement with Trevaskis.

Outraged clerics and county councillors let fly. The documents from the archives show that Minister for Posts and Telegraphs Joe Brennan decided to try to nobble the *Late Late Show*. Joe was a snug man who made his pot of money at the auctioneering game. A GAA stalwart, solid middle class, a card-carrying tribune of Real Ireland, Joe was a man who knew which side to butter his bishop on.

It is notable that those attacking the *Late Late Show*, including Joe, weren't so much upset about Brian Trevaskis as with Gay Byrne's defence of Trevaskis's right to speak. Impertinent troublemakers of the likes of Trevaskis could be expected to pop up from time to time and there wasn't much anyone could do about that. But something, surely, could be done about the fact that they were being allowed to express their opinions to the common herd, and using 'our station' to do it. There was no saying where that kind of thing could lead. Trevaskis, therefore, wasn't the enemy. The enemy was the Telefís Éireann flyboys who didn't know that their role in life was to recognise how perfect things were in the smug republic and to keep the airwaves clean of any riffraff who might think different.

Joe Brennan, with the full weight of his authority as Minister for Posts and Telegraphs, wrote to the chairman of the RTÉ Authority, Eamonn Andrews: 'I must take exception to the view expressed last Saturday night by the Compere when he implied, or, indeed, explicitly stated that anybody is free to say anything they like on this programme.' We must, Joe insisted, guard against providing 'a forum for every crank to vent his grievance'. And the 'first step towards exercising the type of control I have in mind' would be keeping the likes of Trevaskis off the show. And the implied threat: 'If this programme is to be allowed to develop along the lines on which it is moving in recent times, it would be better it were taken off the air.'

In the time that was in it, that was as good as an instruction. Eamonn Andrews was a professional broadcaster with middle-of-the-road politics and a private, unshowy commitment to his Catholic beliefs (much the same could be said of Gay Byrne, a Synge Street boy who always had a good word for the Christian Brothers). An experienced broadcaster in Britain, Andrews saw nothing remarkable in having people express unconventional opinions. Andrews held his nerve. It wouldn't be a good thing, he gently replied to Joe Brennan, if RTÉ was to respond to external pressures. 'A live programme with a good record of information and entertainment for the great bulk of the country's population is a rarity in broadcasting and should be nurtured now that we have it established.'

What was as significant as Andrews's letter was the fact that by the time he wrote it Brian Trevaskis had been brought back on the *Late Late Show*, the week after the row, where there was another controversial discussion of bishop power. And, to make sure no one missed the point, Trevaskis was brought back for a third week. The quiet resolution of a small number of broadcasters that they would exercise editorial freedom regardless of the snarls coming from their political masters or the clerics was a pointer to the future.

Poor Joe Brennan found a second front on which to fight the good fight for the Ireland of the bishops. Not alone was RTÉ impertinently promoting free speech but there were proposals to install cable systems which would bring the British TV channels to Irish viewers. Instead of the snowy, unreliable pictures captured by chimneytop aerials, the pictures from pagan England would come in bright and clear on coaxial cable. The archives contain a document in which Joe suggests that if cable has to come it might still be possible to force viewers to watch the home channel. This would be done by interfering with the signals from the English channels, to make them fuzzy and unclear. If we had to choose a moment which summed up the arrival of a new Ireland and the ill-judged flailing of the grumpy old Ireland, this surely was it.

* * *

It's only now, with perspective, with people speaking more freely, with the knowledge of what has been turned up in research, that we can see the true shape of that time we experienced as the best years of our lives. There were things that were not talked about back then, though they were no secret. For instance, there was a right way to be born, and a wrong way. And those who came here the wrong way, and their mothers, were risking stone-faced rejection and years of misery. The bastard kids mostly had no one to stick up for them. The father usually didn't want to know; the mother, weakened with guilt, was bullied by nuns and priests and by her family; the state and the Church alike betrayed such

205

children, dismissing them as unfortunate chaff to be disentangled from the respectable wheat.

A significant piece of the truth can be found in the archives, in a scribble at the bottom of a government file, noting the bishops' objection to a cabinet move to set up an adoption process: 'We had better drop the matter.' Catholic kids might end up adopted by Protestants, said the bishops, and that wouldn't do. 'We had better drop the matter', said the politicians, their knees permanently bent and oiled to facilitate immediate genuflection towards Maynooth should the occasion demand. Seán McEntee, big, tough Seán who had faced down the Brits, dropped the adoption proposal. And Gerry Boland, who had shown no hesitation in endorsing executions, timidly bowed the knee. Later, Archbishop McQuaid would draw up proposals for the kind of adoption legislation which would be acceptable to him and the politicians would obligingly translate the proposals into law.

Today, when up to a quarter of births are to unwed women, we accept children for what they are. Back then, such kids were mere bastards. They had souls that must be saved for God, but kids not a product of wedlock were not 'legitimate', they were genuinely believed to be different, as though made from an inferior material. Young girls hurried off in shame to England to have their babies, or were consigned to years of slave labour in laundries and convents. A few were despatched to insane asylums and left there for decades. Virtually all bastard children were consigned to the orphanages. Unmarried mothers, confused, fearful, drenched in guilt, were pressured to surrender their babies to the nuns, who draped the children's subsequent whereabouts in layers of bureaucracy and lies.

Not until the publication of Mike Milotte's heartbreaking book *Banished Babies* in 1997 was the full story brought out about the cynical way in which the Church arranged, with state collusion and in secrecy, for many of the kids to be offloaded to American couples desperate for children. There was only minimal checking of the credentials of these people—as long as they were Catholic the job was oxo.

While there may have been the odd headbanger among the nuns, they were on the whole no more malicious than the rest of the population. They were doing what, by the Catholic 'ethos' of the time, they thought best. Society's shame must be concealed; the respectability of the woman's family must be protected; the sinful woman must confess her iniquity and beg God for forgiveness; the baby—a flawed thing made of inferior material—must be whisked away. The politicians were happy to have the Catholic Church handle this unfortunate business. The greater public didn't want to know.

My mother gave birth to me in the Coombe hospital, in Dublin's Liberties, the day before her thirty-ninth birthday. Unlike most of the younger unmarried women who got pregnant, she'd had time to be toughened by the normal ups and downs of life. She had come through hard times, afflictions and bereavements, and she was quietly strong. She was a devout Catholic, respectful of her bishops and her priests, but despite the fierce pressures of the day she wasn't letting go of her baby. On the day I was born, her younger sister Eileen discharged herself from the TB hospital and together the two set up a family. With no resources, no support, amid an 'ethos' hostile to the very existence of such a family, they carved out a space for the three of us.

I was named after Eugenio Pacelli, the given name of the then pontiff, Pope Pius XII. Thank Christ they didn't call me Pius.

It has become traditional, in memoirs of that surly age, to expose the author's angst-ridden early years and dysfunctional background. I have been burdened in this enterprise by the memories of a happy and loving childhood. The warmth of that family life provided a reference point against which the pretensions and cruelties of the larger society could be measured. The routine upsets and disappointments and rejections of childhood leave their marks, but as long as they are delivered by other kids we can usually absorb them and struggle on. It's when adults, with their power and their knowledge, abuse their positions of strength, trust or authority that kids face real trouble. It's when such adults let loose their anger, fear, frustration, need or passion that kids get marked for life.

I can remember suffering just one bastard taunt throughout the years of growing up. It came from a teacher at Tech. 'What's your mother's maiden name?', he asked me, for no reason at all.

'Kerrigan', I said.

'No.' He shook his head, as if dealing with a moron. 'I know that's her name now, but what was her name before she got married?'

'Kerrigan', I said, truthfully, for the want of anything better to say.

'No, her maiden name', he said, and he looked right at me and we both knew that he knew what the score was and that he wanted me to say it.

'Kerrigan.' My cheeks were red. He persisted, I stonewalled. Eventually, unable to get what he wanted, having amused himself, he shrugged and dismissed me. I turned away, my whole face straining successfully to hold back the tears. I told no one what he had done.

That's the worst I can remember. Bridie and Eileen withstood the initial pressures to give me up to an orphanage, held us together, then got on with it, ignoring any disapproval. It was just the way things were, they didn't expect anything better. They did what they knew to be right, and after the initial pressures we suffered no great consequences and evolved into a happy little family. Possessing the strength to do what you know to be right in such matters was uncommon back then. And not just among the bullied, frightened, unmarried pregnant women. Many who were better placed to assert their right to follow either their conscience or simple common sense buckled under the slightest pressure from the small-minded clerics, and bent the knee.

Seán Lemass is remembered as a tough man. Out in 1916, as a kid, fighting the British. Backing up de Valera through the decades, finally taking the office of Taoiseach. Shrugging off the old restrictions, determined to turn the country's face to the future. It's part of the picture, but only part. The evidence shows that when push came to shove Lemass could get down on all fours in front of the nearest powerful cleric and grovel with the rest of his colleagues.

It's in the archives. It was 1960, Lemass had recently become Taoiseach. Richard Hayes, director of the National Library, had come up with a money-saving idea. Both his library and Trinity College Dublin's library needed extensions. Why not link the two libraries on the grounds of TCD, saving state money and eliminating duplication? It was a plausible solution to a mundane problem which had to do with books, documents and space. So, of course, the Taoiseach on 31 March 1960 wrote to Dr John Charles McQuaid, Archbishop of Dublin, informing him of Hayes's idea and crawling: 'I should be glad to have the benefit of Your Grace's advice.'

It was as if His Grace had some special qualifications in librarianship. Or architecture. Or interior decoration. John Charles Interiors, Libraries a Speciality.

But Lemass wasn't asking for advice. He was acknowledging McQuaid's power, asking for permission before taking a simple decision. Trinity was a touchy subject. It was full of Protestants. McQuaid maintained a ban on Catholics attending TCD, to protect them, said the hierarchy in 1956, from the 'dangers of perversion' by Protestants. To break the ban was to risk eternal damnation in the fires of hell.

McQuaid and his fellow bishops informed Lemass that they would rather the link-up didn't go ahead. Siting the National Library extension at Protestant Trinity might give the impression that TCD was somehow more prestigious than UCD, and in Catholic Ireland, McQuaid felt, the main university 'should manifestly be a Catholic institution'.

Lemass promptly informed his secretary he was dropping the idea, because of McQuaid's response. Five days after the archbishop put the clappers on the proposal Lemass informed the TCD provost that there were 'such substantial difficulties that the particular scheme of Dr Hayes must be regarded as impractical'. For a Taoiseach, no less than for a Confraternity member who was having trouble meeting his commitments, the word of the mullahs had to be respected.

Here's Lemass in an interview a few years later, declaring that the influence of the bishops was greatly exaggerated: 'Oh, yes. As Taoiseach I never had the slightest problem in this regard, nor do I recollect any occasion when the Church tried to pressurise me in any area affecting government policy.' Thus the strong men airbrushed from their own minds the ease with which they bent the knee when the bishops said boo.

* * *

That day the plainclothes cops challenged us on the Navan Road, when Frankie and I had been annoying a telephone operator, we climbed a gate into the Bogies to escape. That was the gate my mother and Eileen climbed one afternoon almost twenty years later. Pope John Paul II was in town and he was staying at the Papal Nuncio's place on the far side of the Bogies. Bridie, almost seventy, and Eileen, a couple of years off sixty, climbed over the gate and made their way to a position within a few feet of their pontiff when he returned from one of his appointments. They were delighted. All those people trudging up to the Phoenix Park at dawn, and all they had to do was go over to the Bogies and climb a gate.

Bridie and Eileen had for decades worked mostly behind shop counters. When I was four, my mother, who was then working in a shop in O'Connell Street, came home one mid-morning, white-faced and silent, and Eileen told me to play out on the front steps for a while and the two went inside and talked. My mother wasn't due home until that evening, so I knew there was something wrong. She stayed home for a few weeks and then she began working again, in a shop near Phibsboro. Years later I found out that an old vagrant had come into the O'Connell Street shop, sickly and fading. He asked for a drink of water and was told to get out. My mother followed him into the street, brought him back and gave him a glass of water. Reprimanded, she told them where to shove their job and walked out in tears.

Eileen had, before the TB ended her employment, worked in one of the clothing sweatshops in town, at a sewing machine. The aftermath of the TB kept her at home, where she looked after me until she was sufficiently recovered and I had started school. She went to work in a factory in Coolock (up at dawn, two buses to work, heavy work all day, two buses home that evening, for button wages). She got a job in a supermarket way over on the southside. The wages were, as ever, toy money. Eileen made inquiries about joining a union. The gobshite union official walked into the supermarket a week later and announced that he was the man from the union, where would he find Eileen Kerrigan?

Next day, Eileen was put standing outside the supermarket, stacking heavy sacks of potatoes and weighing vegetables and selling them to passing trade. She quit. She got a job in a northside grocery store, where she worked ridiculous shifts, for more toy money. After years of this, she joined a union. The owner closed the store on a Friday, making everyone redundant. And opened it the following Monday, hiring everyone from the old staff, except Eileen. She went for other jobs but after a while she got tired of being told by shop owners that they wouldn't stamp cards, of how she could make up for the low wages by remaining on the dole. She decided she wasn't going back to work. Eileen and Bridie lived on state pensions and benefits for the rest of their lives, getting back some of the money they had paid in taxes over the previous fifty years or so. They found it amusing that their income from the state, about £30 or £40 a week in the 1980s, exceeded any wages they had ever been paid.

When Eileen died, the priests of the Church of the Most Precious Blood were kind and helpful. As I knelt with my mother at the top of the church, at Eileen's funeral, a priest asked God to forgive Eileen her sins. It was the routine funeral ritual and Eileen would have totally approved. I felt bemused. What sins had that innocent, wholly decent woman committed, and wasn't it an impertinence to presume that she had been anything other than the fine, gracious, courageous person that she was? What kind of culture routinely assumes that seven-year-old kids are sinners, that good people who have died must have had secretly stained souls?

As the funeral left Cabra West for Glasnevin cemetery, driving down past the site of the old turf depot, a Dublin Corporation bin lorry came towards us and the men in the cab saw the hearse and simultaneously blessed themselves. You didn't have to be a believer to find comfort in the decency and dignity of that gesture of respect, the traditional salute to a troubled neighbour.

Three years later my mother's heart failed. She made it to the Mater hospital, where Eileen had spent her last weeks, and in a cubicle of the casualty ward, while she waited for medical attention, we had our final words. She had had a couple of warnings over the previous year, she knew the score. She was ready. Although too frail to attend Mass each week, she watched it on TV on Sunday mornings and a good friend, a Minister of the Eucharist, had for some time been bringing Communion to the house. My mother's concern now was not for her soul but for the fact that she, who had been there for me from my first breath, would no longer be around to break my fall. She leaned forward and looked at me like I was still the twelve-year-old who jumped from bus platforms, the ten-year-old who wouldn't bother to button his overcoat in the winter, the six-year-old who came home with both knees scabbed and bloody. And she said, 'You look after yourself, do you hear me?' Then she lay back and I thought she was dozing but she had drifted into unconsciousness. A doctor and a nurse arrived and I had to leave the cubicle and after a while the doctor came out and shook his head and that was that.

*   *   *

212

She was buried in the same grave as Eileen, which is the grave in which their parents were buried, in Glasnevin cemetery. Their brother Joe lies quite close, and not too far away is the grave of my Uncle Larry and his wife Mary.

On the morning my mother was buried I stood beside the priest, a kind man who had often visited my mother during her last years. He leaned forward and looked down into the grave. Then, purely as a matter of observed fact, just making small talk, he turned to me and he said, 'There's room for one more.' I looked into the grave and I nodded and I said, 'So there is.'

* * *

We led simple lives, and when we sinned it was sin born of anger, of frustration or need. The sins born of greed and power were beyond us. Macker, the neighbourhood predator, eventually settled down and raised a family. His total take from his years of climbing in through people's windows wouldn't pay for the brown envelopes in which certain of our entrepreneurs wrap the backhanders that give them an edge. In our respect for our alleged betters, in our readiness to accept the guilt assigned to us by the holy men, we were true innocents.

There were occasions when I wore a new jacket, or succeeded at something, and my mother would look at me with satisfaction and say quietly, 'You're as good as any of them.' It was a compliment, but the phrasing was also an acknowledgment of the culture which with great solemnity had attempted to convince her that she was a sinner who had given birth to a lesser breed of child.

The fear and the guilt that were routinely inculcated in decent people gave the Church its power. But that power depended on the credibility of the bishops, and that in turn placed a great burden on Their Graces. They might burble on modestly about how they too are mere sinners, but we knew that was all for show. They might indulge in the odd glass too many of port, they might too easily sink into the soft seats of their limos, but they were men of moral certitude. They were our moral betters. That belief was as deeply imbedded in we who were sceptical of the political role of the holy men as it was in the most devout Confraternity member.

The innocence started dying that May morning in 1992 when we all lay rigid in our beds, or spluttered over our cornflakes, as we listened to RTÉ's *Morning Ireland* tell us about Bishop Casey and his lover, Annie Murphy, and their son Peter.

The other bishops hummed and hawed, and days passed. Morality was their business, but they couldn't bring themselves to say the words which we said amongst ourselves: this is not how anyone, let alone a bishop, should treat his child, or his lover. The bishops stunned us with their obvious lack of a moral compass. When Bishop Casey eventually gave an interview, to Veronica Guerin, he was asked why he hadn't used contraception when having sex with Annie Murphy. The bishop didn't bridle at the suggestion of an episcopal condom. 'Because of the fact that any time it happened it was impulsive, it never was premeditated', he said. It wasn't religious qualms which stopped him using a condom, but the fact that when he and Annie had sex it was on the spur of the moment. Had he had notice of an upcoming lustful romp he could have had his condom ready. It was so casual, so thoughtless, this exposure that the beliefs he supposedly espoused through those long years of preaching at us had no meaning at all.

The avalanche of scandals followed. Father Michael Cleary, who had condemned those who questioned Bishop Casey's behaviour, turned out to be a father in more than name. He too denied his flesh and blood, he too lived a lie. And we learned about the kids mistreated in the orphanages. About the priest who died of a heart attack in a gay club and received the last rites from another couple of gay priests who happened to be on the premises. Most of all, the long, drawn-out procession of child abusers who began to emerge from behind their clerical collars.

The gay priests thing didn't matter so much, it was like the Casey affair: people caught breaking the rules they laid down for others. There was more heartfelt anger at the savage treatment of children in the orphanages, at the contemptuous treatment of bastard children taken from their mothers and despatched to America, the kids treated not as children but as problems to be hidden away and sorted out. Above all, at the revelations of the sexual abuse of children and of how the bishops had handled that.

The percentage of priests who abused children was small. But there was no such accumulation of abusers in other areas of life, among lawyers or builders or teachers or binmen or policemen. In that time and that place when we were innocent kids, respectful, guilty and shamed in our alleged sinfulness, people with serious sexual problems were gravitating towards the religious life, seeing security there. And opportunities. Through those pious years, the best years of our lives, as the Classic Religious Anthems of Ireland soared up to heaven, as we packed the churches from porch to altar rail, children were being groped and stroked and raped and buggered. The Confession Box, with its dark intimacy, suddenly seemed a symbol of a twisted relationship between the vulnerable and the powerful.

When the Church authorities copped on that this priest or that brother was sexually abusing children the cleric was quietly transferred, from one opportunity to the next. They were moved on, as though the children they had abused were occasions of sin. The Church authorities cared about the children, but they also cared—and more so—about the Church's reputation, about its position of influence, about its financial liability. One bishop, twenty years ago, became aware of a priest's sexual abuse of children. His response was to forbid the priest to hear Confession, and the abuser was left to continue abusing, year after year, decade after decade. What would that bishop have done had he found out the priest was holding up banks? Perhaps he'd have taken away the priest's Rosary beads? Just what did a priest have to do before his colleagues picked up a phone and called the police?

It was the hierarchy's response to its priests' sexual abuse of children, more than anything else, that changed the relationship between the bishops and their people. It suggested that the Casey

215

scandal and those that followed were not aberrations but symptoms of moral stagnation. Between 1989 and 1996 weekly Mass-going fell from 69 per cent of Dublin Catholics to 41 per cent. At the end of 1996 a poll showed that only 21 per cent of Irish Catholics look to the Church for guidance in the making of serious moral decisions, while 78 per cent said they follow their conscience. It is not a matter of great celebration but of relief that we have at last chosen to allow ourselves this simple human liberty, this freedom of mind which is the very thing that makes us human.

The fear and the guilt inculcated in childhood made us quiescent too long, allowed us to accept for too long a cocky-eyed vision of how life should be lived. In the end, though, their crude head-fixing was as effective as their efforts to beat the Irish language into us. In short: not very.

* * *

On a wall around the corner from where I live now there is graffiti mourning the death of Tupac Shakur, a black American rap singer with a gangster image, who was shot dead in Las Vegas a while back. Further down the wall his name has the hip spelling: 2Pac. Kids here went through a phase of wearing their trainers without laces, wearing oversized jeans with the crotch almost down to their knees. Probably they don't know it (maybe they do), but that's a fashion born in the black ghettoes of America. Black teenagers imitated the style forced on the boyz in the 'hood who had been arrested and were being held on remand, their laces removed, their trousers loose at the crotch because their belt had been taken away in case they would hang themselves.

On that wall in the heart of a comfortable Dublin estate some kid has scrawled his yearning for 'Thug Life', a phrase tattooed across the late Tupac Shakur's midriff. Such yearning has nothing to do with criminal intent. It's a bit like the way we used to imagine ourselves to be hardened riflemen resting from a showdown with the Germans. Or the Apaches. Kids let their fantasies reach out beyond the limits of their experience, to identify with the exotic, in an effort to define themselves as special. And if that shocks their elders, so much the better. Drop them on East LA gang turf and they'd shit themselves.

Today's kids have a wider world from which to choose their fantasies, an easy familiarity through television and music with the culture of far-off places. Their fantasies are more varied than ours were, more risky. And have a better chance of coming to life. In sport and music and movies and books these kids have role models such as we never had, who suggest that anything is possible.

Adults more easily take or leave the religious ethos still drilled into kids in the schools. Decent people choose to believe in God, and people just as decent find they can not. Many now learn Irish for the love of it (though we still stick the schoolkids with the burden of reviving the language, taking vital time away from other subjects). People flock as eagerly as ever to GAA games, come home and knowledgably read an analysis of Manchester United's latest adventure. Things are looser. There is much about today's slick, superficial Ireland, with its café society pretensions, which grates. It's not the bishops who today lecture us on the evils of intervention by the 'nanny state' but the economic rightwingers, their faith in market forces every bit as religious as that of John Charles McQuaid's belief in transubstantiation. Today it is not the Real Irish who dominate, appropriate and exclude, it is the Nouveaux Gombeens. The ghettoes sink deeper into despair while southside gobshites chatter inanely about the Celtic Tiger. Racism is more easily tolerated, and decency dismissed as political correctness. But alongside all this there is a confidence and tolerance foreign to those raised under the thumb of the same John Charles McQuaid.

Despite the smug boasts of the liberals, we are not living in 'post-Catholic Ireland'. The bishops insist on retaining what they call their stake in education. They use that term without irony, despite the fact that only one of them has claimed parenthood. It's just a dozen years since Eileen Flynn lost her teaching job because an unmarried woman getting pregnant is offensive to the 'ethos' of the Catholic Church (and no cracks, please, about the Blessed Virgin). And that 'ethos' is the law of the land. Politicians still bow to it, citizens acquiesce. Few seem to see anything bizarre about bishops—celibate, childless, privileged men with a questionable record in protecting children against predators—insisting on their 'stake' in education. Not their interest or their concern but their stake; their right, world without end, to use the state education system to inculcate their 'ethos' in the young.

On my way back from the supermarket this afternoon three kids were practising their rollerblading, doing intricate 'grinds' on a kerbside, each manoeuvre with its own name and precise moves. We who could deadeye a wing from ten feet when playing the mowl—a lost art—today wouldn't know a Rocky Back Slide from a Soul Roll. And that's how it should be. Kids need their privacy. They need the games and rituals and achievements that exclude the uninitiated and help them feel good about themselves while they're learning how to make sense of the world. They need to have customs and ceremonies they can master, in which they can feel superior to grownups. That's how they survive the imposition of the older generation's 'ethos'. With a few casualties here and there.

*　　*　　*

Mr Hingerty, in Tech, told us that time is relative. For Hingo, a year was just one forty-somethingth of his life. For us it was one-fourteenth. So a year might seem a long time to us, he said, but it sped by for him. The Hingo Theory of Relativity.

Those smalltime years, in which we longed to be grownup and have some sort of control, seemed endless. Now, when you go back and parse your childhood, separate the toddler days from the rest, there were just a few short years when all that happened. We can see the speed of it as our own children shed phases, jumping from one stage to the next. We put aside locks of hair, tiny shoes, photographs and more photographs, storing them away as though trying to put a little bit of time in a box. We store the keepsakes so we can retrieve bits of the past, stare at them, fondle them, odds and sods from the debris of childhood, trying to hold onto something that won't stay still.

The period of time from losing faith in Santa to the onset of puberty is shockingly short. There are ten-year-olds giving Santa one last sceptical chance. And two years later they are experiencing the sexual feelings which underlie so much human passion, feelings which too often leave adults floundering. I'm not sure what age I was when I gave up on Santa, probably when I was ten. But I know that the following year, so great was my love for the magic that I willed myself to discard my knowledge that the whole thing was a myth and to believe again, and to proclaim my belief. So, when I was eleven, for one last season I believed, and for one last time he came, with a gun or an airplane, almost certainly an annual and a flashlamp.

The journey from that last touch of magic to my solemn belief that I had committed adultery took only a year. The ease with which guilt is implanted, the strength with which we cling to magic, the flexibility of the childish mind which can simultaneously embrace the magic and the guilt, the fragility of the whole thing, is both wondrous and disconcerting.

The stern old men saw the insecurities of childhood as fertile ground in which to sow the seeds of guilt. That the best years of our lives were presided over by celibates whose first loyalty was not to us but to their vision of Heaven was—let us search for the gentlest word appropriate in the circumstances—unfortunate. Shaped by their own stern childhoods, they arrogantly poked their reckless fingers into our searching, confused, trusting minds, with often painful consequences. Now, they are where they belong, in the black and white past, out of reach of our anger, beyond our forgiveness, capable now only of being understood. And that—understanding what they were and what they did—is all we can now do to them. And for them.

*   *   *

It's April now, we've reached the other side of winter. We danced up and down and the Sun God brought back the golden ball. It rains occasionally, but the chill is gone out of the air. The cherry blossom is being blown from the trees and gathering like pink snow along the kerbs.

Back in January, the *Faith of Our Fathers* people put on a stage show of the album, at the Point Theatre in Dublin. Now, the video of the concert of the CD is on sale. Nostalgia goes multimedia. The Glenstal Monks have brought out their own album of hymns.

There was a time when those hymns were the carefully crafted accompaniment to the exercise of power. Some people, when they hear *Faith of Our Fathers*, bristle with longing for what was. For most of us such hymns are artefacts to be appreciated for their form, or as aids to the indulgence of nostalgia. Throughout the best years of our lives they echoed through our weekly routine, celebrating the power that looked over our shoulders and into our very minds. Now we have them safely filed away on a CD, to be brought to life at our command, with the touch of a remote control.

Up in the shopping centre the Easter eggs were on sale six weeks before Easter. God be with the days when we marched to church to marvel at Christ's resurrection. Now Easter week is another marketing opportunity. Not a patch on Christmas, but a nice little earner. All the Buzz Lightyear Easter eggs sold out within a couple of days.

The courts continue to deal with the cases of child sexual abuse unearthed with relentless regularity. Priests feature in enough of them to repeatedly renew the dismay of the faithful.

A few days ago I went back to the Church of the Most Precious Blood, in Cabra West, mostly to check my memory of Latin spelling. The words are there, carved above the altar: *Redemisti Nos, Domine, In Sanguine Tuo*. I got it spot on. All those years, it never bothered me to wonder what the words meant. Probably because all of those slogans and prayers and imprecations, whatever

220

the particular phrase might be, say the same thing: You are great, I am unworthy, I prostrate myself before You. And they weren't just referring to relationships between individuals and their god. It was a power thing, between the Church and us, and we were to be convinced that we were the unworthy whose deference must be taken for granted.

At a guess: *Redemisti* is 'Redeem' and *Sanguine* is 'Blood'; *Domine* has the same root as dominate, which would make it a passable stand-in for 'Lord'; *Nos*, *In* and *Tuo* fill things out.

> *Redemisti Nos, Domine, In Sanguine Tuo.*
> Redeem Us, Lord, With Your Blood?

Or, to put it another way: You are great, I am unworthy, I prostrate myself before You.

Now that there's a thick foam covering on the kneelers in the church, Catholicism is easier on the knees. In the Church of the Most Precious Blood pews have been taken out and a new altar has been installed down in the body of the church. It makes for a more intimate setting for the Mass. The change couldn't have happened in the good old days, when every spare yard was needed for a pew, and on Sunday the faithful filled every seat, lined the side walls, stood four deep at the back and overflowed out onto the porch (and the hard chaws leaned on the wall outside, their arms folded). Congregations have shrunk, there's now lots of space to spare and a number of pews can be dispensed with to accommodate a more intimate layout.

I visited Canon Burke's grave, behind the church. He was a tough man who never sought our affection, just our respect for his authority. I've always thought it surprising that he wanted to be buried amongst us. The role of parish priest gave a man a strong presence, fed his ego, assured him of his worth before his people and before his God. But it must have been a lonely life, all those fifty-four years of priesthood, keeping a distance so as to maintain authority. It's a bit of a shock to realise that it's thirty years since he died. There are now three more parish priests, Canon Burke's successors, buried alongside him.

The current parish priest, Father Cecil Johnson, has presided over a deepening of the community welfare involvement of the Church in Cabra West. There's a parish centre in the grounds of the church, and the Church sold some of the land to facilitate the building of fine new flats for pensioners.

Off to one side of the church there's a little shop selling religious artefacts, crosses and holy water fonts and pictures of the Sacred Heart and the like. There I bought a booklet, *The West's Awake*, published to celebrate fifty years of the Parish of the Most Precious Blood. It's by Bernard Neary, Cabra West's local historian, who has published several books about the northside. If you want a date or a name relating to anything that happened in Cabra West, Bernard's fine history of the parish, *Waiting for the 22*, has it. In *The West's Awake*, Bernard writes of the current parish priest, Father Johnson, that he expressed a desire to retire on reaching the age of sixty-five, but that proved impossible. The steady fall in vocations, the national shortage of priests, has put pressure on the older clergy to hang on, imposing on them an increasing workload, sacrificing their years of retirement, rest and reflection.

I left the church and strolled down past Prenderville's shop. The neighbourhood doesn't look like its old self. It seems like every shopfront has changed. Many of the houses have extensions and there are fewer eight-children families being raised in two-bed-and-a-boxroom houses. There are brick driveways and double-glazing and more cars on one street than you'd once-upon-a-time see in all of Cabra West. Where once there were few private phones and most of us depended on a kiosk ten minutes' walk away, and that as often as not with the handset torn off, phones now are commonplace. The old neighbourhood had a look, a feel, and when we were kids every shop and house seemed as fixed and unchangeable as the GPO or the Bank of Ireland at College Green. The neighbourhood looks and feels different now, amended, impermanent; but for the current generation of kids it no doubt

222

seems as fixed and unchangeable as our Cabra West, our time and our place, once seemed.

I walked out of the parish, down the hill where the turf depot used to be, the depot that marked where Cabra West ended and everything else began. It used to have large graffiti on the side facing our neighbourhood, the wording adapted from the old Checkpoint Charlie sign at the Berlin wall: 'Achtung! You are now leaving Cabra West!' On the other side, facing Old Cabra, Phibsboro and the rest of the world, was the warning: 'Townies Keep Out!' The depot is gone now, along with the Berlin wall.

I took care crossing the road. These days I wouldn't dream of darting in and out of the traffic. And not just because I'm middle-aged and slow, not just because I have developed to a brow-clenching degree the sense of my own mortality that children lack. The traffic in this new Ireland is heavier, faster, over-impressed with its own status and skills and not a little ruthless.

Around to the left and down towards the bridge at the top of Connaught Street. I was surprised to see how low the parapet of the bridge is, inviting kids to climb up onto it. We must have been mad, walking along that parapet, open to the push of a strong wind. I looked down at the railway track onto which I might so easily have fallen thirty-five years ago. The tracks are gone now, taken up, probably sold as scrap. Years ago a metal barrier was installed along the length of the parapet, to make it more difficult for kids to climb up. It's rusting but still strong. The bridge is a little safer now.